AUSTRALIAN VERSE
AN ILLUSTRATED TREASURY

AUSTRALIAN VERSE
AN ILLUSTRATED TREASURY

Chosen by Beatrice Davis

Revised by Jamie Grant

STATE LIBRARY OF NEW SOUTH WALES
PRESS

Dedication
To the memory of Beatrice Davis
1909–1992

Australian Verse
An Illustrated Treasury
Chosen by Beatrice Davis

Published in 1996 by the State Library of New South Wales Press ©
Macquarie Street, Sydney 2000

First published in 1984 as The Illustrated Treasury of Australian Verse
Chosen by Beatrice Davis
Designed by Barbara Beckett
Picture research Don Chapman
Copyright in this selection © Estate of Beatrice Davis 1996

This edition revised by Jamie Grant
Cover design by Brian Robson
Additional picture research Judy Nelson
Production co-ordinator Carol Devcich
Printed by South China Printing Company, Hong Kong

National Library of Australia
Cataloguing-in-publication data

Australian verse, an illustrated treasury
New ed.
Bibliography.
Includes index.

ISBN 0 7305 8906 4

1. Australian poetry. I. Davis, Beatrice, 1909–1992. Grant, Jamie, 1949—
II. Title: Illustrated treasury of Australian verse.
A821.008

Cover: Summer at Carcoar, 1977
      By Brett Whiteley
      Collection of the Newcastle Region Art Gallery
Back cover: Beatrice Davis, 1982

CONTENTS

7

INTRODUCTION

POETRY is to be enjoyed, and this selection, scanning the Australian scene from first settlement to the present day, has several simple aims: to give pleasure to those with a nostalgic affection for favourite ballads and favourite poems they've known since their schooldays; to introduce Australian poetry as a whole to those unaware of the riches they have missed; and to present modern poets from Kenneth Slessor (1901–1971) to Les Murray (1938–) in poems that are memorable and immediately understandable.

I shall not attempt an essay on the development of Australian writing since the convicts and outback workers began the ballad tradition – and Harpur and Kendall the poetry – that first expressed our Australian attitudes: it has all been said before by people more competent than I am. Suffice to say that the verse reflects our social and literary history since 1788; and the chronological arrangement clearly shows the growth and maturing of talent as the poets explored and rediscovered and reassessed the Australian environment and their response to it.

Anthologies have often been scorned: yet they may serve a useful purpose in giving a wide assortment from which the reader may choose according to temperament and taste; and if mind, heart and imagination are stirred by certain poems this may lead to an enriching exploration of the poets' other work.

For advice generously given, I am grateful to Douglas Stewart, Geoffrey Lehmann and Les Murray.

B.D.

THE WILD COLONIAL BOY

'TIS OF a wild Colonial boy, Jack Doolan was his name,
Of poor but honest parents he was born in Castlemaine.
He was his father's only hope, his mother's only joy,
And dearly did his parents love the wild Colonial boy.

Chorus Come, all my hearties, we'll roam the mountains high,
Together we will plunder, together we will die.
We'll wander over valleys, and gallop over plains,
And we'll scorn to live in slavery, bound down with iron chains.

He was scarcely sixteen years of age when he left his father's home,
And through Australia's sunny clime a bushranger did roam.
He robbed those wealthy squatters, their stock he did destroy,
And a terror to Australia was the wild Colonial boy.

ANONYMOUS

In sixty-one this daring youth commenced his wild career,
With a heart that knew no danger, no foeman did he fear.
He stuck up the Beechworth mail coach, and robbed Judge MacEvoy,
Who trembled and gave up his gold to the wild Colonial boy.

He bade the judge 'Good morning', and told him to beware,
That he'd never rob a hearty chap that acted on the square,
And never to rob a mother of her son and only joy,
Or else you may turn outlaw, like the wild Colonial boy.

One day as he was riding the mountain-side along,
A-listening to the little birds, their pleasant laughing song,
Three mounted troopers rode along—Kelly, Davis, and FitzRoy—
They thought that they would capture him, the wild Colonial boy.

'Surrender now, Jack Doolan, you see there's three to one.
Surrender now, Jack Doolan, you daring highwayman.'
He drew a pistol from his belt, and shook the little toy.
'I'll fight, but not surrender,' said the wild Colonial boy.

He fired at Trooper Kelly and brought him to the ground,
And in return from Davis received a mortal wound.
All shattered through the jaws he lay still firing at FitzRoy,
And that's the way they captured him—the wild Colonial boy.

THE DYING STOCKMAN

(Air—'The Old Stable Jacket')

ANONYMOUS

A STRAPPING young stockman lay dying,
His saddle supporting his head;
His two mates around him were crying,
As he rose on his elbow and said:

Chorus 'Wrap me up with my stockwhip and blanket,
        And bury me deep down below,
        Where the dingoes and crows can't molest me,
        In the shade where the coolibahs grow.

'Oh! had I the flight of the bronzewing,
Far o'er the plains would I fly,
Straight to the land of my childhood,
And there I would lay down and die.

'Then cut down a couple of saplings,
Place one at my head and my toe,
Carve on them cross, stockwhip, and saddle,
To show there's a stockman below.

'Hark! there's the wail of a dingo,
Watchful and weird—I must go,
For it tolls the death-knell of the stockman
From the gloom of the scrub down below.

'There's tea in the battered old billy;
Place the pannikins out in a row,
And we'll drink to the next merry meeting,
In the place where all good fellows go.

'And oft in the shades of the twilight,
When the soft winds are whispering low,
And the darkening shadows are falling,
Sometimes think of the stockman below.'

CLICK GO THE SHEARS, BOYS

ANONYMOUS

OUT on the board the old shearer stands,
Grasping his shears in his long, bony hands,
Fixed is his gaze on a bare-bellied 'joe',
Glory if he gets her, won't he make the ringer go.

Chorus Click go the shears boys, click, click, click,
  Wide is his blow and his hands move quick,
  The ringer looks around and is beaten by a blow,
  And curses the old snagger with the blue-bellied 'joe'.

In the middle of the floor in his cane-bottomed chair
Is the boss of the board, with eyes everywhere;
Notes well each fleece as it comes to the screen,
Paying strict attention if it's taken off clean.

The colonial-experience man, he is there, of course,
With his shiny leggin's, just got off his horse,
Casting round his eye like a real connoisseur,
Whistling the old tune, 'I'm the Perfect Lure'.

Now Mister Newchum for to begin,
In number seven paddock bring all the sheep in;
Don't leave none behind, whatever you may do,
And then you'll be fit for a jackeroo.

The tarboy is there, awaiting in demand,
With his blackened tar pot, and his tarry hand;
Sees one old sheep with a cut upon its back,
Hears what he's waiting for, 'Tar here, Jack!'

Shearing is all over and we've all got our cheques,
Roll up your swag for we're off on the tracks;
The first pub we come to, it's there we'll have a spree,
And everyone that comes along it's, 'Come and drink with me!'

Down by the bar the old shearer stands,
Grasping his glass in his thin bony hands;
Fixed is his gaze on a green-painted keg,
Glory, he'll get down on it, ere he stirs a peg.

There we leave him standing, shouting for all hands,
Whilst all around him every shouter stands;
His eyes are on the cask, which is now lowering fast,
He works hard, he drinks hard, and goes to hell at last!

THE NUMERELLA SHORE

THERE'S a nice green little gully on the Numerella shore   'COCKATOO JACK'
Which I have ridden over many a day
Under Free Selection there I'll have acres by the score
Where I unyoke my bullocks from the dray.

Chorus To my bullocks I will say, Here for ever you may stay;
         You will never be impounded any more;
         For you're running, running, running on your owner's piece of ground,
         Free-selected on the Numerella shore.

When the moon's behind the mountain and the stars are very bright
My horse and I will saddle and away;
I'll duff the squatter's cattle in the darkness of the night
And the calves I'll have all branded ere the day.

Chorus O my pretty little calf, at the squatter we will laugh,
   For he'll never be your owner any more
   While you're running, running, running on the duffer's piece of ground
   Free-selected on the Numerella shore.

And when we've got our swags we'll steal the squatter's nags
And drive them to the nearest market town;
And when we've got the cash oh won't we cut a dash
And laugh at having done the squatter brown!

Chorus And won't the bullocks bellow when to work they seldom go
   And they think they won't be wanted any more
   While they're running, running, running on the duffer's piece of ground
   Free-selected on the Numerella shore.

Then as to growing grain on the bleak Maneroo Plain
Where we've free-selected from our master's run
Old hands up here will say 'tis a game will never pay,
So we'll go in for no work and lots of fun.

Chorus To my bullocks I will say, Here for ever you may stay
   For you'll never now be wanted any more;
   Your master'll get a living more easily by thieving
   Than by farming on the Numerella shore.

Is my judgment getting blunted that I cannot see my way?
Are there no vessels loading any more?
Oh! it's no use my debating for I only have to say
Farewell now to the Numerella shore.

Chorus To Jack Robertson, I'll say, You've been leading us astray,
   You will never be believed any more;
   And when next you take an airing try nothing half so daring
   As a visit to the Numerella shore.

S.T. GILL

BOLD JACK DONAHOE

'TWAS of a valiant highwayman and outlaw of disdain   ANONYMOUS
Who'd scorn to live in slavery or wear a convict's chain;
His name it was Jack Donahoe of courage and renown—
He'd scorn to live in slavery or humble to the Crown.

This bold, undaunted highwayman, as you may understand,
Was banished for his natural life from Erin's happy land.
In Dublin city of renown, where his first breath he drew,
It's there they titled him the brave and bold Jack Donahoe.

He scarce had been a twelvemonth on the Australian shore,
When he took to the highway, as oft he had before.
Brave Macnamara, Underwood, Webber and Walmsley too,
These were the four associates of bold Jack Donahoe.

As Jack and his companions roved out one afternoon,
Not thinking that the pains of death would overcome so soon,
To their surprise five horse police appeared all in their view,
And in quick time they did advance to take Jack Donahoe.

'Come, come, you cowardly rascals, oh, do not run away!
We'll fight them man to man, my boys, their number's only three;
For I'd rather range the bush around, like dingo or kangaroo,
Than work one hour for Government,' said bold Jack Donahoe.

'Oh, no,' said cowardly Walmsley, 'to that I won't agree;
I see they're still advancing us—their number's more than three.
And if we wait we'll be too late, the battle we will rue.'
'Then begone from me, you cowardly dog,' replied Jack Donahoe.

The Sergeant of the horse police discharged his car-a-bine,
And called aloud to Donahoe, 'Will you fight or resign?'
'Resign, no, no! I never will, until your cowardly crew,
For today I'll fight with all my might,' cried bold Jack Donahoe.

The Sergeant then, in a hurry his party to divide,
Placed one to fire in front of him, and another on each side;
The Sergeant and the Corporal, they both fired too,
Till the fatal ball had pierced the heart of bold Jack Donahoe.

Six rounds he fought those horse police before the fatal ball,
Which pierced his heart with cruel smart, caused Donahoe to fall;
And as he closed his mournful eyes he bade this world adieu,
Saying, 'Good people all, pray for the soul of poor Jack Donahoe.'

There were Freincy, Grant, bold Robin Hood, Brennan and O'Hare;
With Donahoe this highwayman none of them could compare.
But now he's gone to Heaven, I hope, with saints and angels too—
May the Lord have mercy on the soul of brave Jack Donahoe.

from YE WEARY WAYFARER

ADAM LINDSAY GORDON
1833–1870

HARK! the bells on distant cattle
    Waft across the range,
Through the golden-tufted wattle
    Music low and strange;
Like the marriage peal of fairies
    Comes the tinkling sound,
Or like chimes of sweet St Mary's
    On far English ground.

How my courser champs the snaffle,
    And with nostrils spread,
Snorts and scarcely seems to ruffle
    Fern leaves with his tread;
Cool and pleasant on his haunches
    Blows the evening breeze,
Through the overhanging branches
    Of the wattle trees;

Onward! to the Southern Ocean
   Glides the breath of Spring.
Onward! with a dreamy motion,
   I, too, glide and sing—
Forward! forward! still we wander—
   Tinted hills that lie
In the red horizon yonder—
   Is the goal so nigh?

Whisper, spring-wind, softly singing,
   Whisper in my ear;
Respite and nepenthe bringing,
   Can the goal be near?
Laden with the dew of vespers,
   From the fragrant sky,
In my ear the wind that whispers
   Seems to make reply—

'Question not, but live and labour
   Till yon goal be won,
Helping every feeble neighbour,
   Seeking help from none;
Life is mostly froth and bubble,
   Two things stand like stone,
Kindness in another's trouble,
   Courage in your own.'

THE SICK STOCKRIDER

ADAM LINDSAY
GORDON

HOLD HARD, Ned! Lift me down once more, and lay me in the shade.
Old man, you've had your work cut out to guide
Both horses, and to hold me in the saddle when I swayed,
All through the hot, slow, sleepy, silent ride.

The dawn at Moorabinda was a mist-wrack dull and dense;
The sunrise was a sullen, sluggish lamp;
I was dozing in the gateway at Arbuthnot's boundary fence;
I was dreaming on the Limestone cattle camp.

We crossed the creek at Carricksford and, sharply through the haze,
And suddenly, the sun shot flaming forth:
To southward lay Katâwa, with the sand-peaks all ablaze,
And the flushed fields of Glen Lomond lay to north.

Now westward winds the bridle-path that leads to Lindisfarm,
And yonder looms the double-headed Bluff:
From the far side of the first hill, when the skies are clear and calm,
You can see Sylvester's woolshed fair enough.

Five miles we used to call it from our homestead to the place
Where the big tree spans the roadway like an arch;
'Twas here we ran the dingo down that gave us such a chase
Eight years ago—or was it nine?—last March.

'Twas merry in the glowing morn, among the gleaming grass,
To wander as we've wandered many a mile,
And blow the cool tobacco cloud and watch the white wreaths pass,
Sitting loosely in the saddle all the while.

'Twas merry 'mid the backwoods, when we spied the station roofs,
To wheel the wild scrub cattle at the yard,
With a running fire of stockwhips and a fiery run of hoofs
—Oh, the hardest day was never then too hard!

Ay, we had a glorious gallop after Starlight and his gang
When they bolted from Sylvester's on the flat!
How the sun-dried reed-beds crackled, how the flint-strewn ranges rang
To the strokes of Mountaineer and Acrobat!

Hard behind them in the timber—harder still across the heath—
Close beside them through the tea-tree scrub we dashed;
And the golden-tinted fern leaves, how they rustled underneath,
And the honeysuckle osiers, how they crashed!

We led the hunt throughout, Ned, on the chestnut and the grey,
And the troopers were three hundred yards behind
While we emptied our six-shooters on the bushrangers at bay
In the creek, with stunted box-tree for a blind.

26

There you grappled with the leader, man to man and horse to horse,
And you rolled together when the chestnut reared:
He blazed away and missed you in that shallow water-course—
A narrow shave!—his powder singed your beard.

In these hours when life is ebbing, how those days when life was young
Come back to us! how clearly I recall
Even the yarns Jack Hall invented, and the songs Jem Roper sung
—And where are now Jem Roper and Jack Hall?

Ay, nearly all our comrades of the old colonial school,
Our ancient boon companions, Ned, are gone:
Hard livers for the most part! somewhat reckless as a rule!—
It seems that you and I are left alone.

There was Hughes, who got in trouble through that business with the cards—
It matters little what became of him;
But a steer ripped up MacPherson in the Cooraminta yards
And Sullivan was drowned at Sink-or-Swim.

And Mostyn—poor Frank Mostyn!—died at last a fearful wreck,
In the horrors at the upper Wandinong;
And Carisbrooke, the rider, at the Horsefall broke his neck—
Faith, the wonder was he saved his neck so long!

Ah, those days and nights we squandered at the Logans' in the glen!
The Logans, man and wife, have long been dead:
Elsie's tallest girl seems taller than your 'little Elsie' then
And Ethel is a woman grown and wed.

I've had my share of pastime, and I've done my share of toil,
And life is short—the longest life a span:
I care not now to tarry for the corn or for the oil,
Or for the wine that maketh glad the heart of man.

For good undone, and gifts misspent, and resolutions vain
'Tis somewhat late to trouble: this I know—
I should live the same life over, if I had to live again;
And the chances are I go where most men go.

The deep blue skies wax dusky, and the tall green trees grow dim,
The sward beneath me seems to heave and fall;
And sickly, smoky shadows through the sleepy sunlight swim
And on the very sun's face weave their pall.

Let me slumber in the hollow where the wattle blossoms wave,
With never stone or rail to fence my bed:
Should the sturdy station children pull the bush flowers on my grave
I may chance to hear them romping overhead.

A MIDSUMMER NOON IN THE AUSTRALIAN FOREST

NOT a sound disturbs the air,
There is quiet everywhere;
Over plains and over woods
What a mighty stillness broods!

CHARLES HARPUR
1813–1868

All the birds and insects keep
Where the coolest shadows sleep;
Even the busy ants are found
Resting in their pebbled mound;
Even the locust clingeth now
Silent to the barky bough:
Over hills and over plains
Quiet, vast and slumbrous, reigns.

Only there's a drowsy humming
From yon warm lagoon slow coming:
'Tis the dragon-hornet—see!
All bedaubed resplendently,
Yellow on a tawny ground—
Each rich spot nor square nor round,
Rudely heart-shaped, as it were

The blurred and hasty impress there
Of a vermeil-crusted seal
Dusted o'er with golden meal.
Only there's a droning where
Yon bright beetle shines in air,
Tracks it in its gleaming flight
With a slanting beam of light,
Rising in the sunshine higher,
Till its shards flame out like fire.

Every other thing is still,
Save the ever-wakeful rill,
Whose cool murmur only throws
Cooler comfort round repose;
Or some ripple in the sea
Of leafy boughs, where, lazily,
Tired summer, in her bower
Turning with the noontide hour,
Heaves a slumbrous breath ere she
Once more slumbers peacefully.

O 'tis easeful here to lie
Hidden from noon's scorching eye,
In this grassy cool recess
Musing thus of quietness.

29

BELLBIRDS

HENRY KENDALL
1839–1892

BY CHANNELS of coolness the echoes are calling,
And down the dim gorges I hear the creek falling;
It lives in the mountain, where moss and the sedges
Touch with their beauty the banks and the ledges;
Through brakes of the cedar and sycamore bowers
Struggles the light that is love to the flowers.
And, softer than slumber, and sweeter than singing,
The notes of the bellbirds are running and ringing.

The silver-voiced bellbirds, the darlings of daytime,
They sing in September their songs of the Maytime.
When shadows wax strong, and the thunderbolts hurtle,
They hide with their fear in the leaves of the myrtle:
When rain and the sunbeams shine mingled together
They start up like fairies that follow fair weather,
And straightway the hues of their feathers unfolden
Are the green and the purple, the blue and the golden.

October, the maiden of bright yellow tresses,
Loiters for love in these cool wildernesses;
Loiters knee-deep in the grasses to listen,
Where dripping rocks gleam and the leafy pools glisten
Then is the time when the water-moons splendid
Break with their gold, and are scattered or blended
Over the creeks, till the woodlands have warning
Of songs of the bellbird and wings of the morning.

Welcome as waters unkissed by the summers
Are the voices of bellbirds to thirsty far-comers.
When fiery December sets foot in the forest,
And the need of the wayfarer presses the sorest,
Pent in the ridges for ever and ever,
The bellbirds direct him to spring and to river,
With ring and with ripple, like runnels whose torrents
Are toned by the pebbles and leaves in the currents.

Often I sit, looking back to a childhood
Mixt with the sights and the sounds of the wildwood,
Longing for power and the sweetness to fashion
Lyrics with beats like the heartbeats of passion—
Songs interwoven of lights and of laughters
Borrowed from bellbirds in far forest rafters;
So I might keep in the city and alleys
The beauty and strength of the deep mountain valleys,
Charming to slumber the pain of my losses
With glimpses of creeks and a vision of mosses.

from SEPTEMBER IN AUSTRALIA

GREY winter hath gone, like a wearisome guest,   HENRY KENDALL
    And, behold, for repayment,
September comes in with the wind of the West
    And the Spring in her raiment!
The ways of the frost have been filled of the flowers,
    While the forest discovers
Wild wings, with a halo of hyaline hours,
    And the music of lovers.

September, the maid with the swift, silver feet!
    She glides, and she graces
The valleys of coolness, the slopes of the heat,
    With her blossomy traces;
Sweet month, with a mouth that is made of a rose,
    She lightens and lingers
In spots where the harp of the evening glows,
    Attuned by her fingers.
                    .   .   .   .

Oh, season of changes—of shadow and shine—
    September the splendid!
My song hath no music to mingle with thine,
    And its burden is ended;
But thou, being born of the winds and the sun,
    By mountain, by river,
Mayst lighten and listen, and loiter and run,
    With thy voices for ever!

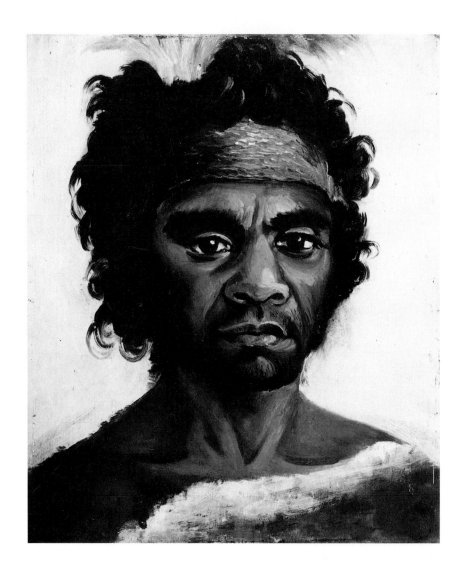

THE LAST OF HIS TRIBE

HENRY KENDALL

HE CROUCHES, and buries his face on his knees,
    And hides in the dark of his hair;
For he cannot look up to the storm-smitten trees,
    Or think of the loneliness there—
    Of the loss and the loneliness there.

The wallaroos grope through the tufts of the grass,
    And turn to their coverts for fear;
But he sits in the ashes and lets them pass
    Where the boomerangs sleep with the spear—
    With the nullah, the sling, and the spear.

Uloola, behold him! The thunder that breaks
On the tops of the rocks with the rain,
And the wind which drives up with the salt of the lakes,
Have made him a hunter again—
A hunter and fisher again.

For his eyes have been full with a smouldering thought;
But he dreams of the hunts of yore,
And of foes that he sought, and of fights that he fought
With those who will battle no more—
Who will go to the battle no more.

It is well that the water which tumbles and fills
Goes moaning and moaning along;
For an echo rolls out from the sides of the hills,
And he starts at a wonderful song—
At the sound of a wonderful song.

And he sees through the rents of the scattering fogs
The corroboree warlike and grim,
And the lubra who sat by the fire on the logs,
To watch, like a mourner, for him—
Like a mother and mourner for him.

Will he go in his sleep from these desolate lands,
Like a chief, to the rest of his race,
With the honey-voiced woman who beckons and stands,
And gleams like a dream in his face—
Like a marvellous dream in his face?

HOW McDOUGAL TOPPED THE SCORE

A PEACEFUL SPOT is Piper's Flat. The folk that live around—
They keep themselves by keeping sheep and turning up the ground;
But the climate is erratic, and the consequences are
The struggle with the elements is everlasting war.
We plough, and sow, and harrow—then sit down and pray for rain;
And then we all get flooded out and have to start again.
But the folk are now rejoicing as they ne'er rejoiced before,
For we've played Molongo cricket, and McDougal topped the score!

Molongo had a head on it, and challenged us to play
A single-innings match for lunch—the losing team to pay.
We were not great guns at cricket, but we couldn't well say no,
So we all began to practise, and we let the reaping go.
We scoured the Flat for ten miles round to muster up our men,
But when the list was totalled we could only number ten.
Then up spoke big Tim Brady: he was always slow to speak,
And he said—'What price McDougal, who lives down at Cooper's Creek?'

THOMAS E.
SPENCER
1845–1910

So we sent for old McDougal, and he stated in reply
That he'd never played at cricket, but he'd half a mind to try.
He couldn't come to practise—he was getting in his hay,
But he guessed he'd show the beggars from Molongo how to play.
Now, McDougal was a Scotchman, and a canny one at that,
So he started in to practise with a paling for a bat.
He got Mrs Mac to bowl to him, but she couldn't run at all,
So he trained his sheep-dog, Pincher, how to scout and fetch the ball.

Now, Pincher was no puppy; he was old, and worn, and grey;
But he understood McDougal, and—accustomed to obey—
When McDougal cried out 'Fetch it!' he would fetch it in a trice,
But until the word was 'Drop it!' he would grip it like a vice.
And each succeeding night they played until the light grew dim:
Sometimes McDougal struck the ball—sometimes the ball struck him.
Each time he struck, the ball would plough a furrow in the ground;
And when he missed, the impetus would turn him three times round.

The fatal day at length arrived—the day that was to see
Molongo bite the dust, or Piper's Flat knocked up a tree!
Molongo's captain won the toss, and sent his men to bat,
And they gave some leather-hunting to the men of Piper's Flat.
When the ball sped where McDougal stood, firm planted in his track,
He shut his eyes, and turned him round, and stopped it—with his back!
The highest score was twenty-two, the total sixty-six,
When Brady sent a yorker down that scattered Johnson's sticks.

Then Piper's Flat went in to bat, for glory and renown,
But, like the grass before the scythe, our wickets tumbled down.
'Nine wickets down for seventeen, with fifty more to win!'
Our captain heaved a heavy sigh, and sent McDougal in.
'Ten pounds to one you'll lose it!' cried a barracker from town;
But McDougal said, 'I'll tak' it, mon!' and planked the money down.
Then he girded up his moleskins in a self-reliant style,
Threw off his hat and boots and faced the bowler with a smile.

He held the bat the wrong side out, and Johnson with a grin
Stepped lightly to the bowling crease, and sent a 'wobbler' in;
McDougal spooned it softly back, and Johnson waited there,
But McDougal, crying 'Fetch it!' started running like a hare.
Molongo shouted 'Victory! He's out as sure as eggs',
When Pincher started through the crowd, and ran through Johnson's legs.
He seized the ball like lightning; then he ran behind a log,
And McDougal kept on running, while Molongo chased the dog!

They chased him up, they chased him down, they chased him round, and then
He darted through the sliprail as the scorer shouted 'Ten!'
McDougal puffed; Molongo swore; excitement was intense;
As the scorer marked down twenty, Pincher cleared a barbed-wire fence.
'Let us head him!' shrieked Molongo. 'Brain the mongrel with a bat!'
'Run it out! Good old McDougal!' yelled the men of Piper's Flat.
And McDougal kept on jogging, and then Pincher doubled back,
And the scorer counted 'Forty' as they raced across the track.

McDougal's legs were going fast, Molongo's breath was gone—
But still Molongo chased the dog—McDougal struggled on.
When the scorer shouted 'fifty' then they knew the chase could cease;
And McDougal gasped out 'Drop it!' as he dropped within his crease.
Then Pincher dropped the ball, and as instinctively he knew
Discretion was the wiser plan, he disappeared from view;
And as Molongo's beaten men exhausted lay around
We raised McDougal shoulder-high, and bore him from the ground.

We bore him to McGinniss's, where lunch was ready laid,
And filled him up with whisky-punch, for which Molongo paid.
We drank his health in bumpers and we cheered him three times three,
And when Molongo got its breath Molongo joined the spree.
And the critics say they never saw a cricket match like that,
When McDougal broke the record in the game at Piper's Flat;
And the folk are jubilating as they never did before;
For we played Molongo cricket—and McDougal topped the score!

WHERE THE PELICAN BUILDS

MARY HANNAY
FOOTT
1846–1918

THE HORSES were ready, the rails were down,
  But the riders lingered still—
    One had a parting word to say,
  And one had his pipe to fill.
Then they mounted, one with a granted prayer,
  And one with a grief unguessed.
    'We are going,' they said as they rode away,
  'Where the pelican builds her nest!'

They had told us of pastures wide and green,
  To be sought past the sunset's glow;
    Of rifts in the ranges by opal lit;
  And gold 'neath the river's flow.
And thirst and hunger were banished words
  When they spoke of the unknown West;
    No drought they dreaded, no flood they feared,
  Where the pelican builds her nest!

The creek at the ford was but fetlock deep
  When we watched them crossing there;
    The rains have replenished it twice since then,
  And thrice has the rock lain bare.
But the waters of Hope have flowed and fled,
  And never from blue hill's breast
    Come back—by the sun and the sands devoured—
  Where the pelican builds her nest.

NINE MILES FROM GUNDAGAI

JACK MOSES
1860–1945

I'VE DONE my share of shearing sheep,
  Of droving and all that,
  And bogged a bullock-team as well,
  On a Murrumbidgee flat.
  I've seen the bullock stretch and strain,
  And blink his bleary eye,
  And the dog sit on the tucker box,
  Nine miles from Gundagai.

  I've been jilted, jarred, and crossed in love,
  And sand-bagged in the dark,
  Till if a mountain fell on me
  I'd treat it as a lark.
  It's when you've got your bullocks bogged
  That's the time you flog and cry,
  And the dog sits on the tucker box,
  Nine miles from Gundagai.

We've all got our little troubles,
In life's hard, thorny way.
Some strike them in a motor car
And others in a dray.
But when your dog and bullocks strike
It ain't no apple pie,
And the dog sat on the tucker box
Nine miles from Gundagai.

But that's all past and dead and gone,
And I've sold the team for meat,
And perhaps some day where I was bogged,
There'll be an asphalt street.
The dog, ah! well he got a bait,
And thought he'd like to die,
So I buried him in the tucker box,
Nine miles from Gundagai.

THE CALL OF THE CITY

VICTOR DALEY
1858–1905

THERE IS a saying of renown—
'God made the country, man the town.'
Well, everybody to his trade!
But man likes best the thing he made.
The town has little space to spare;
The country has both space and air;
The town's confined, the country free—
Yet, spite of all, the town for me.

For when the hills are grey and night is falling,
*   And the winds sigh drearily,*
I hear the city calling, calling, calling,
*   With a voice like the great sea.*

I used to think I'd like to be
A hermit living lonesomely,
Apart from human care or ken,
Afar from all the haunts of men:
Then I would read in Nature's book,
And drink clear water from the brook,
And live a life of sweet content,
In hollow tree, or cave, or tent.

This was a dream of callow Youth
Which always overleaps the truth,
And thinks, fond fool, it is the sum
Of things that are and things to come.
But now, when youth has gone from me,
I crave for genial company.
For Nature wild I still have zest,
But human nature I love best.

I know that hayseed in the hair
Than grit and grime is healthier,
And that the scent of gums is far
More sweet than reek of pavement-tar.
I know, too, that the breath of kine
Is safer than the smell of wine;
I know that here my days are free—
But, ah! the city calls to me.

Let Zimmerman and all his brood
Proclaim the charms of Solitude,
I'd rather walk down Hunter-street
And meet a man I like to meet,
And talk with him about old times,
And how the market is for rhymes,
Between two drinks, than hold commune
Upon a mountain with the moon.

A soft wind in the gully deep
Is singing all the trees to sleep;
And in the sweet air there is balm,
And Peace is here, and here is Calm.
God knows how these I yearned to find!
Yet I must leave them all behind,
And rise and go—come sun, come rain—
Back to the Sorceress again.

For at the dawn or when the night is falling,
Or at noon when shadows flee,
I hear the city calling, calling, calling,
Through the long lone hours to me.

WALTZING MATILDA

A.B. PATERSON
1864–1941

OH! THERE ONCE was a swagman camped in the billabong,
Under the shade of a coolibah-tree;
And he sang as he looked at his old billy boiling,
'Who'll come a-waltzing Matilda with me?'

Chorus Who'll come a-waltzing Matilda, my darling,
    Who'll come a-waltzing Matilda with me?
    Waltzing Matilda and leading a water-bag—
    Who'll come a-waltzing Matilda with me?

Down came a jumbuck to drink at the water-hole,
Up jumped the swagman and grabbed him in glee;
And he sang as he stowed him away in his tucker-bag,
'You'll come a-waltzing Matilda with me!'

Down came the squatter a-riding his thoroughbred;
Down came policemen—one, two, and three.
'Whose is the jumbuck you've got in the tucker-bag?
You'll come a-waltzing Matilda with me'

But the swagman he up and he jumped in the water-hole,
Drowning himself by the coolibah-tree;
And his ghost may be heard as it sings in the billabong,
'Who'll come a-waltzing Matilda with me?'

S.T. GILL

THE MAN FROM SNOWY RIVER

THERE WAS MOVEMENT at the station, for the word had passed around   A.B. PATERSON
    That the colt from old Regret had got away,
And had joined the wild bush horses—he was worth a thousand pound,
    So all the cracks had gathered to the fray.
All the tried and noted riders from the stations near and far
    Had mustered at the homestead overnight,
For the bushmen love hard riding where the wild bush horses are,
    And the stock-horse snuffs the battle with delight.

There was Harrison, who made his pile when Pardon won the cup,
    The old man with his hair as white as snow;
But few could ride beside him when his blood was fairly up—
    He would go wherever horse and man could go.
And Clancy of the Overflow came down to lend a hand,
    No better horseman ever held the reins;
For never horse could throw him while the saddle-girths would stand—
    He learnt to ride while droving on the plains.

And one was there, a stripling on a small and weedy beast;
    He was something like a racehorse undersized,
With a touch of Timor pony—three parts thoroughbred at least—
    And such as are by mountain horsemen prized.
He was hard and tough and wiry—just the sort that won't say die—
    There was courage in his quick impatient tread;
And he bore the badge of gameness in his bright and fiery eye,
    And the proud and lofty carriage of his head.

But still so slight and weedy, one would doubt his power to stay,
    And the old man said, 'That horse will never do
For a long and tiring gallop—lad, you'd better stop away,
    Those hills are far too rough for such as you.'
So he waited, sad and wistful—only Clancy stood his friend—
    'I think we ought to let him come,' he said;
'I warrant he'll be with us when he's wanted at the end,
    For both his horse and he are mountain bred.

'He hails from Snowy River, up by Kosciusko's side,
    Where the hills are twice as steep and twice as rough;
Where a horse's hoofs strike firelight from the flint stones every stride,
    The man that holds his own is good enough.
And the Snowy River riders on the mountains make their home,
    Where the river runs those giant hills between;
I have seen full many horsemen since I first commenced to roam,
    But nowhere yet such horsemen have I seen.'

So he went; they found the horses by the big mimosa clump,
    They raced away towards the mountain's brow,
And the old man gave his orders, 'Boys, go at them from the jump,
    No use to try for fancy riding now.
And, Clancy, you must wheel them, try and wheel them to the right.
    Ride boldly, lad, and never fear the spills,
For never yet was rider that could keep the mob in sight,
    If once they gain the shelter of those hills.'

So Clancy rode to wheel them—he was racing on the wing
    Where the best and boldest riders take their place,
And he raced his stock-horse past them, and he made the ranges ring
    With the stockwhip, as he met them face to face.
Then they halted for a moment, while he swung the dreaded lash,
    But they saw their well-loved mountain full in view,
And they charged beneath the stockwhip with a sharp and sudden dash,
    And off into the mountain scrub they flew.

Then fast the horsemen followed, where the gorges deep and black
    Resounded to the thunder of their tread,
And the stockwhips woke the echoes, and they fiercely answered back
    From cliffs and crags that beetled overhead.
And upward, ever upward, the wild horses held their way,
    Where mountain ash and kurrajong grew wide;
And the old man muttered fiercely, 'We may bid the mob good day,
    No man can hold them down the other side.'

When they reached the mountain's summit, even Clancy took a pull—
    It well might make the boldest hold their breath;
The wild hop scrub grew thickly, and the hidden ground was full
    Of wombat holes, and any slip was death.
But the man from Snowy River let the pony have his head,
    And he swung his stockwhip round and gave a cheer,
And he raced him down the mountain like a torrent down its bed,
    While the others stood and watched in very fear.

He sent the flint-stones flying, but the pony kept his feet,
    He cleared the fallen timber in his stride,
And the man from Snowy River never shifted in his seat—
    It was grand to see that mountain horseman ride.
Through the stringy barks and saplings, on the rough and broken ground,
    Down the hillside at a racing pace he went;
And he never drew the bridle till he landed safe and sound
    At the bottom of that terrible descent.

He was right among the horses as they climbed the farther hill,
    And the watchers on the mountain, standing mute,
Saw him ply the stockwhip fiercely; he was right among them still,
    As he raced across the clearing in pursuit.
Then they lost him for a moment, where two mountain gullies met
    In the ranges—but a final glimpse reveals
On a dim and distant hillside the wild horses racing yet,
    With the man from Snowy River at their heels.

And he ran them single-handed till their sides were white with foam;
    He followed like a bloodhound on their track,
Till they halted, cowed and beated; then he turned their heads for home,
    And alone and unassisted brought them back.
But his hardy mountain pony he could scarcely raise a trot,
    He was blood from hip to shoulder from the spur;
But his pluck was still undaunted, and his courage fiery hot,
    For never yet was mountain horse a cur.

And down by Kosciusko, where the pine-clad ridges raise
    Their torn and rugged battlements on high,
Where the air is clear as crystal, and the white stars fairly blaze
    At midnight in the cold and frosty sky,
And where around the Overflow the reed-beds sweep and sway
    To the breezes, and the rolling plains are wide,
The Man from Snowy River is a household word today,
    And the stockmen tell the story of his ride.

THE MAN FROM IRONBARK

A.B. PATERSON

IT WAS the man from Ironbark who struck the Sydney town,
He wandered over street and park, he wandered up and down,
He loitered here, he loitered there, till he was like to drop,
Until at last in sheer despair he sought a barber's shop.
''Ere! shave my beard and whiskers off, I'll be a man of mark,
I'll go and do the Sydney toff up home in Ironbark.'

The barber man was small and flash, as barbers mostly are,
He wore a strike-your-fancy sash, he smoked a huge cigar:
He was a humorist of note and keen at repartee,
He laid the odds and kept a 'tote', whatever that may be,
And when he saw our friend arrive, he whispered 'Here's a lark!
Just watch me catch him all alive, this man from Ironbark.'

There were some gilded youths that sat along the barber's wall.
Their eyes were dull, their heads were flat, they had no brains at all;
To them the barber passed the wink, his dexter eyelid shut,
'I'll make this bloomin' yokel think his bloomin' throat is cut.'
And as he soaped and rubbed it in he made a rude remark:
'I s'pose the flats is pretty green up there in Ironbark.'

A grunt was all reply he got; he shaved the bushman's chin,
Then made the water boiling hot and dipped the razor in.
He raised his hand, his brow grew black, he paused awhile to gloat,
Then slashed the red-hot razor-back across his victim's throat;
Upon the newly shaven skin it made a livid mark—
No doubt it fairly took him in—the man from Ironbark.

He fetched a wild up-country yell might wake the dead to hear,
And though his throat, he knew full well, was cut from ear to ear,
He struggled gamely to his feet, and faced the murderous foe:
'You've done for me! you dog, I'm beat! one hit before I go
I only wish I had a knife, you blessed murderous shark!
But you'll remember all your life the man from Ironbark.'

He lifted up his hairy paw, with one tremendous clout
He landed on the barber's jaw, and knocked the barber out.
He set to work with tooth and nail, he made the place a wreck;
He grabbed the nearest gilded youth, and tried to break his neck.
And all the while his throat he held to save his vital spark,
And 'Murder! Bloody murder!' yelled the man from Ironbark.

A peeler man who heard the din came in to see the show;
He tried to run the bushman in, but he refused to go.
And when at last the barber spoke, and said, 'Twas all in fun—
'Twas just a little harmless joke, a trifle overdone.'
'A joke!' he cried. 'By George, that's fine; a lively sort of lark;
I'd like to catch that murdering swine some night in Ironbark.'

And now while round the shearing floor the listening shearers gape,
He tells the story o'er and o'er, and brags of his escape.
'Them barber chaps what keeps a tote, by George, I've had enough,
One tried to cut my bloomin' throat, but thank the Lord it's tough.'
And whether he's believed or not, there's one thing to remark,
That flowing beards are all the go way up in Ironbark.

THE TRAVELLING POST OFFICE

THE ROVING BREEZES come and go, the reed-beds sweep and sway,   A.B. PATERSON
The sleepy river murmurs low, and loiters on its way,
It is the land of lots o' time along the Castlereagh.

The old man's son had left the farm, he found it dull and slow,
He drifted to the great North-west, where all the rovers go.
'He's gone so long,' the old man said, 'he's dropped right out of mind,
But if you'd write a line to him I'd take it very kind;
He's shearing here and fencing there, a kind of waif and stray—
He's droving now with Conroy's sheep along the Castlereagh.

'The sheep are travelling for the grass, and travelling very slow;
They may be at Mundooran now, or past the Overflow,
Or tramping down the black-soil flats across by Waddiwong
But all those little country towns would send the letter wrong.
The mailman, if he's extra tired, would pass them in his sleep;
It's safest to address the note to "Care of Conroy's sheep",
For five and twenty thousand head can scarcely go astray,
You write to "Care of Conroy's sheep along the Castlereagh".'

By rock and ridge and riverside the western mail has gone
Across the great Blue Mountain Range to take that letter on.
A moment on the topmost grade, while open fire-doors glare,
She pauses like a living thing to breathe the mountain air,
Then launches down the other side across the plains away
To bear that note to 'Conroy's sheep along the Castlereagh'.

And now by coach and mailman's bag it goes from town to town,
And Conroy's Gap and Conroy's Creek have marked it 'Further down'.
Beneath a sky of deepest blue, where never cloud abides,
A speck upon the waste of plain the lonely mailman rides.
Where fierce hot winds have set the pine and myall boughs asweep
He hails the shearers passing by for news of Conroy's sheep.
By big lagoons where wildfowl play and crested pigeons flock,
By camp fires where the drovers ride around their restless stock,
And past the teamster toiling down to fetch the wool away
My letter chases Conroy's sheep along the Castlereagh.

CLANCY OF THE OVERFLOW

A.B. PATERSON

I HAD written him a letter which I had, for want of better
   Knowledge, sent to where I met him down the Lachlan years ago;
He was shearing when I knew him, so I sent the letter to him.
   Just on spec, addressed as follows, 'Clancy, of The Overflow'

And an answer came directed in a writing unexpected
   (And I think the same was written with a thumb-nail dipped in tar);
'Twas his shearing mate who wrote it, and verbatim I will quote it:
   'Clancy's gone to Queensland droving, and we don't know where he are.'

In my wild erratic fancy visions come to me of Clancy
   Gone a-droving down the Cooper where the Western drovers go;
As the stock are slowly stringing, Clancy rides behind them singing,
   For the drover's life has pleasures that the townsfolk never know.

And the bush has friends to meet him, and their kindly voices greet him
   In the murmur of the breezes and the river on its bars,
And he sees the vision splendid of the sunlit plains extended,
   And at night the wondrous glory of the everlasting stars.

I am sitting in my dingy little office, where a stingy
    Ray of sunlight struggles feebly down between the houses tall,
And the foetid air and gritty of the dusty, dirty city,
    Through the open window floating, spreads its foulness over all.

And in place of lowing cattle, I can hear the fiendish rattle
    Of the tramways and the buses making hurry down the street;
And the language uninviting of the gutter children fighting
    Comes fitfully and faintly through the ceaseless tramp of feet.

And the hurrying people daunt me, and their pallid faces haunt me
    As they shoulder one another in their rush and nervous haste,
With their eager eyes and greedy, and their stunted forms and weedy,
    For townsfolk have no time to grow, they have no time to waste.

And I somehow rather fancy that I'd like to change with Clancy,
    Like to take a turn at droving where the seasons come and go,
While he faced the round eternal of the cash-book and the journal—
    But I doubt he'd suit the office, Clancy, of The Overflow.

OVER THE RANGE

A.B. PATERSON

LITTLE bush maiden, wondering-eyed,
    Playing alone in the creek bed dry,
In the small green flat on every side
    Walled in by the Moonbi ranges high;
Tell me the tale of your lonely life
    'Mid the great grey forests that know no change.
'I never have left my home,' she said.
    'I have never been over the Moonbi Range.'

'Father and mother are both long dead,
    And I live with granny in yon wee place.'
'Where are your father and mother?' I said.
    She puzzled awhile with thoughtful face,
Then a light came into the shy brown eye,
    And she smiled, for she thought the question strange
On a thing so certain—'When people die
    They go to the country over the range.'

'And what is this country like, my lass?'
    'There are blossoming trees and pretty flowers,
And shining creeks where the golden grass
    Is fresh and sweet from the summer showers.
They never need work, nor want, nor weep;
    No troubles can come their hearts to estrange.
Some summer night I shall fall asleep,
    And wake in the country over the range.'

Child, you are wise in your simple trust,
    For the wisest man knows no more than you.
Ashes to ashes, and dust to dust:
    Our views by a range are bounded too;
But we know that God hath this gift in store,
    That, when we come to the final change,
We shall meet with our loved ones gone before
    To the beautiful country over the range.

S.T. GILL

THE WOMEN OF THE WEST

G. ESSEX
EVANS
1863–1909

THEY LEFT the vine-wreathed cottage and the mansion on the hill,
The houses in the busy streets where life is never still,
The pleasures of the city, and the friends they cherished best:
For love they faced the wilderness—the Women of the West.

The roar, and rush, and fever of the city died away,
And the old-time joys and faces—they were gone for many a day;
In their place the lurching coach-wheel, or the creaking bullock-chains,
O'er the everlasting sameness of the never-ending plains.

In the slab-built, zinc-roofed homestead of some lately taken run,
In the tent beside the bankment of a railway just begun,
In the huts on new selections, in the camps of man's unrest,
On the frontiers of the Nation, live the Women of the West.

The red sun robs their beauty and, in weariness and pain,
The slow years steal the nameless grace that never comes again;
And there are hours men cannot soothe, and words men cannot say—
The nearest woman's face may be a hundred miles away.

The wide bush holds the secrets of their longing and desires,
When the white stars in reverence light their holy altar fires,
And silence, like the touch of God, sinks deep into the breast—
Perchance He hears and understands the Women of the West.

For them no trumpet sounds the call, no poet plies his arts,
They only hear the beating of their gallant, loving hearts.
But they have sung with silent lives the song all songs above—
The holiness of sacrifice, the dignity of love.

Well have we held our fathers' creed. No call has passed us by.
We faced and fought the wilderness, we sent our sons to die.
And we have hearts to do and dare, and yet, o'er all the rest,
The hearts that made the Nation were the Women of the West.

THE OLD WHIM-HORSE

HE'S AN old grey horse, with his head bowed sadly,
And with dim old eyes and a queer roll aft,
With the off-fore sprung and the hind screwed badly
And he bears all over the brands of graft;
And he lifts his head from the grass to wonder
Why by night and day now the whim is still,
Why the silence is, and the stampers' thunder
Sounds forth no more from the shattered mill.

In that whim he worked when the night winds bellowed
On the riven summit of Giant's Hand,
And by day when prodigal Spring had yellowed
All the wide, long sweep of enchanted land;
And he knew his shift, and the whistle's warning,
And he knew the calls of the boys below;
Through the years, unbidden, at night or morning,
He had taken his stand by the old whim bow.

But the whim stands still, and the wheeling swallow
In the silent shaft hangs her home of clay,
And the lizards flirt and the swift snakes follow
O'er the grass-grown brace in the summer day;
And the corn springs high in the cracks and corners
Of the forge, and down where the timber lies;
And the crows are perched like a band of mourners
On the broken hut on the Hermit's Rise.

EDWARD DYSON
1865–1931

All the hands have gone, for the rich reef paid out,
And the company waits till the calls come in;
But the old grey horse, like the claim, is played out,
And no market's near for his bones and skin.
So they let him live, and they left him grazing
By the creek, and oft in the evening dim
I have seen him stand on the rises, gazing
At the ruined brace and the rotting whim.

The floods rush high in the gully under,
And the lightnings lash at the shrinking trees,
Or the cattle down from the ranges blunder
As the fires drive by on the summer breeze.
Still the feeble horse at the right hour wanders
To the lonely ring, though the whistle's dumb,
And with hanging head by the bow he ponders
Where the whim-boy's gone—why the shifts don't come.

But there comes a night when he sees lights glowing
In the roofless huts and the ravaged mill,
When he hears again the stampers going
Though the huts are dark and the stampers still:
When he sees the steam to the black roof clinging
As its shadows roll on the silver sands,
And he knows the voice of his driver singing,
And the knocker's clang where the braceman stands.

See the old horse take, like a creature dreaming,
On the ring once more his accustomed place;
But the moonbeams full on the ruins streaming
Show the scattered timbers and grass-grown brace.
Yet he hears the sled in the smithy falling
And the empty truck as it rattles back,
And the boy who stands by the anvil, calling;
And he turns and backs, and he takes up slack.

While the old drum creaks, and the shadows shiver
As the wind sweeps by and the hut doors close,
And the bats dip down in the shaft or quiver
In the ghostly light, round the grey horse goes;
And he feels the strain on his untouched shoulder,
Hears again the voice that was dear to him,
Sees the form he knew—and his heart grows bolder
As he works his shift by the broken whim.

He hears in the sluices the water rushing
As the buckets drain and the doors fall back:
When the early dawn in the east is blushing,
He is limping still round the old, old track.
Now he pricks his ears, with a neigh replying
To a call unspoken, with eyes aglow,
And he sways and sinks in the circle, dying;
From the ring no more will the grey horse go.

In a gully green, where a dam lies gleaming,
And the bush creeps back on a worked-out claim,
And the sleepy crows in the sun sit dreaming
On the timbers grey and a charred hut frame,
Where the legs slant down, and the hare is squatting
In the high rank grass by the dried-up course,
Nigh a shattered drum and a king-post rotting
Are the bleaching bones of the old grey horse.

EVE-SONG

MARY GILMORE
1865–1962

I SPAN and Eve span
A thread to bind the heart of man;
But the heart of man was a wandering thing
That came and went with little to bring:
Nothing he minded what we made,
As here he loitered, and there he stayed.

I span and Eve span
A thread to bind the heart of man;
But the more we span the more we found
It wasn't his heart but ours we bound.
For children gathered about our knees:
The thread was a chain that stole our ease.
And one of us learned in our children's eyes
That more than man was love and prize.
But deep in the heart of one of us lay
A root of loss and hidden dismay.

He said he was strong. He had no strength
But that which comes of breadth and length.
He said he was fond. But his fondness proved
The flame of an hour when he was moved.
He said he was true. His truth was but
A door that winds could open and shut.

And yet, and yet, as he came back,
Wandering in from the outward track,
We held our arms, and gave him our breast,
As a pillowing place for his head to rest.
I span and Eve span,
A thread to bind the heart of man!

S.T. GILL

OLD BOTANY BAY

MARY GILMORE

I'M old
Botany Bay;
Stiff in the joints,
Little to say.

I am he
Who paved the way,
That you might walk
At your ease today;

I was the conscript
Sent to hell
To make in the desert
The living well;

I bore the heat,
I blazed the track—
Furrowed and bloody
Upon my back.

I split the rock;
I felled the tree:
The nation *was*—
Because of me!

Old Botany bay
Taking the sun
From day to day. . . .
Shame on the mouth
That would deny
The knotted hands
That set us high!

NATIONALITY

MARY GILMORE

I HAVE grown past hate and bitterness,
I see the world as one;
But though I can no longer hate,
My son is still my son.

All men at God's round table sit,
And all men must be fed;
But this loaf in my hand,
This loaf is my son's bread.

FOURTEEN MEN

FOURTEEN MEN,
And each hung down
Straight as a log
From his toes to his crown.

Fourteen men,
Chinamen they were,
Hanging on the trees
In their pig-tailed hair

Honest poor men,
But the diggers said 'Nay!'
So they strung them all up
On a fine summer's day.

There they were hanging
As we drove by,
Grown-ups on the front seat,
On the back seat I.

That was Lambing Flat,
And still I can see
The straight up and down
Of each on his tree.

MARY GILMORE

S T. GILL

57

NEVER ADMIT THE PAIN

MARY GILMORE

NEVER admit the pain,
 Bury it deep;
Only the weak complain,
 Complaint is cheap.

Cover thy wound, fold down
 Its curtained place;
Silence is still a crown,
 Courage a grace.

NURSE NO LONG GRIEF

MARY GILMORE

OH, could we weep,
And weeping bring relief!
But life asks more than tears
And falling leaf.

Though year by year
Tears fall and leaves are shed,
Spring bids new sap arise,
And blood run red.

Nurse no long grief,
Lest the heart flower no more;
Grief builds no barns; its plough
Rusts at the door.

THE BRUCEDALE SCANDAL

MARY GILMORE

HIMSELF and me put in the trap
   And daundered into town,
And there we found a whirlygig,
   A circus and a clown;
We took a ticket for the two,
   Without a thought of shame,
And never knew till we got home
   The loss of our good name.

'Twas Mrs Dinny met us first;
   Says she, 'What's this I hear?
Ye're gaddin' round like young gossoons
   Instid of sixty year!'
Says she, 'I heard a shockin' thing
   About a horse ye rid! . . .'
Says I, 'The divel take your ears—
   I don't care if ye did!'

Says she, 'I've had respect for you;
   I've held ye up to all;
And now my heart is broke in two
   To think ye've had a fall;
For sure I never thought to find
   The frivolous in you . . . .'
Says I, for I was feelin' warm,
   'I don't care if ye do!'

We turned and left her where she stood,
   A poor astonished thing,
Whose wildest dissipation was
   A sober Highland Fling;
But when we came to Kelly's gate
   We got another knock,
For there was John O'Brien's Joe,
   Who looked his naked shock!

Says he (to Dan he whispers it)
   'They say—' says he, 'they say . . . .'
'Be damned to what they say,' says Dan;
   Says I, 'Do asses bray?'
The poor misfortune stared at me
   As if he thought me daft,
But, me, I looked him eye for eye,
   Until he felt a draught.

But dear old Gran O'Shaughnessy
    She met us at the door,
And said, 'Since first I heard the news
    My foot's wore out the floor!
I never laughed so much,' says she,
    'Not once in all me days,
As when I heard that you and Dan
    Was took to shameless ways.

'I'm keepin' up the fire,' she said,
    'Through all this blessed day.
My wan eye on the kittle, and
    Me other up the way;
And when I heard ye on the road,
    And thought of what ye'd done,
I felt me longest years slip off
    For thinkin' of your fun!'

'Sure then,' says I, 'it's not myself
  That would begrudge the tale,
And jokes, like butter on the shelf,
  If left too long grow stale.'
I told her how I rid the horse
  In that there jig-ma-gee,
And when I said how I fell off,
  'A-w-w, did ye now!' says she.

The next was Mrs Tracy's Mick;
  Who said, 'I'm hearin' things!'
Says I, 'We'd never need to ride
  If gossipin' was wings!'
Says he, 'There's decency you know;
  Ye mustn't go too far.
I'm that much shocked....' 'Tut, tut,' says I,
  'I don't care if ye are!'

I told her of the circus clown,
  And all the things he did.
She said, 'He wasn't half the fun
  Of that there horse ye rid;
And though my bones is eighty-six,
  I wisht I was wi' ye!'
Says I, 'Myself, I wisht it, too!'
  'I bet ye did!' says she.

'Aw, girl,' she said, 'ye've had your day,
  If Brucedale has the talk;
Ye've ate the apple to the core,
  So let them chew the stalk!'
They chewed the stalk from Rapley's gate
  To Cartwright's on the hill—
'Bedad,' says Dan, 'though years is gone,
  There's some that's chewin' still!'

THE SHEPHERD

OLD SAM SMITH   MARY GILMORE
Lived by himself so long,
He thought three people
A 'turruble throng'.

But he loved Old Shep,
Who could open and shut
The hide-hinged door
Of his old bark hut;

And he loved the trees,
The sun and the sky,
And the sound of the wind,
Though he couldn't tell why.

But besides all these,
He loved, to the full,
The smell of the sheep,
And the greasy wool.

So they buried him out
(For at last he died)
Out, all alone,
On a bleak hill side,

And there's never a sound
But the bleat of the sheep,
As they nibble the mound
That marks his sleep.

WHERE THE DEAD MEN LIE

BARCROFT BOAKE
1866–1892

OUT on the wastes of the Never-Never—
 That's where the dead men lie!
There where the heat waves dance for ever—
 That's where the dead men lie!
That's where the Earth's loved sons are keeping
Endless tryst: not the west wind sweeping
Feverish pinions can wake their sleeping—
 Out where the dead men lie!

Where brown Summer and Death have mated—
 That's where the dead men lie!
Loving with fiery lust unsated—
 That's where the dead men lie!
Out where the grinning skulls bleach whitely
Under the saltbush sparkling brightly;
Out where the wild dogs chorus nightly—
 That's where the dead men lie!

Deep in the yellow, flowing river—
 That's where the dead men lie!
Under the banks where the shadows quiver—
 That's where the dead men lie!
Where the platypus twists and doubles,
Leaving a train of tiny bubbles;
Rid at last of their earthly troubles—
 That's where the dead men lie!

East and backward pale faces turning—
 That's how the dead men lie!
Gaunt arms stretched with a voiceless yearning—
 That's how the dead men lie!
Oft in the fragrant hush of nooning
Hearing again their mother's crooning,
Wrapt for aye in a dreamful swooning—
 That's how the dead men lie!

Only the hand of Night can free them—
 That's when the dead men fly!
Only the frightened cattle see them—
 See the dead men go by!
Cloven hoofs beating out one measure,
Bidding the stockmen know no leisure—
That's when the dead men take their pleasure!
 That's when the dead men fly!

Ask, too, the never-sleeping drover:
    He sees the dead pass by;
Hearing them call to their friends—the plover,
    Hearing the dead men cry;
Seeing their faces stealing, stealing,
Hearing their laughter, pealing, pealing,
Watching their grey forms wheeling, wheeling
    Round where the cattle lie!

Strangled by thirst and fierce privation—
    That's how the dead men die!
Out on Moneygrub's farthest station—
    That's how the dead men die!
Hard-faced greybeards, youngsters callow;
Some mounds cared for, some left fallow;
Some deep down, yet others shallow;
    Some having but the sky.

Moneygrub, as he sips his claret,
    Looks with complacent eye
Down at his watch-chain, eighteen carat—
    There, in his club, hard by:
Recks not that every link is stamped with
Names of the men whose limbs are cramped with
Too long lying in grave mould, cramped with
    Death where the dead men lie.

S.T. GILL

THE FISHER

ALL NIGHT a noise of leaping fish
Went round the bay,
And up and down the shallow sands
Sang waters at their play.

The mangroves drooped on salty creeks,
And through the dark,
Making a pale patch in the deep,
Gleamed, as it swam, a shark.

In streaks and twists of sudden fire
Among the reeds
The bream went by, and where they passed
The bubbles shone like beads.

All night the full deep drinking song
Of nature stirred,
And nought beside, save leaping fish
And some forlorn night-bird.

No lost wind wandered down the hills
To tell of wide
Wild waterways; on velvet moved
The silky, sucking tide.

RODERIC QUINN
1867–1949

Deep down there sloped in shadowy mass
A giant hill;
And midway, mirrored in the tide,
The stars burned large and still.

The fisher, dreaming on the rocks,
Heard Nature say
Strange secret things that none may hear
Upon the beaten way,

And whisperings and wonder stirred,
And hopes and fears,
And sadness touched his heart, and filled
His eyes with star-stained tears:

And so, thrilled through with joy and love
And sweet distress,
He stood entranced, enchained by her
Full-breasted loveliness.

FACES IN THE STREET

HENRY LAWSON
1867–1922

THEY LIE, the men who tell us, for reasons of their own,
That want is here a stranger, and that misery's unknown;
For where the nearest suburb and the city proper meet
My windowsill is level with the faces in the street—
          Drifting past, drifting past,
          To the beat of weary feet—
While I sorrow for the owners of those faces in the street.

And cause I have to sorrow, in a land so young and fair,
To see upon those faces stamped the marks of Want and Care;
I look in vain for traces of the fresh and fair and sweet
In sallow, sunken faces that are drifting through the street— —
          Drifting on, drifting on,
          To the scrape of restless feet;
I can sorrow for the owners of the faces in the street.

In hours before the dawning dims the starlight in the sky
The wan and weary faces first begin to trickle by,
Increasing as the moments hurry on with morning feet,
Till like a pallid river flow the faces in the street—
          Flowing in, flowing in,
          To the beat of hurried feet—
Ah! I sorrow for the owners of those faces in the street.

The human river dwindles when 'tis past the hour of eight,
Its waves go flowing faster in the fear of being late;
But slowly drag the moments, whilst beneath the dust and heat
The city grinds the owners of the faces in the street—
                Grinding body, grinding soul,
                Yielding scarce enough to eat—
Oh! I sorrow for the owners of the faces in the street.

And then the only faces till the sun is sinking down
Are those of outside toilers and the idlers of the town,
Save here and there a face that seems a stranger in the street
Tells of the city's unemployed upon their weary beat—
                Drifting round, drifting round,
                To the tread of listless feet—
Ah! my heart aches for the owner of that sad face in the street.

And when the hours on lagging feet have slowly dragged away,
And sickly yellow gaslights rise to mock the going day,
Then, flowing past my window, like a tide in its retreat,
Again I see the pallid stream of faces in the street—
                Ebbing out, ebbing out,
                To the drag of tired feet,
While my heart is aching dumbly for the faces in the street.

And now all blurred and smirched with vice the day's sad end is seen,
For where the short 'large hours' against the longer 'small hours' lean,
With smiles that mock the wearer, and with words that half entreat,
Delilah pleads for custom at the corner of the street—
                Sinking down, sinking down,
                Battered wreck by tempests beat—
A dreadful, thankless trade is hers, that Woman of the Street.

But, ah! to dreader things than these our fair young city comes,
For in its heart are growing thick the filthy dens and slums,
Where human forms shall rot away in sties for swine unmeet
And ghostly faces shall be seen unfit for any street—
>> Rotting out, rotting out,
>> For the lack of air and meat—
In dens of vice and horror that are hidden from the street.

I wonder would the apathy of wealthy men endure
Were all their windows level with the faces of the Poor?
Ah! Mammon's slaves, your knees shall knock, your hearts in terror beat,
When God demands a reason for the sorrows of the street.
>> The wrong things and the bad things
>> And the sad things that we meet
In the filthy lane and alley, and the cruel, heartless street.

I left the dreadful corner where the steps are never still,
And sought another window overlooking gorge and hill;
But when the night came dreary with the driving rain and sleet,
They haunted me—the shadows of those faces in the street,
>> Flitting by, flitting by,
>> Flitting by with noiseless feet,
And with cheeks that scarce were paler than the real ones in the street.

Once I cried: 'O God Almighty! if Thy might doth still endure,
Now show me in a vision for the wrongs of Earth a cure.'
And, lo, with shops all shuttered I beheld a city's street,
And in the warning distance heard the tramp of many feet,
>> Coming near, coming near,
>> To a drum's dull distant beat—
'Twas Despair's conscripted army that was marching down the street!

Then, like a swollen river that has broken bank and wall,
The human flood came pouring with the red flags over all,
And kindled eyes all blazing bright with revolution's heat,
And flashing swords reflecting rigid faces in the street—
>> Pouring on, pouring on,
>> To a drum's loud threatening beat,
And the war hymns and the cheering of the people in the street.

And so it must be while the world goes rolling round its course,
The warning pen shall write in vain, the warning voice grow hoarse.
For not until a city feels Red Revolution's feet
Shall its sad people miss awhile the terrors of the street—
>> The dreadful, everlasting strife
>> For scarcely clothes and meat
In that pent track of living death—the city's cruel street.

BALLAD OF THE DROVER

ACROSS the stony ridges,
  Across the rolling plain,
Young Harry Dale, the drover,
  Comes riding home again.
And well his stock-horse bears him,
  And light of heart is he,
And stoutly his old packhorse
  Is trotting by his knee.

HENRY LAWSON

Up Queensland way with cattle
  He's travelled regions vast,
And many months have vanished
  Since home-folks saw him last.
He hums a song of someone
  He hopes to marry soon;
And hobble-chains and camp-ware
  Keep jingling to the tune.

Beyond the hazy dado
  Against the lower skies
And yon blue line of ranges
  The station homestead lies.
And thitherward the drover
  Jogs through the lazy noon,
While hobble chains and camp-ware
  Are jingling to a tune.

An hour has filled the heavens
  With storm-clouds inky black;
At times the lightning trickles
  Around the drover's track;
But Harry pushes onward,
  His horses' strength he tries,
In hope to reach the river
  Before the flood shall rise.

The thunder, pealing o'er him,
  Goes rumbling down the plain;
And sweet on thirsty pastures
  Beats fast the plashing rain;
Then every creek and gully
  Sends forth its tribute flood—
The river runs a banker,
  All stained with yellow mud.

Now Harry speaks to Rover,
    The best dog on the plains,
And to his hardy horses,
    And strokes their shaggy manes:
'We've breasted bigger rivers
    When floods were at their height,
Nor shall this gutter stop us
    From getting home tonight!'

The thunder growls a warning
    The blue, forked lightnings gleam;
The drover turns his horses
    To swim the fatal stream.
But, oh! the flood runs stronger
    Than e'er it ran before;
The saddle-horse is failing,
    And only half-way o'er!

When flashes next the lightning,
    The flood's grey breast is blank;
A cattle dog and packhorse
    Are struggling up the bank.
But in the lonely homestead
    The girl shall wait in vain—
He'll never pass the stations
    In charge of stock again.

The faithful dog a moment
    Lies panting on the bank,
Then plunges through the current
    To where his master sank.
And round and round in circles
    He fights with failing strength,
Till, gripped by wilder waters,
    He fails and sinks at length.

Across the flooded lowlands
    And slopes of sodden loam
The packhorse struggles bravely
    To take dumb tidings home;
And mud-stained, wet, and weary,
    He goes by rock and tree,
With clanging chains and tinware
    All sounding eerily.

The floods are in the ocean,
    The creeks are clear again,
And now a verdant carpet
    Is stretched across the plain.
But bleaching on the desert
    Or in the river reeds
The bones lie of the bravest
    That Wide Australia breeds.

WHEN YOUR PANTS BEGIN TO GO

WHEN you wear a cloudy collar and a shirt that isn't white,
And you cannot sleep for thinking how you'll reach tomorrow night,
You may be a man of sorrow, and on speaking terms with Care,
But as yet you're unacquainted with the Demon of Despair;
For I rather think that nothing heaps the trouble on your mind
Like the knowledge that your trousers badly need a patch behind.

I have noticed when misfortune strikes the hero of the play
That his clothes are worn and tattered in a most unlikely way;
And the gods applaud and cheer him while he whines and loafs around,
But they never seem to notice that his pants are mostly sound;
Yet, of course, he cannot help it, for our mirth would mock his care
If the ceiling of his trousers showed the patches of repair.

HENRY
LAWSON

You are none the less a hero if you elevate your chin
When you feel the pavement wearing through the leather, sock and skin;
You are rather more heroic than are ordinary folk
If you scorn to fish for pity under cover of a joke;
You will face the doubtful glances of the people that you know;
But—of course, you're bound to face them when your pants begin to go.

If, when flush, you took your pleasure, failed to make a god of Pelf—
Some will say that for your troubles you can only thank yourself;
Some will swear you'll die a beggar, but you only laugh at that
While your garments hang together and you wear a decent hat;
You may laugh at their predictions while your soles are wearing through—
But a man's an awful coward when his pants are going too!

Though the present and the future may be anything but bright,
It is best to tell the fellows that you're getting on all right.
And a man prefers to say it—'tis a manly lie to tell,
For the folks may be persuaded that you're doing very well;
But it's hard to be a hero, and it's hard to wear a grin,
When your most important garment is in places very thin.

Get some sympathy and comfort from the chum who knows you best,
Then your sorrows won't run over in the presence of the rest;
There's a chum that you can go to when you feel inclined to whine;
He'll declare your coat is tidy, and he'll say: 'Just look at mine!'
Though you may be patched all over he will say it doesn't show,
And he'll swear it can't be noticed when your pants begin to go.

Brother mine, and of misfortune! Times are hard, but do not fret,
Keep your courage up and struggle, and we'll laugh at these things yet.
Though there is no corn in Egypt, surely Africa has some—
Keep your smile in working order for the better days to come!
We shall often laugh together at the hard times that we know,
And get measured by the tailor when our pants begin to go.

REEDY RIVER

HENRY LAWSON

TEN MILES down Reedy River
    A pool of water lies,
And all the year it mirrors
    The changes in the skies.
Within that pool's broad bosom
    Is room for all the stars;
Its bed of sand has drifted
    O'er countless rocky bars.

Around the lower edges
  There waves a bed of reeds,
Where water-rats are hidden
  And where the wild duck breeds;
And grassy slopes rise gently
  To ridges long and low,
Where groves of wattle flourish
  And native bluebells grow.

Beneath the granite ridges
  The eye may just discern
Where Rocky Creek emerges
  From deep green banks of fern;
And standing tall between them,
  The drooping she-oaks cool
The hard, blue-tinted waters
  Before they reach the pool.

Ten miles down Reedy River
    One Sunday afternoon,
I rode with Mary Campbell
    To that broad, bright lagoon;
We left our horses grazing
    Till shadows climbed the peak,
And strolled beneath the she-oaks
    On the banks of Rocky Creek.

Then home along the river
    That night we rode a race,
And the moonlight lent a glory
    To Mary Campbell's face;
I pleaded for my future
    All through that moonlight ride,
Until our weary horses
    Drew closer side by side.

Ten miles from Ryan's Crossing
    And five below the peak,
I built a little homestead
    On the banks of Rocky Creek;
I cleared the land and fenced it
    And ploughed the rich red loam;
And my first crop was golden
    When I brought Mary home.

.   .   .   .

Now still down Reedy River
    The grassy she-oaks sigh;
The water-holes still mirror
    The pictures in the sky;
The golden sand is drifting
    Across the rocky bars;
And over all for ever
    Go sun and moon and stars.

But of the hut I builded
    There are no traces now,
And many rains have levelled
    The furrows of my plough.
The glad bright days have vanished;
    For sombre branches wave
Their wattle-blossom golden
    Above my Mary's grave.

S.T. GILL

ANDY'S GONE WITH CATTLE

OUR Andy's gone with cattle now—
Our hearts are out of order—
With drought he's gone to battle now
Across the Queensland border.

HENRY LAWSON

He's left us in dejection now,
Our thoughts with him are roving;
It's dull on this selection now,
Since Andy went a-droving.

Who now shall wear the cheerful face
In times when things are slackest?
And who shall whistle round the place
When Fortune frowns her blackest?

Oh, who shall cheek the squatter now
When he comes round us snarling?
His tongue is growing hotter now
Since Andy crossed the Darling.

Oh, may the showers in torrents fall,
And all the tanks run over;
And may the grass grow green and tall
In pathways of the drover;

And may good angels send the rain
On desert stretches sandy;
And when the summer comes again
God grant 'twill bring us Andy.

WARATAH AND WATTLE

HENRY
LAWSON

THOUGH poor and in trouble I wander alone,
   With a rebel cockade in my hat;
Though friends may desert me, and kindred disown,
   My country will never do that!
You may sing of the shamrock, the thistle, and rose,
   Or the three in a bunch if you will;
But I know of a country that gathered all those,
And I love the great land where the waratah grows,
   And the wattle-bough blooms on the hill.

Australia! Australia! so fair to behold—
   While the blue sky is arching above;
The stranger should never have need to be told
That the wattle-bloom means that her heart is of gold
   And the waratah red blood of love.

Australia! Australia! most beautiful name,
   Most kindly and bountiful land;
I would die every death that might save her from shame,
   If a black cloud should rise in the strand;
But whatever the quarrel, whoever her foes,
   Let them come! Let them come when they will!
Though the struggle be grim, 'tis Australia that knows,
That her children shall fight while the waratah grows,
   And the wattle blooms out on the hill.

THE SHEARER'S DREAM

OH, I DREAMT I shore in a shearin'-shed, and it was a dream of joy,
For every one of the rouseabouts was a girl dressed up as a boy—
Dressed up like a page in a pantomime, and the prettiest ever seen—
They had flaxen hair, they had coal-black hair—and every shade between.
There was short, plump girls, there was tall, slim girls, and the handsomest ever seen—
They was four-foot-five, they was six-foot high, and every height between.

The shed was cooled by electric fans that was over every shoot;
The pens was of polished ma-ho-gany, and everything else to suit;
The huts had springs to the mattresses, and the tucker was simply grand,
And every night by the billerbong we danced to a German band.

Our pay was the wool on the jumbucks' backs, so we shore till all was blue—
The sheep was washed afore they was shore (and the rams was scented too);
And we all of us wept when the shed cut out, in spite of the long, hot days,
For every hour them girls waltzed in with whisky and beer on tr-a-a-a-ys!

There was three of them girls to every chap, and as jealous as they could be—
There was three of them girls to every chap, and six of 'em picked on me;
We was draftin' them out for the homeward track and sharin' 'em round like steam,
When I woke with me head in the blazin' sun to find 'twas a shearer's dream.

HENRY
LAWSON

THE NEVER-NEVER LAND

BY hut, homestead, and shearing-shed,
   By railroad, coach, and track—
By lonely graves where rest our dead,
   Up-Country and Out-Back:
To where beneath the clustered stars
   The dreamy plains expand—
My home lies wide a thousand miles
   In the Never-Never Land.

It lies beyond the farming belt,
   Wide wastes of scrub and plain,
A blazing desert in the drought,
   A lake-land after rain;
To the skyline sweeps the waving grass,
   Or whirls the scorching sand—
A phantom land, a mystic realm!
The Never-Never Land.

HENRY
LAWSON

Where lone Mount Desolation lies,
   Mounts Dreadful and Despair—
'Tis lost beneath the rainless skies
   In hopeless deserts there;
It spreads nor'-west by No-Man's-Land—
   Where clouds are seldom seen—
To where the cattle-stations lie
   Three hundred miles between.

The drovers of the Great Stock Routes
   The strange Gulf country know—
Where, travelling from the southern droughts,
   The big lean bullocks go;
And camped by night where plains lie wide,
   Like some old ocean's bed,
The watchmen in the starlight ride
   Round fifteen hundred head.

       ·   ·   ·   ·

Lest in the city I forget
   True mateship after all,
My water-bag and billy yet
   Are hanging on the wall;
And I, to save my soul again,
   Would tramp to sunsets grand
With sad-eyed mates across the plain
   In the Never-Never Land.

J. WOLINSKI

TO JIM

I GAZE upon my son once more,
   With eyes and heart that tire,
As solemnly he stands before
   The screen drawn round the fire;
With hands behind clasped hand in hand,
   Now loosely and now fast—
Just as his fathers used to stand
   For generations past.

A fair and slight and childish form,
   And big brown dreamy eyes—
God help him! for a life of storm
   And strife before him lies:
A wanderer and a gipsy wild,
   I've learnt the world and know,
For I was such another child—
   Ah, many years ago!

HENRY LAWSON

79

But in those dreamy eyes of him
    There is no hint of doubt—
I wish that you could tell me, Jim,
    The things you dream about.
Dream on, and dream the world is true
    And things not what they seem—
'Twill be a bitter day for you
    When wakened from your dream.

      ·   ·   ·   ·

But O beware of bitterness
    When you are wronged, my lad—
I wish I had the faith in men
    And women that I had!
'Tis better far (for I have felt
    The sadness in my song)
To trust all men and still be wronged
    Than to trust none, and wrong.

Be generous and still do good
    And banish while you live
The spectre of ingratitude
    That haunts the ones who give.
But if the crisis comes at length
    That your future might be marred,
Strike hard, my son, with all your strength!
    For your own self's sake, strike hard!

BILL

HENRY
LAWSON

HE SHALL LIVE to the end of this mad old world as he's lived since the world began;
He never has done any good for himself, but was good to every man.
He never has done any good for himself, and I'm sure that he never will;
He drinks, and he swears, and he fights at times, and his name is mostly Bill.

He carried a freezing mate to his cave, and nursed him, for all I know,
When Europe was mainly a sheet of ice, thousands of years ago.
He has stuck to many a mate since then, he is with us everywhere still—
He loves and gambles when he is young, and the girls stick up for Bill.

He has rowed to a wreck, when the lifeboat failed, with Jim in a crazy boat;
He has given his lifebelt many a time, and sunk that another might float.
He has 'stood 'em off' while others escaped, when the niggers rushed from the hill,
And rescue parties that came too late have found what was left of Bill.

He has thirsted on deserts that others might drink, he has given lest others should lack,
He has staggered half-blinded through fire or drought with a sick man on his back.
He is first to the rescue in tunnel or shaft, from Bulli to Broken Hill,
When the water breaks in or the fire breaks out, a leader of men is Bill!

He wears no Humane Society's badge for the fearful deaths he braved;
He seems ashamed of the good he did, and ashamed of the lives he saved.
If you chance to know of a noble deed he has done, you had best keep still;
If you chance to know of a kindly act, you mustn't let on to Bill.

He is fierce at a wrong, he is firm in right, he is kind to the weak and mild;
He will slave all day and sit up all night by the side of a neighbour's child.
For a woman in trouble he'd lay down his life, nor think as another man will;
He's a man all through, and no other man's wife has ever been worse for Bill.

He is good for the noblest sacrifice, he can do what few men can;
He will break his heart that the girl he loves may marry a better man.
There's many a mother and wife tonight whose heart and eyes will fill
When she thinks of the days of the long-ago when she well might have stuck to Bill.

Maybe he's in trouble or hard up now, and travelling far for work,
Or fighting a dead past down tonight in a lone camp west of Bourke.
When he's happy and flush, take your sorrow to him and borrow as much as you will;
But when he's in trouble or stony-broke, you never will hear from Bill.

And when, because of its million sins, this earth is cracked like a shell,
He will stand by a mate at the Judgment Seat and comfort him down in—Well,—
I haven't much sentiment left to waste, but let cynics sneer as they will,
Perhaps God will fix up the world again for the sake of the likes of Bill.

J.A. MACARTNEY

E. MORRIS

LOVERS

MARY FULLERTON ('E')
1868–1946

TO BE unloved brings sweet relief:
The strong adoring eyes
Play the eternal thief
With the soul's fit disguise.

He will not sleep, and let be drawn
The screen of thy soul's ark;
They keep, those lidless eyes,
Thy sanctuary stark.

God, when he made each separate
Unfashioned his own act,
Giving the lover eyes,
So his love's soul be sacked.

To be unloved gives sweet relief;
The one integrity
Of soul is to be lone,
Inviolate, and free.

STUPIDITY

Stupidity achieves the crime
Not less than sheer malevolence;
Praying for virtue time and time,
Pray too for *sense*.

I fear the dullard, for the knave
One's own quick wit can circumvent,
But how beware the fool that has,
No ill intent?

MARY FULLERTON ('E')

THE COACHMAN'S YARN

THIS a tale that the coachman told,
As he flicked the flies from Marigold
And flattered and fondled Pharaoh.
The sun swung low in the western skies:
Out on a plain, just over a rise,
   Stood Nimitybell, on Monaro;
Cold as charity, cold as hell,
Bleak, bare, barren Nimitybell—
   Nimitybell on Monaro.

'Now this 'ere 'appened in 'Eighty-three,
The coldest winter *ever* we see;
Strewth, it was cold, as cold as could be,
   Out 'ere on Monaro;
It froze the blankets, it froze the fleas,
It froze the sap in the blinkin' trees,
It made a grindstone out of cheese,
   Right 'ere in Monaro.

'Freezin' an' snowin'—ask the old hands;
They seen, they knows, an' they understands.
The ploughs was froze, and the cattle brands,
   Down 'ere in Monaro;
It froze our fingers and froze our toes;
I seen a passenger's breath so froze
Icicles 'ung from 'is bloomin' nose
   Long as the tail on Pharaoh!

E.J. BRADY
1869–1952

'I ketched a curlew down by the creek;
His feet was froze to his blessed beak;
'E stayed like that for over a week—
    That's *cold* on Monaro.
Why, even the *air* got froze that tight
You'd 'ear the awfullest sounds at night,
When things was put to a fire or light,
    Out 'ere on Monaro.

'For the *sounds* was froze. At Haydon's Bog
A cove 'e cross-cut a big back-log,
An' carted 'er 'ome ('e wants to jog—
    Stiddy, go stiddy there, Pharaoh!).
As soon as his log begins to thaw
They 'ears the sound of the crosscut saw
A-thawin' out. Yes, his name was Law.
    Old hands, them Laws, on Monaro.

'The second week of this 'ere cold snap
I'm drivin' the coach. A Sydney chap,
'E strikes this part o' the bloomin' map,
    A new hand 'ere on Monaro;
'Is name or game I never heard tell,
But 'e gets off at Nimitybell;
Blowin' like Bluey, freezin' like 'ell
    At Nimitybell on Monaro.

'The drinks was froze, o' course, in the bar;
They *breaks* a bottle of old Three Star,
An' the barman sez, 'Now, there y' are,
    You can't beat *that* for Monaro!'
The stranger bloke, 'e was tall an' thin,
Sez, 'Strike me blue, but I think you win;
We'll 'ave another an' I'll turn in—
    It's blitherin' cold on Monaro.'

''E borrowed a book an' went to bed
To read awhile, so the missus said,
By the candlelight. 'E must ha' read
    (These nights is long on Monaro)
Past closin' time. Then 'e starts an' blows
The candle out; but the wick 'ad froze!
Leastways, that's what folks round 'ere suppose,
    Old hands as lived on Monaro.

'So bein' tired, an' a stranger, new
To these mountain ways, they think he threw
'Is coat on the wick; an' maybe, too,
    Any old clothes 'e'd to spare. Oh,
This ain't no fairy, an' don't you fret!
Next day came warmer, an' set in wet—
There's some out 'ere as can mind it yet,
    The real old 'ands on Monaro.

'The wick must ha' thawed. The fire began
At breakfast time. The neighbours all ran
To save the pub . . . an' forgot the man
    (Stiddy, go stiddy there, mare-oh).
The pub was burned to the blanky ground;
'Is buttons was all they ever found.
The blinkin' cow, 'e *owed me a pound*—
    From Cooma his blinkin' fare, oh!

'That ain't no fairy, not what I've told;
I'm gettin' shaky an' growin' old,
An' I hope I never again see cold,
    Like that down 'ere on Monaro! . . . '
He drives his horses, he drives them well,
And this is the tale he loves to tell
Nearing the town of Nimitybell,
    Nimitybell on Monaro.

THE DEATH OF BEN HALL

WILL H. OGILVIE
1869–1963

BEN HALL was out on the Lachlan side
With a thousand pounds on his head;
A score of troopers were scattered wide
And a hundred more were ready to ride
Wherever a rumour led.

They had followed his track from the Weddin heights
And north by the Weelong yards;
Through dazzling days and moonlit nights
They had sought him over their rifle-sights,
With their hands on their trigger guards.

The outlaw stole like a hunted fox
Through the scrub and stunted heath,
And peered like a hawk from his eyrie rocks
Through the waving boughs of the sapling box
On the troopers riding beneath.

His clothes were rent by the clutching thorn
And his blistered feet were bare;
Ragged and torn, with his beard unshorn,
He hid in the woods like a beast forlorn,
With a padded path to his lair.

But every night when the white stars rose
He crossed by the Gunning Plain
To a stockman's hut where the Gunning flows,
And struck on the door three swift light blows,
And a hand unhooked the chain—

And the outlaw followed the lone path back
With food for another day;
And the kindly darkness covered his track
And the shadows swallowed him deep and black
Where the starlight melted away.

But his friend had read of the Big Reward,
And his soul was stirred with greed;
He fastened his door and window board,
He saddled his horse and crossed the ford,
And spurred to the town at speed.

You may ride at a man's or a maid's behest
When honour or true love call
And steel your heart to the worst or best,
But the ride that is ta'en on a traitor's quest
Is the bitterest ride of all.

A hot wind blew from the Lachlan bank
And a curse on its shoulder came;
The pine-trees frowned at him, rank on rank,
The sun on a gathering storm-cloud sank
And flushed his cheek with shame.

He reined at the Court; and the tale began
That the rifles alone should end;
Sergeant and trooper laid their plan
To draw the net on a hunted man
At the treacherous word of a friend.

False was the hand that raised the chain
And false was the whispered word:
'The troopers have turned to the south again,
You may dare to camp on the Gunning Plain.'
And the weary outlaw heard.

He walked from the hut but a quarter-mile
Where a clump of saplings stood
In a sea of grass like a lonely isle;
And the moon came up in a little while
Like silver steeped in blood.

Ben Hall lay down on the dew-wet ground
By the side of his tiny fire;
And a night breeze woke, and he heard no sound
As the troopers drew their cordon round—
And the traitor earned his hire.

And nothing they saw in the dim grey light,
But the little glow in the trees;
And they crouched in the tall cold grass all night,
Each one ready to shoot at sight,
With his rifle cocked on his knees.

When the shadows broke and the dawn's white sword
Swung over the mountain wall,
And a little wind blew over the ford,
A sergeant sprang to his feet and roared:
'In the name of the Queen, Ben Hall!'

Haggard, the outlaw leapt from his bed
With his lean arms held on high.
'Fire!' And the word was scarcely said
When the mountains rang to a rain of lead—
And the dawn went drifting by.

They kept their word and they paid his pay
Where a clean man's hand would shrink;
And that was the traitor's master day
As he stood by the bar on his homeward way
And called on the crowd to drink.

He banned no creed and he barred no class,
And he called to his friends by name;
But the worst would shake his head and pass
And none would drink from the bloodstained glass
And the goblet red with shame.

And I know when I hear the last grim call
And my mortal hour is spent,
When the light is hid and the curtains fall
I would rather sleep with the dead Ben Hall
Than go where that traitor went.

I AM SHUT OUT OF MINE OWN HEART

I AM shut out of mine own heart
because my love is far from me,
nor in the wonders have I part
that fill its hidden empery:

the wildwood of adventurous thought
and lands of dawn my dream had won,
the riches out of Faery brought
are buried with our bridal sun.

And I am in a narrow place,
and all its little streets are cold,
because the absence of her face
has robb'd the sullen air of gold.

My home is in a broader day:
at times I catch it glistening
thro' the dull gate, a flower'd play
and odour of undying spring:

the long days that I lived alone,
sweet madness of the springs I miss'd,
are shed beyond, and thro' them blown
clear laughter, and my lips are kiss'd:

—and here, from mine own joy apart,
I wait the turning of the key:—
I am shut out of mine own heart
because my love is far from me.

CHRISTOPHER
BRENNAN
1870–1932

CONRAD MARTENS

MY HEART WAS WANDERING IN THE SANDS

MY HEART was wandering in the sands,
a restless thing, a scorn apart;
Love set his fire in my hands,
I clasped the flame unto my heart.

Surely, I said, my heart shall turn
one fierce delight of pointed flame;
and in that holocaust shall burn
its old unrest and scorn and shame:

surely my heart the heavens at last
shall storm with fiery orisons,
and know, enthroned in the vast,
the fervid peace of molten suns.

The flame that feeds upon my heart
fades or flares, by wild winds controll'd:
my heart still walks a thing apart,
my heart is restless as of old.

CHRISTOPHER
BRENNAN

SONG BE DELICATE

LET your song be delicate.
  The skies declare
No war—the eyes of lovers
  Wake everywhere.

Let your voice be delicate.
  How faint a thing
Is Love, little Love crying
  Under the Spring.

Let your song be delicate.
  The flowers can hear:
Too well they know the tremble
  Of the hollow year.

Let your voice be delicate.
  The bees are home:
All their day's love is sunken
  Safe in the comb.

Let your song be delicate.
  Sing no loud hymn:
Death is abroad.... Oh, the black season!
  The deep—the dim!

SHAW NEILSON
1872–1942

LOVE'S COMING

SHAW NEILSON

QUIETLY as rosebuds
  Talk to the thin air,
Love came so lightly
  I knew not he was there.

Quietly as lovers
  Creep at the middle moon,
Softly as players tremble
  In the tears of a tune;

Quietly as lilies
  Their faint vows declare
Came the shy pilgrim:
  I knew not he was there.

Quietly as tears fall
  On a wild sin,
Softly as griefs call
  In a violin;

Without hail or tempest,
  Blue sword or flame,
Love came so lightly
  I knew not that he came.

THE ORANGE TREE

SHAW NEILSON

THE YOUNG GIRL stood beside me. I
  Saw not what her young eyes could see:
—A light, she said, not of the sky
  Lives somewhere in the Orange Tree.

—Is it, I said, of east or west?
  The heartbeat of a luminous boy
Who with his faltering flute confessed
  Only the edges of his joy?

Was he, I said, borne to the blue
  In a mad escapade of Spring
Ere he could make a fond adieu
  To his love in the blossoming?

—Listen! the young girl said. There calls
  No voice, no music beats on me;
But it is almost sound: it falls
  This evening on the Orange Tree.

—Does he, I said, so fear the Spring
　　Ere the white sap too far can climb?
See in the full gold evening
　　All happenings of the olden time?

Is he so goaded by the green?
　　Does the compulsion of the dew
Make him unknowable but keen
　　Asking with beauty of the blue?

—Listen! the young girl said. For all
　　Your hapless talk you fail to see
There is a light, a step, a call
　　This evening on the Orange Tree.

—Is it, I said, a waste of love
　　Imperishably old in pain,
Moving as an affrighted dove
　　Under the sunlight or the rain?

Is it a fluttering heart that gave
　　Too willingly and was reviled?
Is it the stammering at a grave,
　　The last word of a little child?

—Silence! the young girl said. Oh, why,
　　Why will you talk to weary me?
Plague me no longer now, for I
　　Am listening like the Orange Tree.

BEAUTY IMPOSES

SHAW NEILSON

BEAUTY imposes reverence in the Spring.
Grave as the urge within the honeybuds,
It wounds us as we sing.

Beauty is joy that stays not overlong.
Clad in the magic of sincerities,
It rides up in a song.

Beauty imposes chastenings on the heart,
Grave as the birds in last solemnities
Assembling to depart.

MAY

SHAW NEILSON

SHYLY the silver-hatted mushrooms make
  Soft entrance through,
And undelivered lovers, half awake,
  Hear noises in the dew.

Yellow in all the earth and in the skies,
  The world would seem
Faint as a widow mourning with soft eyes
  And falling into dream.

Up the long hill I see the slow plough leave
  Furrows of brown;
Dim is the day and beautiful: I grieve
  To see the sun go down.

But there are suns a many for mine eyes
  Day after day:
Delightsome in grave greenery they rise,
  Red oranges in May.

'TIS THE WHITE PLUM TREE

SHAW NEILSON

IT IS the white Plum Tree
  Seven days fair
As a bride goes combing
  Her joy of hair.

As a peacock dowered
  With golden eyes
Ten paces over
  The Orange lies.

It is the white Plum Tree
  Her passion tells
As a young maid rustling
  She so excels.

The birds run outward,
  The birds are low,
Whispering in manna
  The sweethearts go.

It is the white Plum Tree
  Seven days fair
As a bride goes combing
  Her joy of hair.

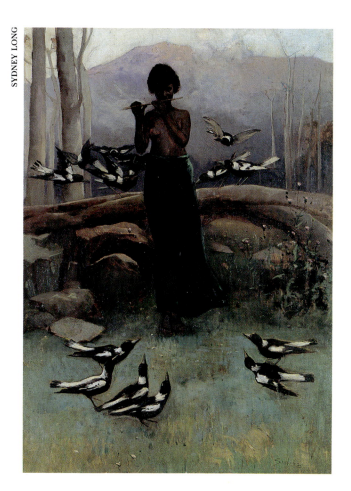

SYDNEY LONG

I BLOW MY PIPES

I BLOW my pipes, the glad birds sing,
The fat young nymphs about me spring,
The sweaty centaur leaps the trees
And bites his dryad's splendid knees;
The sky, the water, and the earth
Repeat aloud our noisy mirth ...
Anon, tight-bellied bacchanals,
With ivy from the vineyard walls,
Lead out and crown with shining glass
The wine's red baby on the grass.

I blow my pipes, the glad birds sing,
The fat young nymphs about me spring,
I am the lord,
I am the lord,
I am the lord of everything!

HUGH McCRAE
1876–1958

97

SONG OF THE RAIN

HUGH McCRAE

NIGHT,
And the yellow pleasure of candlelight . . .
Old brown books and the kind fine face of the clock
Fogged in the veils of the fire—its cuddling tock.

The cat,
Greening her eyes on the flame-litten mat;
Wickedly wakeful she yawns at the rain
Bending the roses over the pane,
And a bird in my heart begins to sing
Over and over the same sweet thing—

Safe in the house with my boyhood's love,
And our children asleep in the attic above.

THE INTRO

C.J. DENNIS
1876–1938

'ER NAME'S DOREEN. . . . Well, spare me bloomin days!
    You could er knocked me down wiv 'arf a brick!
Yes, me, that kids meself I know their ways,
    An' 'as a name for smoogin' in our click!
I just lines up an' tips the saucy wink.
But strike! The way she piled on dawg! Yer'd think
    A bloke was givin' back-chat to the Queen. . . .
        'Er name's Doreen.

I seen er in the markit first uv all,
Inspectin' brums at Steeny Isaacs' stall.
    I backs me barrer in—the same ole way—
    An' sez, 'Wot O! It's been a bonzer day.
'Ow is it fer a walk?' . . . Oh, 'oly wars!
The sorter *look* she gimme! Jest becors
    I tried to chat 'er, like you'd make a start
        Wiv any tart.

An' I kin take me oaf I wus perlite,
An' never said no word that wasn't right,
    An' never tried to maul 'er, or to do
    A thing yeh might call crook. Ter tell yeh true,
I didn't seem to 'ave the nerve—wiv 'er.
I felt as if I couldn't go that fur,
    An' start to sling off chiack like I used. . . .
        Not intrajuiced!

98

Nex' time I sighted 'er in Little Bourke,
Where she was in a job. I found 'er lurk
   Wus pastin' labels in a pickle joint,
    A game that—any'ow, that ain't the point.
Once more I tried ter chat 'er in the street,
But, bli' me! Did she turn me down a treat!
    The way she tossed 'er 'ead an' swished 'er skirt!
      Oh, I wus dirt!

       .   .   .   .

I know a bloke 'oo knows a bloke 'oo toils
In that same pickle found-ery. ('E boils
   The cabbitch storks or somethink.) Anyway,
    I gives me pal the orfis fer to say
'E 'as a sister in the trade 'oo's been
Out uv a jorb, an' wants ter meet Doreen;
    Then we kin get an intro, if we've luck.
      'E sez, 'Ribuck.'

ME PAL 'E TROTS 'ER UP AN' DOES THE TOFF
'E ALLUS WUS A BLOKE FER SHOWIN' OFF.
"THIS 'ERE'S DOREEN," 'E SEZ. — "THIS 'ERE'S THE KID."
— I DIPS ME LID —

O' course we worked the oricle; you bet!
But, 'struth, I ain't recovered frum it yet!
　　'Twas on a Saturdee, in Colluns Street,
　　An'—quite by accident, o'course—we meet.
Me pal 'e trots 'er up an' does the toff—
'E allus wus a bloke fer showin' off.
　　'This 'ere's Doreen,' 'e sez. 'This 'ere's the Kid.'
　　　　I dips me lid.

'This 'ere's Doreen,' 'e sez. I sez 'Good day.'
An', bli'me, I' ad nothin' more ter say!
　　I couldn't speak a word, or meet 'er eye.
　　Clean done me block! I never been so shy,
Not since I was a tiny little cub,
An' run the rabbit to the corner pub—
　　Wot time the Summer days wus dry an' 'ot—
　　　　Fer me ole pot.

　　　　　.　　　.　　　.　　　.

I dunno 'ow I done it in the end.
I reckerlect I arst ter be 'er friend;
　　An' tried ter play at 'andies in the park,
　　A thing she wouldn't sight. Aw, it's a nark!
I gotter swear when I think wot a mug
I must 'a' seemed to 'er. But still I 'ug
　　That promise that she give me fer the beach.
　　　　The bonzer peach!

Now, as the poit sez, the days drag by
On ledding feet, I wish't they'd do a guy.
　　I dunno 'ow I 'ad the nerve ter speak,
　　An' make that meet wiv 'er fer Sundee week!
But strike! It's funny wot a bloke'll do
When 'e's all out. . . . She's gorn, when I come-to
　　I'm yappin' to me cobber uv me mash. . . .
　　　　I've done me dash!

'Er name's Doreen. . . . An' me—that thort I knoo
　　The ways uv tarts, an' all that smoogin' game!
An' so I ort; fer ain't I known a few?
　　Yet some'ow . . . I dunno. It ain't the same.
I carn't tell wot it is; but, all I know,
I've dropped me bundle—an' I'm glad it's so.
　　Fer when I come ter think uv wot I been. . . .
　　　　'Er name's Doreen.

THE PLAY

C.J. DENNIS

'WOT's in a name?' she sez ... An' then she sighs,
An' clasps 'er little 'ands, an' rolls 'er eyes.
'A rose,' she sez, 'be any other name
Would smell the same.
Oh, w'erefore art you Romeo, young sir?
Chuck yer ole pot, an' change yer moniker!'

Doreen an' me, we bin to see a show—
The swell two-dollar touch. Bong tong, yeh know.
A chain apiece wiv velvit on the seat;
A slap-up treat.
The drarmer's writ be Shakespeare, years ago,
About a barmy goat called Romeo.

'Lady, be yonder moon I swear!' sez 'e.
An' then 'e climbs up on the balkiney;
An' there they smooge a treat, wiv prety words
Like two lovebirds.
I nudge Doreen. She whispers, 'Ain't it grand!'
'Er eyes is shinin'; an' I squeeze 'er 'and.

'Wot's in a name?' she sez. 'Struth, I dunno.
Billo is just as good as Romeo.
She may be Juli-er or Juli-et——
'E loves 'er yet.
If she's the tart 'e wants, then she's 'is queen,
Names never count.... But ar, I like 'Doreen!'

A sweeter, dearer sound I never 'eard;
Ther's music 'angs around that little word,
Doreen!... but wot was this I starts to say
About the play?
I'm off me beat. But when a bloke's in love
'Is thorts turns 'er way, like a 'omin' dove.

This Romeo 'e's lurkin' wiv a crew—
A dead tough crowd o' crooks—called Montague.
'Is cliner's push—wot's nicknamed Capulet—
They 'as 'em set.
Fair narks they are, jist like them back-street clicks,
Ixcep' they fights wiv skewers, 'stid o' bricks.

Wot's in a name? Wot's in a string o' words?
They scraps in ole Verona wiv their swords,
An' never give a bloke a stray dog's chance,
An' that's Romance.
But when they deals it out wiv bricks an' boots
In little Lon., they're low, degraded broots.

Wot's jist plain stoush wiv us, right 'ere today,
Is 'valler' if yer fur enough away.
Some time, some writer bloke will do the trick
Wiv Ginger Mick,
Of Spadger's Lane. 'E'll be a Romeo,
When 'e's bin dead five 'undred years or so

Fair Juli-et, she gives 'er boy the tip.
Sez she: 'Don't sling that crowd o' mine no lip;
An' if you run agin a Capulet,
Jist do a get.'
'E swears 'e's done wiv lash; 'e'll chuck it clean.
(Same as I done when I first met Doreen.)

They smooge some more at that. Ar, strike me blue!
It gimme Joes to sit an' watch them two!
'E'd break away an' start to say goodbye,
An' then she'd sigh
'Ow, Ro-me-o!' an' git a strangleholt,
An' 'ang around 'im like she feared 'e'd bolt.

Nex' day 'e words a gorspil cove about
A secrit weddin'; an' they plan it out.
'E spouts a piece about 'ow 'e's bewitched:
Then they git 'itched....
Now, 'ere's the place where I fair git the pip!
She's 'is for keeps, an' yet 'e lets 'er slip!

Ar! but 'e makes me sick! A fair gazob!
'E's jist the glarssy on the soulful sob,
'E'll sigh and spruik, an' 'owl a lovesick vow—
(The silly cow!)
But when 'e's got 'er, spliced an' on the straight,
'E crools the pitch, an' tries to kid it's Fate.

Aw! Fate me foot! Instid of slopin' soon
As 'e was wed, off on 'is 'oneymoon,
'Im an' 'is cobber, called Mick Curio,
They 'ave to go
An' mix it wiv that push o' Capulets.
They look fer trouble; an' it's wot they gets.

A tug named Tyball (cousin to the skirt)
Sprags 'em an' makes a start to sling off dirt.
Nex' minnit there's a reel ole ding-dong go—
'Arf round or so.
Mick Curio, 'e gets it in the neck,
'Ar rats!' 'e sez, an' passes in 'is check.

Quite natchril, Romeo gits wet as 'ell.
'It's me or you!' 'e 'owls, an' wiv a yell,
Plunks Tyball through the gizzard wiv 'is sword,
'Ow I ongcored!
'Put in the boot!' I sez. 'Put in the boot!'
''Ush!' sez Doreen.... 'Shame!' sez some silly coot

Then Romeo, 'e dunno wot to do.
The cops gits busy, like they allwiz do,
An' nose around until 'e gits blue funk
An' does a bunk.
They wants 'is tart to wed some other guy.
'Ah, strike!' she sez. 'I wish that I could die!'

Now, this 'ere gorspil bloke's a fair shrewd 'ead.
Sez 'e, 'I'll dope yeh, so they'll think yer dead.'
(I tips 'e was a cunnin' sort, wot knoo
A thing or two.)
She takes 'is knock-out drops, up in 'er room:
They think she's snuffed, an' plant 'er in 'er tomb.

Then things gits mixed a treat an' starts to whirl.
'Ere's Romeo comes back an' finds 'is girl
Tucked in 'er little coffing, cold an' stiff,
An' in a jiff,
'E swallers lysol, throws a fancy fit,
'Ead over turkey, an' 'is soul 'as flit.

Then Juli-et wakes up an' sees 'im there,
Turns on the waterworks an' tears 'er 'air,
'Dear love,' she sez, 'I cannot live alone!'
An' wiv a moan,
She grabs 'is pockit knife, an' ends 'er cares. . . .
'*Peanuts or lollies!*' sez a boy upstairs.

THE AUSTRAL ——— AISE

FELLERS of Australier,   C.J. DENNIS
Blokes an' coves an' coots,
Shift yer ——— carcasses,
Move yer ——— boots.
Gird yer ——— loins up,
Get yer ——— gun,
Set the ——— enermy
An' watch the ——— run.

Chorus:
Get a ——— move on.
Have some ——— sense.
Learn the ——— art of
Self de- ——— fence.

Have some ——— brains be-
Neath yer ——— lids.
An' swing a ——— sabre
For the missus an' the kids.
Chuck supportin' ——— posts,
An' strikin' ——— lights,
Support a ——— fam'ly an'
Strike for yer ——— rights.

Chorus:
      Get a ——— move, etc.

      Joy is ——— fleetin',
      Life is ——— short.
      Wot's the use uv wastin' it
      All on ——— sport?
      Hitch yer ——— tip-dray
      To a ——— star.
      Let yer ——— watchword be
      'Australi- ——— ar!'

Chorus:
      Get a ——— move, etc.

      'Ow's the ——— nation
      Goin' to ixpand
      'Lest us ——— blokes an' coves
      Lend a ——— 'and?
      'Eave yer ——— apathy
      Down a ——— chasm;
      'Ump yer ——— burden with
      Enthusi- ——— asm.

Chorus:
      Get a ——— move, etc.

      W'en the ——— trouble
      Hits yer native land
      Take a ——— rifle
      In yer ——— 'and.
      Keep yer ——— upper lip
      Stiff as stiff can be,
      An' speed a ——— bullet for
      Pos- ——— terity.

Chorus:
      Get a ——— move, etc.

      W'en the ——— bugle
      Sounds 'Ad- ——— vance'
      Don't be like a flock uv sheep
      In a ——— trance.
      Biff the ——— foeman
      Where it don't agree.
      Spifler- ——— cate him
      To Eternity.

Chorus:
  Get a ———— move, etc.

  Fellers of Australier,
  Cobbers, chaps an' mates,
  Hear the ———— enermy
  Kickin' at the gates!
  Blow the ———— bugle,
  Beat the ———— drum,
  Upper-cut and out the cow
  To Kingdom ———— come!

Chorus:
  Get a ———— move on,
  Have some ———— sense.
  Learn the ———— art of
  Self de- ————fence!

COUNTRY FELLOWS

C.J. DENNIS

When country fellows come to town,
    And meet to have a chat,
They bring the news from Camperdown,
    Birchip and Ballarat.
Wisely they talk of wheat and wool
    From Boort and Buninyong,
From Warragul and Warrnambool,
    From Junee and Geelong.

Ted tells them how the crops are now
    Well up round Bullarook,
And Fred describes the champion cow
    He bred at Quambatook.
'If rain comes soon 'twill be a boon,'
    Says Clive of Koo-wee-rup.
'Too right,' says Nick of Nar-nar-goon;
    'The grass wants fetchin' up.'

And I, who have been country bred,
    And love the country still,
I listen wistfully to Ted
    And George and Joe and Bill.
I see again the peaceful scene,
I hear them talk of paddocks green,
    At Yea and Grogan's Dam,
Koroit, Kerang and Moulamein;
Then, dreaming of the might-have-been,
    I go home in a tram.

JOHN D. MOORE

SAID HANRAHAN

'WE'LL all be rooned,' said Hanrahan
In accents most forlorn
Outside the church ere Mass began
One frosty Sunday morn.

The congregation stood about,
Coat-collars to the ears,
And talked of stock and crops and drought
As it had done for years.

'It's lookin' crook,' said Daniel Croke;
'Bedad, it's cruke, me lad,
For never since the banks went broke
Has seasons been so bad.'

'It's dry, all right,' said young O'Neil,
With which astute remark
He squatted down upon his heel
And chewed a piece of bark.

And so around the chorus ran
'It's keepin' dry, no doubt.'
'We'll all be rooned,' said Hanrahan,
'Before the year is out.

'The crops are done; ye'll have your work
To save one bag of grain;
From here way out to Back-o'-Bourke
They're singin' out for rain.

'They're singin' out for rain,' he said,
'And all the tanks are dry.'
The congregation scratched its head,
And gazed around the sky.

'There won't be grass, in any case,
Enough to feed an ass;
There's not a blade on Casey's place
As I came down to Mass.'

'If rain don't come this month,' said Dan,
And cleared his throat to speak—
'We'll all be rooned,' said Hanrahan,
'If rain don't come this week.'

P.J. HARTIGAN
('JOHN O'BRIEN)
1879–1952

A heavy silence seemed to steal
On all at this remark;
And each man squatted on his heel,
And chewed a piece of bark.

'We want an inch of rain, we do,'
O'Neil observed at last;
But Croke maintained we wanted two
To put the danger past.

'If we don't get three inches, man,
Or four to break this drought,
We'll all be rooned,' said Hanrahan,
'Before the year is out.'

In God's good time down came the rain;
And all the afternoon
On iron roof and windowpane
It drummed a homely tune.

And through the night it pattered still,
And lightsome, gladsome elves
On dripping spout and windowsill
Kept talking to themselves.

It pelted, pelted all day long,
A-singing at its work,
Till every heart took up the song
Way out to Back-o'-Bourke.

And every creek a banker ran,
And dams filled overtop;
'We'll all be rooned,' said Hanrahan,
'If this rain doesn't stop.'

And stop it did, in God's good time:
And spring came in to fold
A mantle o'er the hills sublime
Of green and pink and gold.

And days went by on dancing feet,
With harvest hopes immense,
And laughing eyes beheld the wheat
Nid-nodding o'er the fence.

And, oh, the smiles on every face,
As happy lad and lass
Through grass knee-deep on Casey's place
Went riding down to Mass.

While round the church in clothes genteel
Discoursed the men of mark,
And each man squatted on his heel,
And chewed his piece of bark.

'There'll be bushfires for sure, me man,
There will, without a doubt;
We'll all be rooned,' said Hanrahan,
'Before the year is out.'

TANGMALANGALOO

THE BISHOP sat in lordly state and purple cap sublime,
And galvanised the old bush church at Confirmation time;
And all the kids were mustered up from fifty miles around,
With Sunday clothes, and staring eyes, and ignorance profound.
Now was it fate, or was it grace, whereby they yarded too
An overgrown two-storey lad from Tangmalangaloo?

P.J. HARTIGAN
('JOHN
O'BRIEN')

A hefty son of virgin soil, where nature has her fling,
And grows the trefoil three feet high and mats it in the spring;
Where mighty hills uplift their heads to pierce the welkin's rim,
And trees sprout up a hundred feet before they shoot a limb;
There everything is big and grand, and men are giants too—
But Christian Knowledge wilts, alas, at Tangmalangaloo.

The bishop summed the youngsters up, as bishops only can;
He cast a searching glance around, then fixed upon his man.
But glum and dumb and undismayed through every bout he sat;
He seemed to think that he was there, but wasn't sure of that.
The bishop gave a scornful look, as bishops sometimes do,
And glared right through the pagan in from Tangmalangaloo.

'Come, tell me, boy,' his lordship said in crushing tones severe,
'Come, tell me why is Christmas Day the greatest of the year?
How is it that around the world we celebrate that day
And send a name upon a card to those who're far away?
Why is it wandering ones return with smiles and greetings, too?'
A squall of knowledge hit the lad from Tangmalangaloo.

He gave a lurch which set a-shake the vases on the shelf,
He knocked the benches all askew, up-ending of himself.
And oh, how pleased his lordship was, and how he smiled to say,
'That's good, my boy. Come, tell me now; and what is Christmas Day?'
The ready answer bared a fact no bishop ever knew—
'It's the day before the races out at Tangmalangaloo.'

from THE VICTORIA MARKETS RECOLLECTED IN TRANQUILLITY

I

WINDS are bleak, stars are bright,
Loads lumber along the night:
Looming, ghastly white,
A towering truck of cauliflowers sways
Out of the dark, roped over and packed tight
Like faces of a crowd of football jays.

The roads come in, roads dark and long,
To the knock of hubs and a sleepy song.
Heidelberg, Point Nepean, White Horse,
Flemington, Keilor, Dandenong,
Into the centre from the source.

Rocking in their seats
The worn-out drivers droop
When dawn stirs in the streets
And the moon's a silver hoop;
Come rumbling into the silent mart
To put their treasure at its heart,
Wagons, lorries, a lame Ford bus,
Like ants along the arms of an octopus
Whose body is all one mouth; that pays them hard
And drives them back with less than a slave's reward.

When Batman first at Heaven's command
Said, 'This is the place for a peanut-stand'
It must have been grand!

II

'Cheap today, lady; cheap today!'
Jostling watermelons roll
From fountains of Earth's mothering soul.
Tumbling from box and tray
Rosy, cascading apples play
Each with a glowing aureole
Caught from a split sun-ray.
'Cheap today, lady, cheap today.'
Hook the carcasses from the dray!
(Where the dun bees hunt in droves
Apples ripen in the groves.)

'FURNLEY MAURICE'
(FRANK WILMOT)
1881–1942

An old horse broods in a Chinaman's cart
While from the throbbing mart
Go cheese and celery, pears and jam
In barrow, basket, bag or pram
To the last dram the purse affords—
Food, food for the hordes.

Shuffling in the driven crush
The souls and the bodies cry,
Rich and poor, skimped and flush,
'Spend or perish. Buy or die!'

Food, food for the hordes!
Turksheads tumble on the boards.
     ·   ·   ·   ·

Along the shadows furtive, lone,
The unwashed terrier carries his weekend bone.
An old horse with a pointed hip
And dangling disillusioned under-lip
Stands in a harvest-home of cabbage leaves
And grieves.
A lady by a petrol case,
With a far-off wounded look in her face
Says, in a voice of uncertain pitch,
'Muffins' or 'Crumpets', I'm not sure which;
A pavement battler whines with half a sob,
'Ain't anybody got a bloody bob?'

Haunted by mortgages and overdrafts.
The old horse droops between the shafts.
A smiling Chinaman upends a bag
And spills upon the bench with thunder-thud
(A nearby urchin trilling the newest rag)
Potatoes caked with loamy native mud.

Andean pinnacles of labelled jam.
The melting succulence of two-toothed lamb.
The little bands of hemp that truss
The succulent asparagus
That stands like tiny sheaves of purple wheat
Ready to eat!
Huge and alluring hams and rashered swine
In circular repetitive design.
Gobbling turkeys and ducks in crates,
Pups in baskets and trays of eggs;
A birdman turns and gloomily relates
His woes to a girl with impossible legs.

When Batman first at Heaven's command
Stuck flag-staffs in this sacred strand ...
We'll leave all that to the local band

MY COUNTRY

DOROTHEA MACKELLAR
1885–1968

THE love of field and coppice,
Of green and shaded lanes,
Of ordered woods and gardens
Is running in your veins;
Strong love of grey-blue distance,
Brown streams and soft, dim skies—
I know but cannot share it,
My love is otherwise.

I love a sunburnt country,
A land of sweeping plains,
Of ragged mountain ranges,
Of droughts and flooding rains.
I love her far horizons,
I love her jewel sea,
Her beauty and her terror—
The wide brown land for me!

The stark white ringbarked forests,
All tragic to the moon,
The sapphire-misted mountains,
The hot gold hush of noon.
Green tangle of the brushes,
Where lithe lianas coil,
And orchids deck the tree-tops
And ferns the warm dark soil.

Core of my heart, my country!
Her pitiless blue sky,
When sick at heart, around us,
We see the cattle die—
But then the grey clouds gather,
And we can bless again
The drumming of an army,
The steady, soaking rain.

Core of my heart, my country!
Land of the Rainbow Gold,
For flood and fire and famine,
She pays us back threefold;
Over the thirsty paddocks,
Watch, after many days,
The filmy veil of greenness
That thickens as we gaze.

An opal-hearted country,
A wilful, lavish land—
All you who have not loved her,
You will not understand—
Though earth holds many splendours,
Wherever I may die,
I know to what brown country
My homing thoughts will fly.

AFTERNOON IN THE GARDEN

PUT the sun a thought below his prime   ETHEL ANDERSON
1883–1958
Shake the light across the apple-tree.
Let the shadow lengthen on the lawn.

Dent a dimple in a passing cloud.
Show a flight of field-fares on the wing.
Fling a wedge-tailed swallow in the height.

Run an azure ribbon through the wheat.
Where the willows linger by the stream
Dip their weeping tendrils in the blue.

Right beyond the hazy rim of sight
Swathe the amber grasses on the plain.
Lie the folded mountains in a ring.

Hark! The happy tap of bat and ball!
Beat of flitting feet across the court.
Laughter in the precincts of the sun.

See! bright figures flit between the trees!
One picks apples. Someone pats a horse.
Eight play tennis. (Let the Navy win.)

Time, you rogue, be still a little while,
Space, be kind, a moment keep your place,
Call King Joshua, let the sun stand still.

Good King Joshua's dead and turned to clay.
I, evoking pictures from the past,
Do again what lordly Joshua did.

THROUGH A PORTHOLE

LEON GELLERT
1892–1977

IF you could lie upon this berth, this berth whereon I lie,
If you could see a tiny peak uplift its tinged tusk,
If you could see the purple hills against the changing sky,
And see a shadowed pinnace lying in the dusk:
If you could see the sabre-moon shining on the deep:
You'd say the world was not unkind, but just a sleeping child,
You'd say the world had gone to sleep,
And while it slept
It smiled.

ANZAC COVE

LEON GELLERT

THERE'S a lonely stretch of hillocks:
There's a beach asleep and drear:
There's a battered broken fort beside the sea.
There are sunken, trampled graves;
And a little rotting pier:
And winding paths that wind unceasingly.

There's a torn and silent valley:
There's a tiny rivulet
With some blood upon the stones beside its mouth.
There are lines of buried bones:
There's an unpaid waiting debt:
There's a sound of gentle sobbing in the South.

ONLY GODS FORGET

I BELONG to nowhere—
Where do you belong?
Once I loved a lady
And put her in a song.
First we loved with laughter,
Then we loved with tears;
And that's the way a life goes—
Oh, the years and years!

I'm for sun and sea-light.
Do you seek them too?
If there's azure ever,
Then her eyes were blue.
Say there's precious glinting:
So her hair was gold.
Free the captive future,
For it's old now, old!

Love's a pretty poison.
Have you known it fail?
She and I are ghosts now,
Haunting an old tale,
Proud as thwarted marble,
Meek as mignonette.
Only the gods are happy:
Only gods forget!

FREDERICK T.
MACARTNEY
1887–1980

FIVE BELLS

TIME that is moved by little fidget wheels
Is not my Time, the flood that does not flow.
Between the double and the single bell
Of a ship's hour, between a round of bells
From the dark warship riding there below,
I have lived many lives, and this one life
Of Joe, long dead, who lives between five bells.

Deep and dissolving verticals of light
Ferry the falls of moonshine down. Five bells
Coldly rung out in a machine's voice. Night and water
Pour to one rip of darkness, the Harbour floats
In air, the Cross hangs upside down in water.

KENNETH SLESSOR
1901–1971

Why do I think of you, dead man, why thieve
These profitless lodgings from the flukes of thought
Anchored in Time? You have gone from earth,
Gone even from the meaning of a name;
Yet something's there, yet something forms its lips
And hits and cries against the ports of space,
Beating their sides to make its fury heard.

Are you shouting at me, dead man, squeezing your face
In agonies of speech on speechless panes?
Cry louder, beat the windows, bawl your name!

But I hear nothing, nothing . . . only bells,
Five bells, the bumpkin calculus of Time.
Your echoes die, your voice is dowsed by Life,
There's not a mouth can fly the pygmy strait—
Nothing except the memory of some bones
Long shoved away, and sucked away, in mud;
And unimportant things you might have done,
Or once I thought you did; but you forgot,
And all have now forgotten—looks and words
And slops of beer; your coat with buttons off,
Your gaunt chin and pricked eye, and raging tales
Of Irish kings and English perfidy,
And dirtier perfidy of publicans
Groaning to God from Darlinghurst.

                                        Five bells.

Then I saw the road, I heard the thunder
Tumble, and felt the talons of the rain
The night we came to Moorebank in slab-dark,
So dark you bore no body, had no face,
But a sheer voice that rattled out of air
(As now you'd cry if I could break the glass),
A voice that spoke beside me in the bush,
Loud for a breath or bitten off by wind,
Of Milton, melons, and the Rights of Man,
And blowing flutes, and how Tahitian girls
Are brown and angry-tongued, and Sydney girls
Are white and angry-tongued, or so you'd found.
But all I heard was words that didn't join,
So Milton became melons, melons girls,
And fifty mouths, it seemed, were out that night,
And in each tree an Ear was bending down,
Or something had just run, gone behind grass,
When, blank and bone-white, like a maniac's thought,
The naphtha-flash of lightning slit the sky,
Knifing the dark with deathly photographs.
There's not so many with so poor a purse
Or fierce a need, must fare by night like that,
Five miles in darkness on a country track,
But when you do, that's what you think.

                                              Five bells.

In Melbourne, your appetite had gone,
Your angers too; they had been leached away
By the soft archery of summer rains
And the sponge-paws of wetness, the slow damp
That stuck the leaves of living, snailed the mind,
And showed your bones, that had been sharp with rage,
The sodden ecstasies of rectitude.
I thought of what you'd written in faint ink,
Your journal with the sawn-off lock, that stayed behind
With other things you left, all without use,
All without meaning now, except a sign
That someone had been living who now was dead:
'At Labassa. Room 6 x 8
On top of the tower; because of this, very dark
And cold in winter. Everything has been stowed
Into this room—500 books all shapes
And colours, dealt across the floor
And over sills and on the laps of chairs;
Guns, photoes of many differant things
And differant curioes that I obtained. . . .'

In Sydney, by the spent aquarium-flare
Of penny gaslight on pink wallpaper,
We argued about blowing up the world,
But you were living backward, so each night
You crept a moment closer to the breast,
And they were living, all of them, those frames
And shapes of flesh that had perplexed your youth,
And most your father, the old man gone blind,
With fingers always round a fiddle's neck,
That graveyard mason whose fair monuments
And tablets cut with dreams of piety
Rest on the bosoms of a thousand men
Staked bone by bone, in quiet astonishment
At cargoes they had never thought to bear,
These funeral-cakes of sweet and sculptured stone.

Where have you gone? The tide is over you,
The turn of midnight water's over you,
As Time is over you, and mystery,
And memory, the flood that does not flow.
You have no suburb, like those easier dead
In private berths of dissolution laid—
The tide goes over, the waves ride over you
And let their shadows down like shining hair,
But they are Water; and the sea-pinks bend
Like lilies in your teeth, but they are Weed;
And you are only part of an Idea.
I felt the wet push its black thumb-balls in,
The night you died, I felt your eardrums crack,
And the short agony, the longer dream,
The Nothing that was neither long nor short;
But I was bound, and could not go that way,
But I was blind, and could not feel your hand.
If I could find an answer, could only find
Your meaning, or could say why you were here
Who now are gone, what purpose gave you breath
Or seized it back, might I not hear your voice?

I looked out of my window in the dark
At waves with diamond quills and combs of light
That arched their mackerel-backs and smacked the sand
In the moon's drench, that straight enormous glaze,
And ships far off asleep, and Harbour-buoys
Tossing their fireballs wearily each to each,
And tried to hear your voice, but all I heard
Was a boat's whistle, and the scraping squeal
Of seabirds' voices far away, and bells,
Five bells. Five bells coldly ringing out.

                                        Five bells.

COUNTRY TOWNS

COUNTRY towns, with your willows and squares,
And farmers bouncing on barrel mares
To public-houses of yellow wood
With '1860' over their doors,
And that mysterious race of Hogans
Which always keeps General Stores. . . .

At the School of Arts, a broadsheet lies
Sprayed with the sarcasm of flies:
'The Great Golightly Family
Of Entertainers Here Tonight'—
Dated a year and a half ago,
But left there, less from carelessness
Than from a wish to seem polite.

Verandas baked with musky sleep,
Mulberry faces dozing deep,
And dogs that lick the sunlight up
Like paste of gold—or, roused in vain
By far, mysterious buggy wheels,
Lower their ears, and drowse again. . . .

Country towns with your schooner bees,
And locusts burnt in the pepper-trees,
Drown me with syrups, arch your boughs,
Find me a bench, and let me snore,
Till, charged with ale and unconcern,
I'll think it's noon at half-past four!

KENNETH
SLESSOR

CAPTAIN DOBBIN

KENNETH SLESSOR

CAPTAIN DOBBIN, having retired from the South Seas
In the dumb tides of 1900, with a handful of shells,
A few poisoned arrows, a cask of pearls,
And five thousand pounds in the colonial funds,
Now sails the street in a brick villa, 'Laburnum Villa',
In whose blank windows the harbour hangs
Like a fog against the glass,
Golden and smoky, or stoned with a white glitter,
And boats go by, suspended in the pane,
Blue Funnel, Red Funnel, Messageries Maritimes,
Lugged down the port like sea-beasts taken alive
That scrape their bellies on sharp sands,
Of which particulars Captain Dobbin keeps
A ledger sticky with ink,
Entries of time and weather, state of the moon,
Nature of cargo and captain's name,
For some mysterious and awful purpose
Never divulged.
For at night, when the stars mock themselves with lanterns,
So late the chimes blow loud and faint
Like a hand shutting and unshutting over the bells,
Captain Dobbin, having observed from bed
The lights, like a great fiery snake, of the *Comorin*
Going to sea, will note the hour
For subsequent recording in his gazette.

But the sea is really closer to him than this,
Closer to him than a dead, lovely woman,
For he keeps bits of it, like old letters,
Salt tied up in bundles
Or pressed flat,
What you might call a lock of the sea's hair,
So Captain Dobbin keeps his dwarfed memento,
His urn-burial, a chest of mummied waves,
Gales fixed in print, and the sweet dangerous countries
Of shark and casuarina-tree,
Stolen and put in coloured maps,
Like a flask of seawater, or a bottled ship,
A schooner caught in a glass bottle;
But Captain Dobbin keeps them in books,
Crags of varnished leather
Pimply with gilt, by learned mariners
And masters of hydrostatics, or the childish tales
Of simple heroes, taken by Turks or dropsy.
So nightly he sails from shelf to shelf
Or to the quadrants, dangling with rusty screws,
Or the hanging-gardens of old charts,
So old they bear the authentic protractor-lines,
Traced in faint ink, as fine as Chinese hairs.

Over the flat and painted atlas-leaves
His reading glass would tremble,
Over the fathoms, pricked in tiny rows,
Water shelving to the coast.
Quietly the bone-rimmed lens would float
Till, through the glass, he felt the barbéd rush
Of bubbles foaming, spied the albicores,
The blue-finned admirals, heard the wind-swallowed cries
Of planters running on the beach
Who filched their swags of yams and ambergris,
Birds' nests and sandalwood, from pastures numbed
By the sun's yellow, too meek for honest theft;
But he, less delicate robber, climbed the walls,
Broke into dozing houses
Crammed with black bottles, marish wine
Crusty and salt-corroded, fading prints,
Sparkle-daubed almanacs and playing cards,
With rusty cannon, left by the French outside,
Half-buried in sand,
Even to the castle of Queen Pomaree
In the Yankee's footsteps, and found her throne-room piled
With golden candelabras, mildewed swords,
Guitars and fowling-pieces, tossed in heaps
With greasy cakes and flung-down calabashes.

Then Captain Dobbin's eye,
That eye of wild and wispy scudding blue,
Voluptuously prying, would light up
Like mica scratched by gully-suns,
And he would be fearful to look upon
And shattering in his conversation;
Nor would he tolerate the harmless chanty,
No *Shenandoah*, or the dainty mew
That landsmen offer in a silver dish
To Neptune, sung to pianos in candlelight.
Of these he spoke in scorn,
For there was but one way of singing *Stormalong*,
He said, and that was not really singing,
But howling, rather—shrieked in the wind's jaws
By furious men; not tinkled in drawing-rooms
By lap-dogs in clean shirts.
And, at these words,
The galleries of photographs, men with rich beards,
Pea-jackets and brass buttons, with folded arms,
Would scowl approval, for they were shipmates, too,
Companions of no cruise by reading-glass,
But fellows of storm and honey from the past—
'The Charlotte, Java, '93,'
'Knuckle and Fred at Port au Prince,'
'William in his New Rig,'
Even that notorious scoundrel, Captain Baggs,
Who, as all knew, owed Dobbin Twenty Pounds
Lost at fair cribbage, but he never paid,
Or paid 'with the slack of the tops'l sheets'
As Captain Dobbin frequently expressed it.

There were their faces, grilled a trifle now,
Cigar-hued in various spots
By the brown breath of sodium-eating years,
On quarterdecks long burnt to the water's edge,
A resurrection of the dead by chemicals.
And the voyages they had made,
Their labours in a country of water,
Were they not marked by inadequate lines
On charts tied up like skins in a rack?
Or his own Odysseys, his lonely travels,
His trading days, an autobiography
Of angles and triangles and lozenges
Ruled tack by tack across the sheet,
That with a single scratch expressed the stars,
Merak and Alamak and Alpherat,
The wind, the moon, the sun, the clambering sea,
Sails bleached with light, salt in the eyes,

Bamboos and Tahiti oranges,
From some forgotten countless day,
One foundered day from a forgotten month,
A year sucked quietly from the blood,
Dead with the rest, remembered by no more
Than a scratch on a dry chart—
Or when the return grew too choking bitter-sweet
And laburnum-berries manifestly tossed
Beyond the window, not the fabulous leaves
Of Hotoo or canoe-tree or palmetto,
There were the wanderings of other keels,
Magellan, Bougainville and Cook,
Who found no greater a memorial
Than footprints over a lithograph.

For Cook he worshipped, that captain with the sad
And fine white face, who never lost a man
Or flinched a peril; and of Bougainville
He spoke with graceful courtesy, as a rival
To whom the honours of the hunting-field
Must be accorded. Not so with the Spaniard,
Sebastian Juan del Cano, at whom he sneered
Openly, calling him a fool of fortune
Blown to a sailors' abbey by chance winds
And blindfold currents, who slept in a fine cabin,
Blundered through five degrees of latitude,
Was bullied by mutineers a hundred more,
And woke and found himself across the world.

Coldly in the window,
Like a fog rubbed up and down the glass
The harbour, bony with mist
And ropes of water, glittered; and the blind tide
That crawls it knows not where, nor for what gain,
Pushed its drowned shoulders against the wheel,
Against the wheel of the mill.
Flowers rocked far down
And white, dead bodies that were anchored there
In marshes of spent light.
Blue Funnel, Red Funnel,
The ships went over them, and bells in engine-rooms
Cried to their bowels of flaring oil,
And stokers groaned and sweated with burnt skins,
Clawed to their shovels.
But quietly in his room,
In his little cemetery of sweet essences
With fond memorial-stones and lines of grace,
Captain Dobbin went on reading about the sea.

POLARITIES

KENNETH
SLESSOR

SOMETIMES she is like sherry, like the sun through a vessel of glass,
Like light through an oriel window in a room of yellow wood;
Sometimes she is the colour of lions, of sand in the fire of noon,
Sometimes as bruised with shadows as the afternoon.

Sometimes she moves like rivers, sometimes like trees;
Or tranced and fixed like South Pole silences;
Sometimes she is beauty, sometimes fury, sometimes neither,
Sometimes nothing, drained of meaning, null as water.

Sometimes, when she makes pea-soup or plays me Schumann,
I love her one way; sometimes I love her another
More disturbing way when she opens her mouth in the dark;
Sometimes I like her with camellias, sometimes with a parsley-stalk,
Sometimes I like her swimming in a mirror on the wall;
Sometimes I don't like her at all.

SLEEP

KENNETH
SLESSOR

DO YOU give yourself to me utterly,
    Body and no-body, flesh and no-flesh,
Not as a fugitive, blindly or bitterly,
    But as a child might, with no other wish?
Yes, utterly.

Then I shall bear you down my estuary,
Carry you and ferry you to burial mysteriously,
Take you and receive you,
Consume you, engulf you,
In the huge cave, my belly, lave you
With huger waves continually.

And you shall cling and clamber there
And slumber there, in that dumb chamber,
Beat with my blood's beat, hear my heart move
Blindly in bones that ride above you,
Delve in my flesh, dissolved and bedded,
Through viewless valves embodied so—

Till daylight, the expulsion and awakening,
    The riving and the driving forth,
Life with remorseless forceps beckoning—
    Pangs and betrayal of harsh birth.

METEMPSYCHOSIS

KENNETH
SLESSOR

SUDDENLY to become John Benbow, walking down William Street
With a tin trunk and a five-pound note, looking for a place to eat,
And a peajacket the colour of a shark's behind
That a Jew might buy in the morning....

To fry potatoes (God save us!) if you feel inclined,
Or to kiss the landlady's daughter, and no one mind,
In a peel-papered bedroom with a whistling jet
And a picture of the Holy Virgin....

Wake in a shaggy bale of blankets with a fished-up cigarette,
Picking over 'Turfbird's Tattle' for a Saturday morning bet,
With a bottle in the wardrobe easy to reach
And a blast of onions from the landing....

Tattooed with foreign ladies' tokens, a heart and dagger each,
In places that make the delicate female inquirer screech,
And over a chest smoky with gunpowder-blue—
Behold!—a mermaid piping through a coach-horn!

Banjo-playing, firing off guns, and other momentous things to do,
Such as blowing through peashooters at hawkers to improve the view—

Suddenly paid-off and forgotten in Woolloomooloo....

Suddenly to become John Benbow....

BEACH BURIAL

KENNETH
SLESSOR

SOFTLY and humbly to the Gulf of Arabs
The convoys of dead sailors come;
At night they sway and wander in the waters far under,
But morning rolls them in the foam.

Between the sob and clubbing of the gunfire
Someone, it seems, has time for this,
To pluck them from the shallows and bury them in burrows
And tread the sand upon their nakedness;

And each cross, the driven stake of tidewood,
Bears the last signature of men,
Written with such perplexity, with such bewildered pity,
The words choke as they begin—

'*Unknown seaman*'—the ghostly pencil
Wavers and fades, the purple drips,
The breath of the wet season has washed their inscriptions
As blue as drowned men's lips,

Dead seamen, gone in search of the same landfall,
Whether as enemies they fought,
Or fought with us, or neither; the sand joins them together,
Enlisted on the other front.

El Alamein.

LEGEND

ROBERT D.
FitzGERALD
1902–1987

NOW Doctor Bell's portrait is hung in tall Trinity
(so one from far Erin was telling me once)
yet we'll pass him by quickly, his Laws, his Divinity,
or whatever so famed him and finally framed him
up there to be gaped at by scholar and dunce.
Since facts are so scanty to prop up my story,
on all I can find I'm committed to dwell,
but, regarding the Doctor, his chief claim to glory
is that he was the father of Mary Ann Bell.

Were I scribe or historian, sure I could take you
to those days and Dublin and welcome enough,
using brogue in your ears for the magic to make you
smell turf and fine horses, hear jigs and discourses,
see wigs and bright waistcoats, drink porter, take snuff;
as it is—well, imagine a molten variety
of all kinds of gentry and heroes pell-mell,
and know that the toast of that crazy society
and queen of the city was Mary Ann Bell.

There's a miniature somewhere that shows her: beguiling,
bright-featured, red-lipped, and her eyes full of fun—
brown eyes like twin rogues for the dancing and smiling,
matching curls, a rich jumble that laughing winds tumble
and fingers must itch for to tease one by one.

A flirt?—An you will; but too kind to wound greatly.
A wit?—First and foremost, and a madcap as well—
Oh, bedad, the ould town wouldn't strut so sedately
what with pranks and gay doings of Mary Ann Bell!

And my grandfather's father was young, rich and merry,
(it was prior to the Famine: I write in a tent)
and what should he do to be stuck down in Kerry,
with the spring so exciting, the world so inviting,
and gold in his pocket to pay as he went?
So up from Tralee for a spree in the city
to stretch out the cramps—just a lark and a spell,
then a cheery goodbye to the kind girls and pretty;
but I doubt if he'd reckoned on Mary Ann Bell.

See him then, one fine morning, at rest a brief minute
at his club's upstair window, a glass by his side,
well-content to be watching the world and what's in it:
the crowds and the muddles, the cobbles and puddles—
Smash, tumbler! Devil take him, but what has he spied?
'Hey, Steward, Bartender, Gossoon . . . plague upon her,
she's gone . . . there she is! Who's that girl? Death and Hell!
that's the woman I'll marry or none.' . . . 'Save your Honour!
'tis the Doctor's own daughter, Miss Mary Ann Bell.'

No more. That's the tale; that's the little it's built on. . . .
What else? Just some books that she brought overseas,
some books of her schooldays, a Gray and a Milton,
with her name in the covers—but her tale and her lover's,
and the dance that she led him, not a word about these;
and an Aunt—luck be hers!—from a time dim and shady
can recall, when so tiny she hardly could tell,
being taken to visit a very old lady
who she thinks was her grandmother—Mary Ann Bell.

Here alone in the bush and with no one to cheer me
I'll be thinking this evening of days drifted on
and of all the brave past: should the White Knight ride near me,
why! my heart it will name him, my blood will acclaim him,
nor doubt on my stirring and waking anon.
For the rest, there's one ghost less aghast and astounding;
deceits of false Death she is strong to dispel;
should she come to me now through the dark years abounding—
Good night and most welcome . . . dear Mary Ann Bell.

THE WIND AT YOUR DOOR

(*To Mary Gilmore*)

ROBERT D.
FitzGERALD

MY ancestor was called on to go out—
a medical man, and one such must by law
wait in attendance on the pampered knout
and lend his countenance to what he saw,
lest the pet, patting with too bared a claw,
be judged a clumsy pussy. Bitter and hard,
see, as I see him, in that jailhouse yard.

Or see my thought of him: though time may keep
elsewhere tradition or a portrait still,
I would not feel under his cloak of sleep
if beard there or smooth chin, just to fulfil
some canon of precision. Good or ill
his blood's my own; and scratching in his grave
could find me more than I might wish to have.

Let him then be much of the middle style
of height and colouring; let his hair be dark
and his eyes green; and for that slit, the smile
that seemed inhuman, have it cruel and stark,
but grant it could be too the ironic mark
of all caught in the system—who the most,
the doctor or the flesh twined round that post?

There was a high wind blowing on that day;
for one who would not watch, but looked aside,
said that when twice he turned it blew his way
splashes of blood and strips of human hide
shaken out from the lashes that were plied
by one right-handed, one left-handed tough,
sweating at this paid task, and skilled enough.

That wind blows to your door down all these years.
Have you not known it when some breath you drew
tasted of blood? Your comfort is in arrears
of just thanks to a savagery tamed in you
only as subtler fears may serve in lieu
of thong and noose—old savagery which has built
your world and laws out of the lives it spilt.

For what was jailyard widens and takes in
my country. Fifty paces of stamped earth
stretch; and grey walls retreat and grow so thin
that towns show through and clearings—new raw birth
which burst from handcuffs—and free hands go forth
to win tomorrow's harvest from a vast
ploughland—the fifty paces of that past.

But see it through a window barred across,
from cells this side, facing the outer gate
which shuts on freedom, opens on its loss
in a flat wall. Look left now through the grate
at buildings like more walls, roofed with grey slate
or hollowed in the thickness of laid stone
each side the court where the crowd stands this noon.

One there with the officials, thick of build,
not stout, say burly (so this obstinate man
ghosts in the eyes) is he whom enemies killed
(as I was taught) because the monopolist clan
found him a grit in their smooth-turning plan,
too loyally active on behalf of Bligh.
So he got lost; and history passed him by.

But now he buttons his long coat against
the biting gusts, or as a gesture of mind,
habitual; as if to keep him fenced
from stabs of slander sticking him from behind,
sped by the schemers never far to find
in faction, where approval from one source
damns in another clubroom as of course.

This man had Hunter's confidence, King's praise;
and settlers on the starving Hawkesbury banks
recalled through twilight drifting across their days
the doctor's fee of little more than thanks
so often; and how sent by their squeezed ranks
he put their case in London. I find I lack
the hateful paint to daub him wholly black.

Perhaps my life replies to his too much
through veiling generations dropped between.
My weakness here, resentments there, may touch
old motives and explain them, till I lean
to the forgiveness I must hope may clean
my own shortcomings; since no man can live
in his own sight if it will not forgive.

Certainly I must own him whether or not
it be my will. I was made understand
this much when once, marking a freehold lot,
my papers suddenly told me it was land
granted to Martin Mason. I felt his hand
heavily on my shoulder, and knew what coil
binds life to life through bodies, and soul to soil.

There, over to one corner, a bony group
of prisoners waits; and each shall be in turn
tied by his own arms in a human loop
about the post, with his back bared to learn
the price of seeking freedom. So they earn
three hundred rippling stripes apiece, as set
by the law's mathematics against the debt.

These are the Irish batch of Castle Hill,
rebels and mutineers, my countrymen
twice over: first, because of those to till
my birthplace first, hack roads, raise roofs; and then
because their older land time and again
enrolls me through my forbears; and I claim
as origin that threshold whence we came.

One sufferer had my surname, and thereto
'Maurice', which added up to history once;
an ignorant dolt, no doubt, for all that crew
was tenantry. The breed of clod and dunce
makes patriots and true men: could I announce
that Maurice as my kin I say aloud
I'd take his irons as heraldry, and be proud.

Maurice is at the post. Its music lulls,
one hundred lashes done. If backbone shows
then play the tune on buttocks! But feel his pulse;
that's what a doctor's for; and if it goes
lamely, then dose it with these purging blows—
which have not made him moan; though, writhing there,
'Let my neck be,' he says, 'and flog me fair.'

One hundred lashes more, then rest the flail.
What says the doctor now? 'This dog won't yelp;
he'll tire you out before you'll see him fail;
here's strength to spare; go on!' Ay, pound to pulp;
yet when you've done he'll walk without your help,
and knock down guards who'd carry him being bid,
and sing no song of where the pikes are hid.

It would be well if I could find, removed
through generations back—who knows how far?—
more than a surname's thickness as a proved
bridge with that man's foundations. I need some star
of courage from his firmament, a bar
against surrenders: faith. All trials are less
than rain-blacked wind tells of that old distress.

Yet I can live with Mason. What is told,
and what my heart knows of his heart, can sort
much truth from falsehood, much there that I hold
good clearly or good clouded by report;
and for things bad, ill grows where ills resort:
they were bad times. None know what in his place
they might have done. I've my own faults to face.

IMPERIAL ADAM

IMPERIAL ADAM, naked in the dew,
Felt his brown flanks and found the rib was gone.
Puzzled he turned and saw where, two and two,
The mighty spoor of Jahweh marked the lawn.

A.D. HOPE
1907–

Then he remembered through mysterious sleep
The surgeon fingers probing at the bone,
The voice so far away, so rich and deep:
'It is not good for him to live alone.'

Turning once more he found Man's counterpart
In tender parody breathing at his side.
He knew her at first sight, he knew by heart
Her allegory of sense unsatisfied.

The pawpaw drooped its golden breasts above
Less generous than the honey of her flesh;
The innocent sunlight showed the place of love;
The dew on its dark hairs winked crisp and fresh.

This plump gourd severed from his virile root,
She promised on the turf of Paradise
Delicious pulp of the forbidden fruit;
Sly as the snake she loosed her sinuous thighs,

And waking, smiled up at him from the grass;
Her breasts rose softly and he heard her sigh—
From all the beasts whose pleasant task it was
In Eden to increase and multiply

Adam had learned the jolly deed of kind:
He took her in his arms and there and then,
Like the clean beasts, embracing from behind,
Began in joy to found the breed of men.

Then from the spurt of seed within her broke
Her terrible and triumphant female cry,
Split upward by the sexual lightning stroke.
It was the beasts now who stood watching by:

The gravid elephant, the calving hind,
The breeding bitch, the she-ape big with young
Were the first gentle midwives of mankind;
The teeming lioness rasped her with her tongue;

The proud vicuña nuzzled her as she slept
Lax on the grass; and Adam watching too
Saw how her dumb breasts at their ripening wept,
The great pod of her belly swelled and grew,

And saw its water break, and saw, in fear,
Its quaking muscles in the act of birth,
Between her legs a pigmy face appear,
And the first murderer lay upon the earth.

from SONNETS TO BAUDELAIRE

VII

WHY women should outlive men, the wits aver,   A.D. HOPE
Is that the hazards that confront the human
Give men one more to face than women: Woman!
She is the earth: he digs his grave in her,
The insatiate sea that drowns the tallest mast,
The gorgon sky that stares his dreams to stone,
The mould that quietly eats him to the bone,
The long, long night in which he sleeps at last.

Was it your luck or genius to discover
That living is this voyage among the dead,
That poets have one task: to tell the brave
How all his victories must be lost in bed
And in the womb say to each unborn lover:
The hand that rocks the cradle rules the grave.

AUSTRALIA

A.D. HOPE

A NATION of trees, drab green and desolate grey
In the field uniform of modern wars,
Darkens her hills, those endless, outstretched paws
Of Sphinx demolished or stone lion worn away.

They call her a young country, but they lie:
She is the last of lands, the emptiest,
A woman beyond her change of life, a breast
Still tender but within the womb is dry.

Without songs, architecture, history:
The emotions and superstitions of younger lands,
Her rivers of water drown among inland sands,
The river of her immense stupidity

Floods her monotonous tribes from Cairns to Perth.
In them at last the ultimate men arrive
Whose boast is not: 'We live' but 'We survive',
A type who will inhabit the dying earth.

And her five cities, like five teeming sores,
Each drains her: a vast parasite robber-state
Where second-hand Europeans pullulate
Timidly on the edge of alien shores.

Yet there are some like me turn gladly home.
From the lush jungle of modern thought, to find
The Arabian desert of the human mind,
Hoping, if still from the deserts the prophets come,

Such savage and scarlet as no green hills dare
Springs in that waste, some spirit which escapes
The learned doubt, the chatter of cultured apes
Which is called civilisation over there.

CHORALE

Often had I found her fair;   A.D. HOPE
Most when to my bed she came,
Naked as the moving air,
Slender, walking like a flame.
In that grace I sink and drown:
Opening like the liquid wave
To my touch she laid her down,
Drew me to her crystal cave.
   Love me ever, love me long—
   Was the burden of her song.

All divisions vanish there;
Now her eyes grow dark and still;
Now I feel the living air
With contending thunder fill;
Hear the shuddering cry begin,
Feel the heart leap in her breast,
And her moving loins within
Clasp their strong, rejoicing guest.
   Love me now, O now, O long!
   Is the burden of her song.

Now the wave recedes and dies;
Dancing fires descend the hill;
Blessed spirits from our eyes
Gaze in wonder and are still.
Yes, our wondering spirits come
From their timeless anguish freed:
Yet within they hear the womb
Sighing for the wasted seed.
   Love may not delay too long—
   Is the burden of their song.

THE HOUSE OF GOD

A.D. HOPE

MORNING SERVICE! parson preaches;
People all confess their sins:
God's domesticated creatures
Twine and rub against his shins;

Tails erect and whiskers pricking,
Sleeking down their Sunday fur,
Though demure, alive and kicking,
All in unison they purr:

'Lord we praise Thee; hear us Master!
Feed and comfort, stroke and bless!
And not too severely cast a
Glance upon our trespasses:

Yesterday we were not able
To resist that piece of fish
Left upon the kitchen table
While You went to fetch the dish;

Twice this week a scrap with Rover;
Once, at least, we missed a rat;
And we *do* regret, Jehovah,
Having kittens in Your hat!

Sexual noises in the garden,
Smelly patches in the hall—
Hear us, Lord, absolve and pardon,
We are human after all!'

Home at last from work in Heaven,
This is all the rest God gets;
Gladly for one day in seven
He relaxes with His pet.

Looking down He smiles and ponders,
Thinks of something extra nice:
From His beard, O Joy, O wonders!
Falls a shower of little mice.

THE DEATH OF THE BIRD

FOR EVERY BIRD there is this last migration: A.D. HOPE
Once more the cooling year kindles her heart;
With a warm passage to the summer station
Love pricks the course in lights across the chart.

Year after year a speck on the map, divided
By a whole hemisphere, summons her to come;
Season after season, sure and safely guided,
Going away she is also coming home.

And being home, memory becomes a passion
With which she feeds her brood and straws her nest,
Aware of ghosts that haunt the heart's possession
And exiled love mourning within the breast.

The sands are green with a mirage of valleys;
The palm-tree casts a shadow not its own;
Down the long architrave of temple or palace
Blows a cool air from moorland scarps of stone.

And day by day the whisper of love grows stronger;
That delicate voice, more urgent with despair,
Custom and fear constraining her no longer,
Drives her at last on the waste leagues of air.

A vanishing speck in those inane dominions,
Single and frail, uncertain of her place,
Alone in the bright host of her companions,
Lost in the blue unfriendliness of space,

She feels it close now, the appointed season:
The invisible thread is broken as she flies;
Suddenly, without warning, without reason,
The guiding spark of instinct winks and dies.

Try as she will, the trackless world delivers
No way, the wilderness of light no sign,
The immense and complex map of hills and rivers
Mocks her small wisdom with its vast design.

And darkness rises from the eastern valleys,
And the winds buffet her with their hungry breath,
And the great earth, with neither grief nor malice,
Receives the tiny burden of her death.

NATIVE BORN

EVE LANGLEY
1908–1974

IN a white gully among fungus red
Where serpent logs lay hissing at the air,
I found a kangaroo. Tall, dewy, dead,
So like a woman, she lay silent there,
Her ivory hands, black-nailed, crossed on her breast,
Her skin of sun and moon hues, fallen cold.
Her brown eyes lay like rivers come to rest
And death had made her black mouth harsh and old.
Beside her in the ashes I sat deep
And mourned for her, but had no native song
To flatter death, while down the ploughlands steep
Dark young Camelli whistled loud and long,
'Love, liberty and Italy are all.'
Broad golden was his breast against the sun.
I saw his wattle whip rise high and fall
Across the slim mare's flanks, and one by one
She drew the furrows after her as he
Flapped like a gull behind her, climbing high,
Chanting his oaths and lashing soundingly,
While from the mare came once a blowing sigh.
The dew upon the kangaroo's white side
Had melted. Time was whirling high around,
Like the thin woomera, and from heaven wide
He, the bull-roarer, made continuous sound.
Incarnate, lay my country by my hand:
Her long hot days, bushfires and speaking rains,
Her mornings of opal and the copper band
Of smoke around the sunlight on the plains.
Globed in fire bodies the meat-ants ran
To taste her flesh and linked us as we lay,
For ever Australian, listening to a man
From careless Italy, swearing at our day.
When, golden-lipped, the eaglehawks came down
Hissing and whistling to eat of lovely her,
And the blowflies with their shields of purple brown
Plied hatching to and fro across her fur,
I burnt her with the logs, and stood all day
Among the ashes, pressing home the flame
Till woman, logs and dreams were scorched away,
And native with night, that land from where they came.

THE COMMERCIAL TRAVELLER'S WIFE

RONALD McCUAIG
1908–1993

I'M LIVING with a commercial traveller.
He's away, most of the time.
Most I see of him's his wife; as for her:
I'm just home from a show,
And there I am undressing, in my shirt.
I hear midnight chime,
And up flares the curtain at the window.
The door's opened. It's Gert—
That's the wife. Her hair's hanging down.
She's only got her nightgown
Blowing up against her in the wind.
She's fat, and getting fatter.
I said, 'What's the matter?'
'Jack,' she said, 'now's your chance.'
'What chance?' I said. 'You out of your mind?'
She goes over to the bed.
I grab my pants.
'That's enough of that,' I said. 'Now go on; you get out.'
'But Jack,' she said, 'don't you love me?'
'I don't know what you're talking about,'
I said. 'Besides, Jim—
What about him?'
'Yes; Jim,' she said; 'there's always Jim, but he's
Always away. And you don't know
What it's like. I can't stand it. And anyhow,
Jack, don't you want me?'
'Oh, don't be an ass,'
I said. 'Look at yourself in the glass.'
She faced the mirror where she stood
And sort of stiffened there.
Her eyes went still as knots in a bit of wood,
And it all seemed to sigh out of her:
'All right,' she said. 'All right, all right, good night',
As though she didn't know if I heard,
And shuffled out without another word.

Well, I was tired. I went to bed and slept.
In the morning
I thought I'd dreamt the whole thing,
But, at breakfast, I could have wept:
Poor Gert, clattering the dishes
With a dead sort of face
Like a fish's.
I'll have to get a new place.
I'm going out today to have a look.
Trouble is, she's a marvellous cook.

LOVE ME AND NEVER LEAVE ME

LOVE ME, and never leave me,   RONALD McCUAIG
Love, nor ever deceive me,
And I shall always bless you
If I may undress you:
  This I heard a lover say
  To his sweetheart where they lay.

He, though he did undress her,
Did not always bless her;
She, though she would not leave him,
Often did deceive him;
  Yet they loved, and when they died
  They were buried side by side.

THE LETTER

RONALD McCUAIG

DEAR, as I write and think of you,
And several other people too,
The flooring of the flat above,
Creaking with aged, illicit love,
Reminds me, when I was trying to write
These very words the other night,
He spoke from three till half past four
Merely repeating she was a whore.
The boy below has just begun
To find it not precisely fun;
The trouble is, as he explained
The Thursday evening when it rained
To a judicial prig of a friend
(I thought their talk would never end),
The girl is really not the kind
Of girl he really had in mind.
But still he keeps her on, for fear
Of hurting her. And now I hear
The lovely girl who loves to dwell,
And dwells to love, across the well,
Saying, since he is married, he
Should be considerate, in that she

Is taking risks. As for the rent,
She fears, it has been otherwise spent.
The opposite flat is dark and dumb,
Yet I feel certain he will come
Home to his love as drunk as ever
And, in a slowly rising fever,
Noting the whisky bottle gone,
Will trip and curse and stumble on
Into the bathroom, pull the chain,
Fumble the cabinet, curse again;
Will ask the slut where she has hid
His toothbrush; blunder back to bed,
Find his pyjamas tied in knots
And give her, as he puts it, what's
Coming to her. She won't escape
Her deeply meditated rape.
But I must write of love, and all
That once was high, and had a fall,
And how I burn; and I confess
It gives me little happiness:
Encompassed so, my rooms become
A kind of lovers' vacuum,
Dear, as I write, and ache for you,
And dream of all that we could do
If these delights thy mind might move
To live with me and be my love.

THE PASSIONATE CLERK TO HIS LOVE

LIVE with me; be my wife;   RONALD McCUAIG
We'll end flirtations;
You'll find it a slow life,
But with compensations.

And we'll get a flat
Of two witty
Rooms, a bath and kitchenette,
High over the city,

Where, in the evening
When dinner's over,
We'll wash up everything
And I'll be your lover,

And tie knot after knot
Of flesh aching,
Then cut the lot,
And without waking

You'll sleep till sunrise,
And we'll rise early,
And through each other's eyes
We'll see things clearly,

And never be dismayed
To find them shoddy,
And never be afraid
Of anybody;

And on Sunday afternoon
About three or four
I'll play the gramophone
While you pour

Afternoon tea
Into my soul,
And bending to me
With the sugar-bowl

You'll be a priestess
Swaying the sheathing
Of a flower-stained dress
With even breathing,

And in this atmosphere
Charmed from your breast
Half we shall hear
And feel the rest

As we talk scandal and
A kind of wit
We alone understand,
Or maybe just sit

Quiet while the clock chimes
Patient tomorrows,
And smile sometimes
At old sorrows.

THE TRAIN IN THE NIGHT

WHO hears in the night
The train's sharp whistle
Cut off the top
Of chickweed and thistle
Flutter the birds
That drowse in the willow
And rouse the boy
From his frosty pillow?

Who hears in the night
The wheels that mutter
Past mill and grave
Past barn and shutter
Is the boy for whom
All time unravels
Who'll swallow the wind
And go on his travels.

ELIZABETH RIDDELL
1909–

WAKEFUL IN THE TOWNSHIP

ELIZABETH RIDDELL

BARKS the melancholy dog,
Swims in the stream the shadowy fish.
Who would live in a country town
If they had their wish?

When the sun comes hurrying up
I will take the circus train
That cries, cries once in the night
And then not again.

In the stream the shadowy fish
Sleeps below the sleeping fly.
Many around me straitly sleep
But not I.

Near my window a drowsy bird
Flickers its feathers against the thorn.
Around the township's single light
My people die and are born.

I will join the circus train
For mangy leopard and tinsel girl
And the trotting horses' great white haunches
Whiter than a pearl.

When to the dark blue mountains
My captive pigeons flew
I'd no heart to lure them back
With wheat upon the dew.

When the dog at morning
Whines upon the frost
I shall be in another place.
Lost, lost, lost.

HERBERT BADHAM

SUBURBAN SONG

ELIZABETH RIDDELL

NOW all the dogs with folded paws
Stare at the lowering sky.
This is the hour when women hear
Their lives go ticking by.

The baker's horse with rattling hooves
Upon the windy hill
Mocks the thunder in the heart
Of women sitting still.

The poppies in the garden turn
Their faces to the sand
And tears upon the sewing fall
And on the stranger's hand.

Flap flap the washing flies
To meet the starting hail.
Close the door on love and hang
The key upon the nail.

SPACE
from 'Christopher Columbus'

COLUMBUS looks towards the New World,
the sea is flat and nothing breaks the rim
of the world's disc;
he takes the sphere with him.

Day into night the same, the only change
the living variation at the core
of this man's universe;
and silent on the silver ship he broods.

Red gouts of weed, and skimming fish, to crack
the stupefying emptiness of sea,
night, and the unimpassioned gaze of stars. . . .

And God be praised for the compass, oaths
bawled in the fo'c'sle,
broken heads and wine,
song and guitars,

the tramp of boots,
the wash and whip of brine.

WILLIAM
HART-SMITH
1911–1990

157

THE WATERSPOUT
from 'Christopher Columbus'

WILLIAM
HART-SMITH

FORWARD lay sunlight silver on the sea;
behind, the darkness of a cavern;
from it a wind, and cloud-arms over the wind
towards the ship.

They saw a rope of cloud twist down
and a tongue of sea drawn up as the whirlwind blew,
drinking the ocean up in a plume of foam.
'Santa Maria, look!... how far is home!'

And some knelt down, some checked their blasphemy,
eyes wide and mouths wide, dumb.
Columbus watching, touched his brow and breast.
'Christ be with us!' he said, as the ship sped west.

BOOMERANG

WILLIAM
HART-SMITH

BEHOLD! wood into bird and bird to wood again.
A brown-winged bird from the hand of a brown man.

Elbow of wood from flexed elbow of bone
to a swift hawk has amazingly grown

that mounts the sky, sun in its wings,
up, up, over the far tree fluttering

where it turns as if seized with doubt in the air.
Looks back down to the man carved there

and, afraid of the gift of sudden blood,
beats back to his hand and melts once more to wood.

JOHN GLOVER

SHEEP

THEY TEETER with an inane care among the skewbald stones,
plead each other's prison names in grey bewildered tones
and trust their faces—powdered pale and bilious with unease—
against the wires of the fence, like haunted internees:
'Here and here, man, m - a - a - n.'

From off the withers of the slopes the traitor clouds have fled
guerrilla wind's philippic and the sun's assault of red;
the mincing, gelded, godless tribe bleats anguish in a haze
of sacrificial tulles of dust and rings of feckless days:
'Here and here, man, m - a -a - n.'

Disquieted, illusionless, from jibbahs stuck with twigs,
the visors carved with grieving mourn beneath judicial wigs;
upon their brows in horny pride Ionic head-dress coils,
while eyes, opaque with hankering, roll in their timid oils:
'Here and here, man, m - a - a - n.'

About them die the sun-scarred miles, the dams of muddy milk,
the fences sutured on mirage, the ranges ripped from silk;
before them, from the gravel road, their murderer assesses,
their Judas peers at haughty teeth and parts their clumsy dresses:
'Here and here, man, m - a - a - n.'

HAL PORTER
1911–1984

THE MARRIED COUPLE

HAL PORTER

THEY RENDERED what was due, not one tithe more:
The grandee manner, the unriven mind;
Bred enough proper sons—to that resigned
More to prove usual than to hint desire.

Not tied by love but land, they aged while young
From public wearing, without smiles or frowns,
Ancestral leavings, wealth, those weighty crowns—
She queen of caution, he a wary king.

The sons, the world, admired—and ceased there
As sensing warmth's withdrawal, coolness meant
To show them free of unforeseen event,
Perfected, some hard absence at the core.

Their smiles resembled others', yet not quite:
Neither to palliate nor patronise
Theirs fell just short. Locked doors behind those eyes
Hid shut-mouth captives overspent with hate.

Alone in private night, teeth bared to wound,
They balked; like turnkeys, granted hate no pass,
Loving like mimics in a looking-glass,
From themselves severed, to each other blind.

Their statues waltzed at balls, or side by side
Spanked in a landau, letting all perceive
Her hand the seeming heart upon his sleeve—
Rift never left for rumour to intrude.

To lookers-on such warranties of love
Seemed, in their keeping, love's own monument
Whose gloss the years could never dull or dent.
He died. All wondered that she still could live.

She lived for years, elusive, duty done,
Sealed in equivocation. At the last,
Inspired to break truth's long fatiguing fast,
She cried, 'I hate him. Bury me alone.'

To this insuavity sons must sham deaf.
They buried her beside him. Someone came
To carve a stone with decades of her fame,
And in two words exposed it: *Loving Wife.*

Within a chiselled rose-wreath hand clasps hand,
Stone trapped in stone, the costly roses stone.
Below, teeth bared, they lie once more alone,
From themselves severed, to each other blind.

FRIENDSHIP AND LOVE

WHAT was it that you said?—'Friendship, not love,
shall tie us close together'—bodily friendship
you meant; but you and night and wine betrayed me
tenderly into this. But now, being womanly,
out of the summer of our genial bodies
you reap uneasy yearning when all's over—
the sharp-edged sweet fruit of wild regret,
that angry hunger raging in you still.

KENNETH
MACKENZIE
1913–1955

What shall I do? We counted our betrayals
and cancelled them with reason: said, Thus long
and after that, no longer, may we lie
together and about our fierce encounter.
Yet in your distant voice desire is mixed now
with something more than friendship and memory.
I would not want that love should spring from this—
from nights of sleep and pleasure ended lately,
ended on oath, god-bless-you, and one kiss
to seal the bargain. I can love no more,
and no more want it, turning always backward
into the past, where love, being solitary,
is perfect. If you love me, do not say so
but hold your peace: for I cannot love you
and so am not deserving of your love
nor its true object. Be content, content
to wait upon the future and its chances
of our superb resumption—when, I know not,
but be assured I shall not fail you there.
Count the dark nights, and count the shining days,
and in their noble order and declension
let you find comfort, if your heart is troubled
by what we said our union would not mean.
Let your strong body outgrow memory
of all it suffered in the summer nights
whose heat for some great hours we both contained.
Let winter's cool embrace, and sleep, and laughter
and food and labour purge you of me now,
so finally that, if we go again,
your first low cry of passionate surprise
will be your first indeed.
                    All this I beg
in your name and my own: friendship, not love,
has been our bond. So let it be for ever.

HEAT

'WELL, this is where I go down to the river,'
the traveller with me said, and turned aside
out of the burnt road, through the black trees
spiking the slope, and went down, and never
came back into the heat from water's ease
in which he swooned, in cool joy, and died.

Often since then, in brutal days of summer
I have remembered him, with envy too;
thought of him sinking down above his knees
in a cold torrent, senseless of the rumour
of death gone down behind him through the trees,
through the dead grass and bushes he shoved through.

He must have tasted water after walking
miles and miles along that stream of road,
gulping and drooling it out of his mouth
that had for one day been too dry for talking
as we went on through drought into the south
shouldering leaden heat for double load.

Plainly he couldn't bear it any longer.
Like the hand of a bored devil placed
mercilessly upon a man's head,
it maddened him. I was a little stronger
and knew the river, rich with many dead,
lustrous and very cold, but two-faced

like some cold, vigorous, enticing woman
quite at the mercy of her remote source
and past springs. I could not warn him now—
not if he were here now. I could warn no man
while these red winds and summer lightnings blow
frantic with heat across my dogged course

into the south, beside the narrow river
which has that traveller's flesh and bones, and more.
Often I see him walking down that slope
thirsty and mad, never to return, never
quenched quite of his thirst, or of his hope
that heat would be arrested on its shore.

KENNETH
MACKENZIE

WHO — ME, MATE?

IAN MUDIE
1911–1977

WHAT'S wrong with us, what the hell's wrong with us,
for ever saying I'll go droving I'll go bush I'll buy
a little place in the hills with some ducks and apple-trees
and some pigs and some fowls and a cow
and a hive full of bees though God knows I'll be stung
by the bees and the agents and the blasted Government
but at least I'll be set if there's another depression
and I'll grow fat lambs and have goose cheap at Christmas
and butter and pork and eggs and milk for the kids
whatever happens and in the end the shops in the township
will hang black in their windows and be sorry I've gone. . . .

Oh, what the hell's wrong with us, don't you remember
we used to say Sydney or the bush, didn't we didn't we,
but now we say nothing but the bush the bush the bush,
and curse and whinge about the great big wicked cities
sucking like aphis colonies at the juice of the earth,
but we'll only shift out of the big smoke on Sundays
and if it's bitumen bitumen bitumen all the way
from here to when we get back again this evening. . . .

Decentralise. . . .
Back to the Land. . . .
Distribute the People. . . . .

Who, me?
I'd like to, mate,
but, mate, you've got me wrong;
I'll grant that with our population
big cities are a crime,
but me, the big smoke for me mate,
every blovely time.

EAR SHELL

IT LAY like an ear—it lay here on the shore;
strange like a pink right ear iridescent with charm.
The voice of the East it had heard . . . sun's roar
at sunrise, surf-shock and storm's alarm.
And pierced like a cannibal's lobe, its edge,
with neat perforations, passed through the vast surge
of rumour and shock, and captured only the valid
voices of worlds—of the waters, of the solid
rocks. And my hand shook as I picked up the shell
so shaped like my pink right ear. Clapped to a rock
by its living creature, this ear, as of Hell,
Earth's inner hammerings, torment and shock
it had heard; and, when it was dead, then, only in death:
wave's ripple, gull's call, and wind's whispering breath.

JOHN BLIGHT
1913–1995

OLD MAN AND TREE

JOHN BLIGHT

HOW may I live without my friend
the tree, beside me to life's happy
end? If I've a tree that grows with
me to age, I've life's gnarled image
of maturity beside me.

This, I gave courage as the seedling;
now there sits a song for me on
every bough; and longer as
I live, companionship, shade, and
comfort on the hottest day.

I
have no need to move away
to bolder kingdoms. Here has grown all
majesty that earthly thrones may
thrust above the history of
crumbling dust.

I must sit here, old
man beneath my tree, contemplate
how kind—life, time, and place may be.

DEATH OF A WHALE

JOHN BLIGHT

WHEN the mouse died, there was a sort of pity:
the tiny, delicate creature made for grief.
Yesterday, instead, the dead whale on the reef
drew an excited multitude to the jetty.
How must a whale die to wring a tear?
Lugubrious death of a whale: the big
feast for the gulls and sharks; the tug
of the tide simulating life still there,
until the air, polluted, swings this way
like a door ajar from a slaughterhouse.
Pooh! pooh! spare us, give us the death of a mouse
by its tiny hole; not this in our lovely bay.
—Sorry we are, too, when a child dies;
but at the immolation of a race who cries?

from THE WANDERER

ROLAND
ROBINSON
1912–1992

I REACHED that waterhole, its mud designed
by tracks of egret, finch, and jabiru,
while in the coming night the moon declined:
a feather floating from a cockatoo.

Ten paces more and there, in painted mime,
against the mountain like a stone-axe dropped,
the spirit-trees stood stricken from the time
the song-sticks, song-man, and the drone-pipe stopped.

Some thrust their arms and hands out in the air,
and some were struck, contorted, on their knees:
and deep and still the leaves like unbound hair
lay over limbs and torsos of those trees.

Over their limbs their night-still tresses slept;
faint in the stars a wandering night-bird creaked.
Then, as towards their company I stepped,
the whole misshapen tribe awoke and shrieked.

And, beating from limbs and leaves, white birds,
like spirits in a terror of strange birth,
streamed out with harsh and inarticulate words
above the mountains, trees, and plains of earth.

ROCK-LILY

THE ROCK-LILY'S pale spray,
like sunlight, halts my way
up through the unpierced hush
of birdless blue-grey bush.
The rocks crouch on their knees
in earth, torsos of trees
and limb-boughs lead up where
the cliff-face scales the air.
Out from you, rock, my friend,
I lean and, reaching, bend
the scentless pale spray back
to me and see the black
spots in each orchid flower.
O, my love, what power
keeps you curled and bound?
Tormented, the earth's round
begins again. What rock
holds you where you lock
yourself from me? Alone
this spray breaks from the stone.

ROLAND
ROBINSON

THE DOSSER IN SPRINGTIME

DOUGLAS STEWART
1913–1985

THAT girl from the sun is bathing in the creek,
Says the white old dosser in the cave.
It's a sight worth seeing though your old frame's weak;
Her clothes are on the wattle and it's gold all over,
And if I was twenty I'd try to be her lover,
Says the white old dosser in the cave.

If I was twenty I'd chase her back to Bourke,
Says the white old dosser in the cave.
My swag on my shoulder and a haughty eye for work,
I'd chase her to the sunset where the desert burns and reels,
With an old blue dog full of fleas at my heels,
Says the white old dosser in the cave.

I'd chase her back to Bourke again, I'd chase her back to Alice,
Says the white old dosser in the cave.
And I'd drop upon her sleeping like a beauty in a palace
With the sunset wrapped around her and a black snake keeping watch—
She's lovely and she's naked but she's very hard to catch,
Says the white old dosser in the cave.

I've been cooling here for years with the gum-trees wet and weird,
Says the white old dosser in the cave.
My head grew lichens and moss was my beard,
The creek was in my brain and a bullfrog in my belly,
The she-oaks washed their hair in me all down the gloomy gully,
Says the white old dosser in the cave.

My eyes were full of water and my ears were stopped with bubbles,
Says the white old dosser in the cave.
Yabbies raised their claws in me or skulked behind the pebbles.
The water-beetle loved his wife, he chased her round and round—
I thought I'd never see a girl unless I found one drowned,
Says the white old dosser in the cave.

Many a time I laughed aloud to stop my heart from thumping,
Says the white old dosser in the cave.
I saw my laugh I saw my laugh I saw my laugh go jumping
Like a jaunty old goanna with his tail up stiff
Till he dived like a stone in the pool below the cliff,
Says the white old dosser in the cave.

There's a fine bed of bracken, the billy boils beside her,
Says the white old dosser in the cave.
But no one ever ate with me except the loathsome spider;
And no one ever lay with me beside the sandstone wall
Except the pallid moonlight and she's no good at all,
Says the white old dosser in the cave.

But now she's in the creek again, that woman made of flame,
Says the white old dosser in the cave.
By cripes, if I was twenty I'd stop her little game.
Her dress is on the wattle—I'd take it off and hide it;
And when she sought that golden dress, I'd lay her down beside it,
Says the white old dosser in the cave.

TWO ENGLISHMEN

DOUGLAS
STEWART

FAR, FAR from home they rode on their excursions
And looked with much amusement and compassion
On Indians and Africans and Persians,
People indeed of any foreign nation
Who milled in mobs completely uninhibited
In the peculiar lands that they inhabited.

But in their own small island crowded thickly,
Each with his pride of self and race and caste,
They could not help but be a little prickly
And in their wisdom they evolved at last
This simple code to save them from destruction—
One did not speak without an introduction.

So naturally when Kinglake on his camel,
Mounted aloft to see the world or take it,
Saw faint against the sky's hard blue enamel
A solar topee, then a shooting jacket,
Then all too clear an Englishman appearing
He found the prospect anything but cheering.

Merely because the distances were wider
One could not speak with every Dick or Harry,
For all he knew some absolute outsider,
Who trotted up upon his dromedary,
And yet he felt, alone and unprotected:
On these bare sands some talk might be expected.

Of course, he thought, with spirits briefly lightened,
Though ten to one he did not know the fellow
He might be quite all right; but then he mightn't;
And on he came by sandy hill and hollow—
It was a bit too thick thus to arrive at
The desert's core and then not find it private.

For if for one's own reasons one had ridden
By camel through the empty wastes to Cairo
From Gaza in the distance back there hidden
One did not do the thing to play the hero
Or have some chap come dropping from the sky
To ask what one was doing there, and why.

The sweat lay on his camel dank and soapy
And Kinglake too broke out in perspiration
For close and closer in his solar topee
The stranger came with steady undulation;
One could not hide, for shelter there was none,
Nor yet, however tempting, cut and run.

No, if they met, as meet it seemed they must,
Though heartily he wished him at the devil,
Kinglake decided, halting in the dust,
That if the fellow spoke he must be civil;
But then observed, in ultimate dismay,
He could not think of anything to say.

But he, as it fell out, need not have worried.
It was an English military man
Long years in Burma boiled, in India curried,
Who riding home on some deep private plan
Now sat his camel equally embarrassed
To find himself thus hunted out and harassed;

And while their Arab servants rushed together
With leaps and yells to suit the glad occasion
Each Englishman gazed coolly at the other
And briefly touched his hat in salutation
And so passed by, erect, superb, absurd,
Across the desert sands without a word.

But when they'd passed, one gesture yet endures;
Each turned and waved his hand as if to say,
'Well, help yourself to Egypt'—'India's yours',
And so continued grandly on his way;
And as they went, one feels that, truth to tell,
They understood each other pretty well.

PLACE NAMES

ETHADINNA, Mira Mitta,
Mulka, Mungerannie—
Dark shadows blown
With the dust away,
Far from our day
Far out of time,
Fill the land with water.
Where the blue sky flames
On the bare red stone,
Dulkaninna, Koperamanna,
Ooroowilanie, Kilalpaninna—
Only the names
In the land remain
Like a dark well
Like the chime of a bell.

DOUGLAS
STEWART

BRINDABELLA

DOUGLAS
STEWART

ONCE on a silver and green day, rich to remember,
When thick over sky and gully rolled winter's grey wave
And one lost magpie was straying on Brindabella
I heard the mountain talking in a tall green cave
Between the pillars of the trees and the moss below:
It made no sound but talked to itself in snow.

All the white words were falling through the timber
Down from the old grey thought to the flesh of rock
And some were of silence and patience, and spring after winter,
Tidings for leaves to catch and roots to soak,
And most were of being the earth and floating in space
Alone with its weather through all the time there is.

Then it was, struck with wonder at this soliloquy,
The magpie lifting his beak by the frozen fern
Sent out one ray of a carol, softened and silvery,
Strange through the trees as sunlight's pale return,
Then cocked his black head and listened, hunched from the cold,
Watching that white whisper fill his green world.

MARGARET COEN

THE SNOW-GUM

IT IS the snow-gum silently,
In noon's blue and the silvery
Flowering of light on snow,
Performing its slow miracle
Where upon drift and icicle
Perfect lies its shadow.

Leaf upon leaf's fidelity,
The creamy trunk's solidity,
The full-grown curve of the crown,
It is the tree's perfection
Now shown in clear reflection
Like flakes of soft grey stone.

Out of the granite's eternity,
Out of the winters' long enmity,
Something is done on the snow;
And the silver light like ecstasy
Flows where the green tree perfectly
Curves to its perfect shadow.

DOUGLAS
STEWART

LADY FEEDING THE CATS

I

DOUGLAS STEWART

SHUFFLING ALONG in her broken shoes from the slums,
A blue-eyed lady showing the weather's stain,
Her long dress green and black like a pine in the rain,
Her bonnet much bedraggled, daily she comes
Uphill past the Moreton Bays and the smoky gums
With a sack of bones on her back and a song in her brain
To feed those outlaws prowling about the Domain,
Those furtive she-cats and those villainous toms.

Proudly they step to meet her, they march together
With an arching of backs and a waving of plumy tails
And smiles that swear they never would harm a feather.
They rub at her legs for the bounty that never fails,
    They think she is a princess out of a tower,
    And so she is, she is trembling with love and power.

Meat, it is true, is meat, and demands attention
But this is the sweetest moment that they know
Whose courtship even is a hiss, a howl and a blow.
At so much kindness passing their comprehension
—Beggars and rogues who never deserved this pension—
Some recollection of old punctilio
Dawns in their eyes, and as she moves to go
They turn their battered heads in condescension.

She smiles and walks back lightly to the slums.
If she has fed their bodies, they have fed
More than the body in her; they purr like drums,
Their tails are banners and fountains inside her head.
   The times are hard for exiled aristocrats,
    But gracious and sweet it is to be queen of the cats.

From GLENCOE

SIGH, wind in the pine;   DOUGLAS STEWART
River, weep as you flow;
Terrible things were done
Long, long ago.

In daylight golden and mild
After the night of Glencoe
They found the hand of a child
Lying upon the snow.

Lopped by the sword to the ground
Or torn by wolf or fox,
That was the snowdrop they found
Among the granite rocks.

Oh, life is fierce and wild
And the heart of the earth is stone,
And the hand of a murdered child
Will not bear thinking on.

Sigh, wind in the pine,
Cover it over with snow;
But terrible things were done
Long, long ago.

BETWEEN THE NIGHT AND MORNING

DOUGLAS
STEWART

O HEAR the magpie sing, my love,
Between the night and morning,
And if he says it's four or five
That's true enough, my darling.

But there's no thought in the sweet bird
That while the moon's still shining
Would drive us out of our warm bed
With song that's meant for warning.

Oh no, his far faint silver flute
Soft through the moonlight floating
Is only for his own delight
And chimes so with our loving

It seems the whole wide world is one
In light or music ringing,
Now in our love, now in the moon,
Now in the magpie's singing.

So if he says how rich it is
To wake at four or five
In bed or in the moonlit trees
And find oneself alive,

Or if he says in that bright tree
That all things live and breathe
At last in one deep harmony
Of song and light and love,

Then while I hold you so, my dear,
In love's soft music moving,
How right he is this shining hour
Between the night and morning.

DOMESTIC POEM

DOUGLAS
STEWART

MY WIFE, my life, my almost obligatory love,
Heaven forbid that I should seem your slave,
But perhaps I should say I saw you once in the garden
Rounding your arms to hold a most delicate burden
Of violets and lemons, fruits of the winter earth,
Violets and lemons, and as you came up the path—
Dark hair, blue eyes, some dress that has got me beaten—
Noting no doubt as a painter their colour and shape
And bowing your face to their fragrance, the sweet and the sharp,
You were lit with delight that I have never forgotten.

179

DAVID STRACHAN

WOMAN TO MAN

JUDITH WRIGHT
1915–

THE eyeless labourer in the night,
the selfless, shapeless seed I hold,
builds for its resurrection day—
silent and swift and deep from sight
foresees the unimagined light.

This is no child with a child's face;
this has no name to name it by:
yet you and I have known it well.
This is our hunter and our chase,
the third who lay in our embrace.

This is the strength that your arm knows,
the arc of flesh that is my breast,
the precise crystals of our eyes.
This is the blood's wild tree that grows
the intricate and folded rose.

This is the maker and the made;
this is the question and reply;
the blind head butting at the dark,
the blaze of light along the blade.
Oh hold me, for I am afraid.

MAGPIES

ALONG the road the magpies walk
with hands in pockets, left and right.
They tilt their heads, and stroll and talk.
In their well-fitted black and white

they look like certain gentlemen
who seem most nonchalant and wise
until their meal is served—and then
what clashing beaks, what greedy eyes!

But not one man that I have heard
throws back his head in such a song
of grace and praise—no man nor bird.
Their greed is brief; their joy is long,
for each is born with such a throat
as thanks his God with every note.

JUDITH WRIGHT

MAX DUPAIN

CHARLES KERRY

OUR LOVE IS SO NATURAL

JUDITH WRIGHT

OUR love is so natural,
the wild animals move
gentle and light on
the shores of our love.

My eyes rest upon you,
to me your eyes turn
as bee goes to honey,
as fire to fire will burn.

Bird and beast are at home,
and star lives in tree
when we are together
as we should be.

But so silent my heart falls
when you are away,
I can hear the world breathing
where he hides from our day

My heart crouches under,
silent and still,
and the avalanche gathers
above the green hill.

Our love is so natural—
I cannot but fear.
I would reach out and touch you.
Why are you not here?

WOMAN'S SONG

JUDITH WRIGHT

O MOVE in me, my darling,
for now the sun must rise;
the sun that will draw open
the lids upon your eyes.

O wake in me, my darling.
The knife of day is bright
to cut the thread that binds you
within the flesh of night.

Today I lose and find you
whom yet my blood would keep—
would weave and sing around you
the spells and songs of sleep.

None but I shall know you
as none but I have known;
yet there's a death and a maiden
who wait for you alone;

so move in me, my darling,
whose debt I cannot pay.
Pain and the dark must claim you,
and passion and the day.

THE FLAME-TREE

JUDITH WRIGHT

HOW to live, I said, as the flame-tree lives?
—to know what the flame-tree knows; to be
prodigal of my life as that wild tree
and wear my passion so?
That lover's knot of water and earth and sun,
that easy answer to the question baffling reason,
branches out of my heart this sudden season.
I know what I would know.

How shall I thank you, who teach me how to wait
in quietness for the hour to ask or give:
to take and in taking bestow, in bestowing live:
in the loss of myself, to find?
This is the flame-tree; look how gloriously
that careless blossomer scatters, and more and more.
What the earth takes of her, it will restore.
These are the thanks of lovers who share one mind.

AUSTRALIA 1970

JUDITH WRIGHT

DIE, wild country, like the eaglehawk,
dangerous till the last breath's gone,
clawing and striking. Die
cursing your captor through a raging eye.

Die like the tigersnake
that hisses such pure hatred from its pain
as fills the killer's dreams
with fear like suicide's invading stain.

Suffer, wild country, like the ironwood
that gaps the dozer-blade.
I see your living soil ebb with the tree
to naked poverty.

Die like the soldier-ant
mindless and faithful to your million years.
Though we corrupt you with our torturing mind
stay obstinate; stay blind.

For we are conquerors and self-poisoners
more than scorpion or snake
and dying of the venoms that we make
even while you die of us.

I praise the scoring drought, the flying dust,
the drying creek, the furious animal,
that they oppose us still;
that we are ruined by the thing we kill.

FINALE

THE cruellest thing they did
was to send home his teeth from the hospital.
What could she do with those,
arriving as they did days after the funeral?

Wrapped them in one of his clean handkerchiefs
she'd laundered and taken down.
All she could do was cradle them in her hands;
they looked so strange, alone—

utterly jawless in a constant smile
not in the least like his. She could cry no more.
At midnight she took heart and aim and threw
them out of the kitchen-door.

It rocketed out, that finally-parted smile,
into the gully? the scrub? the neighbour's land?
And she went back and fell into stupid sleep,
knowing him dead at last, and by her hand.

JUDITH WRIGHT

THE AUSTRALIAN DREAM

THE DOORBELL buzzed. It was past three o'clock.
The steeple-of-Saint-Andrew's weathercock
Cried silently to darkness, and my head
Was bronze with claret as I rolled from bed
To ricochet from furniture. Light! Light
Blinded the stairs, the hatstand sprang upright,
I fumbled with the lock, and on the porch
Stood the Royal Family with a wavering torch.

'We hope,' the Queen said, 'we do not intrude.
The pubs were full, most of our subjects rude.
We came before our time. It seems the Queen's
Command brings only, "Tell the dead marines!"
We've come to you.' I must admit I'd half
Expected just this visit. With a laugh
That put them at their ease, I bowed my head.

DAVID CAMPBELL
1915-1979

'Your Majesty is most welcome here,' I said.
'My home is yours. There is a little bed
Downstairs, a boiler-room, might suit the Duke.'
He thanked me gravely for it and he took
Himself off with a wave. 'Then the Queen Mother?
She'd best bed down with you. There is no other
But my wide bed. I'll curl up in a chair.'
The Queen looked thoughtful. She brushed out her hair
And folded up *The Garter* on a pouf.
'Distress was the first commoner, and as proof
That queens bow to the times,' she said, 'we three
Shall share the double bed. Please follow me.'

I waited for the ladies to undress—
A sense of fitness, even in distress,
Is always with me. They had tucked away
Their state robes in the lowboy; gold crowns lay
Upon the bedside tables; ropes of pearls
Lassoed the plastic lampshade; their soft curls
Were spread out on the pillows and they smiled.
'Hop in,' said the Queen Mother. In I piled
Between them to lie like a stick of wood.
I could not find a thing to say. My blood
Beat, but like rollers at the ebb of tide.
'I hope your Majesties sleep well,' I lied.
A hand touched mine and the Queen said, 'I am
Most grateful to you, Jock. Please call me Ma'am.'

NIGHT SOWING

DAVID CAMPBELL

O GENTLE, gentle land
Where the green ear shall grow,
Now you are edged with light:
The moon has crisped the fallow,
The furrows run with night.

This is the season's hour:
While couples are in bed,
I sow the paddocks late,
Scatter like sparks the seed
And see the dark ignite.

O gentle land, I sow
The heart's living grain.
Stars draw their harrows over,
Dews send their melting rain:
I meet you as a lover.

WINDY GAP

DAVID CAMPBELL

AS I was going through Windy Gap
A hawk and a cloud hung over the map.

The land lay bare and the wind blew loud
And the hawk cried out from the heart of the cloud,

'Before I fold my wings in sleep
I'll pick the bones of your travelling sheep,

'For the leaves blow back and the wintry sun
Shows the tree's white skeleton.'

A magpie sat in the tree's high top
Singing a song on Windy Gap

That streamed far down to the plain below
Like a shaft of light from a high window.

From the bending tree he sang aloud,
And the sun shone out of the heart of the cloud

And it seemed to me as we travelled through
That my sheep were the notes that trumpet blew.

And so I sing this song of praise
For travelling sheep and blowing days.

HENRI MALLARD

190

ON FROSTY DAYS

ON FROSTY DAYS, when I was young,
I rode out early with the men
And mustered cattle till their long
Blue shadows covered half the plain;

And when we turned our horses round,
Only the homestead's point of light,
Men's voices, and the bridles' sound,
Were left in the enormous night.

And now again the sun has set
All yellow and a greening sky
Sucks up the colour from the wheat—
And here's my horse, my dog and I.

DAVID CAMPBELL

THE STOCKMAN

DAVID CAMPBELL

THE SUN was in the summer grass,
The coolibahs were twisted steel:
The stockman paused beneath their shade
And sat upon his heel,
And with the reins looped through his arm
He rolled tobacco in his palm.

His horse stood still. His cattle dog
Tongued in the shadow of the tree,
And for a moment on the plain
Time waited for the three.
And then the stockman licked his fag
And Time took up his solar swag.

I saw the stockman mount and ride
Across the mirage on the plain;
And still that timeless moment brought
Fresh ripples to my brain:
It seemed in that distorting air
I saw his grandson sitting there.

MOTHERS AND DAUGHTERS

THE cruel girls we loved
Are over forty,
Their subtle daughters
Have stolen their beauty;

And with a blue stare
Of cool surprise,
They mock their anxious mothers
With their mothers' eyes.

DAVID CAMPBELL

THE BUNYIP AND THE WHISTLING KETTLE

JOHN MANIFOLD
1915–1985

I KNEW a most superior camper
  Whose methods were absurdly wrong;
He did not live on tea and damper
  But took a little stove along.

And every place he came to settle
  He spread with gadgets saving toil;
He even had a whistling kettle
  To warn him it was on the boil.

Beneath the waratahs and wattles,
  Boronia and coolibah,
He scattered paper, cans, and bottles,
  And parked his nasty little car.

He camped, this sacrilegious stranger
  (The moon was at the full that week),
Once in a spot that teemed with danger
  Beside a bunyip-haunted creek.

He spread his junk but did not plunder,
    Hoping to stay the weekend long;
He watched the bloodshot sun go under
    Across the silent billabong.

He ate canned food without demurring,
    He put the kettle on for tea.
He did not see the water stirring
    Far out beside a sunken tree.

Then, for the day had made him swelter
    And night was hot and tense to spring,
He donned a bathing suit in shelter
    And left the firelight's friendly ring.

He felt the water kiss and tingle.
    He heard the silence—none too soon!
A ripple broke against the shingle,
    And dark with blood it met the moon.

Abandoned in the hush, the kettle
    Screamed as it guessed its master's plight,
And loud it screamed, the lifeless metal,
    Far into the malicious night.

A PROBLEM OF LANGUAGE

HOW praise a man? She cannot vow
His lips are red, his brow is snow,
Nor celebrate a smooth white breast
While gazing on his hairy chest;
And though a well-turned leg might please,
More often he has knobbly knees;
His hair excites no rapt attention—
If there's enough of it to mention.
She cannot praise his damask skin,
Still less the suit he's wrapped it in;
And even if he's like Apollo
To gaze upon, it does not follow
That she may specify the features
That mark him off from other creatures.
No rime can hymn her great occasion
But by a process of evasion;
And so she gives the problem over,
Describes her love, but not her lover,
Despairs of words to tell us that
Her heart sings his magnificat.

DOROTHY
AUCHTERLONIE
1915–1991

RELEASE

DOROTHY
AUCHTERLONIE

THIS is the last thing—now all is done, all is said,
The house is empty and the far hills glow;
The wine is drunk, and broken all the bread,
The doors are open: it is time to go.

To go—to be able to go:
This is the meaning and the deed,
Cause and effect, to be led and to lead,
To free and to be freed.

To withdraw, and withdrawing, to unfold,
Not to be held, not to hold—
To cast off, like an outgrown garment,
The once-needs, the once-fears.

You are gone: there are no more tears.

BECAUSE

JAMES McAULEY
1917–1976

MY FATHER and my mother never quarrelled.
They were united in a kind of love
As daily as the *Sydney Morning Herald*,
Rather than like the eagle or the dove.

I never saw them casually touch,
Or show a moment's joy in one another.
Why should this matter to me now so much?
I think it bore more hardly on my mother,

Who had more generous feelings to express.
My father had dammed up his Irish blood
Against all drinking praying fecklessness,
And stiffened into stone and creaking wood.

His lips would make a switching sound, as though
Spontaneous impulse must be kept at bay.
That it was mainly weakness I see now,
But then my feelings curled back in dismay.

Small things can pit the memory like a cyst:
Having seen other fathers greet their sons,
I put my childish face up to be kissed
After an absence. The rebuff still stuns

My blood. The poor man's curt embarrassment
At such a delicate proffer of affection
Cut like a saw. But home the lesson went:
My tenderness thenceforth escaped detection.

My mother sang *Because*, and *Annie Laurie*,
White Wings, and other songs; her voice was sweet.
I never gave enough, and I am sorry;
But we were all closed in the same defeat.

People do what they can; they were good people,
They cared for us and loved us. Once they stood
Tall in my childhood as the school, the steeple.
How can I judge without ingratitude?

Judgment is simply trying to reject
A part of what we are because it hurts.
The living cannot call the dead collect:
They won't accept the charge, and it reverts.

It's my own judgment day that I draw near,
Descending in the past, without a clue,
Down to that central deadness: the despair
Older than any hope I ever knew.

PASTORAL

JAMES McAULEY

TREE of grace, the wattle flowers,
Gold against a sapphire sky.
Through and through the book of hours
Cruel white-eyed shadows fly.

Rain-filled ponds and brimming dams
Hold an image of the sky.
Shadows wheel above new lambs
With a dark dismaying cry.

Harsh the hungry ravens' cry,
Brief the wattle's age of gold,
Silent the blue depth of sky
That the brimming waters hold.

MAGPIE

THE magpie's mood is never surly;
Every morning, waking early,
He gargles music in his throat.
The liquid squabble of his note,

Its silver stridencies of sound,
The bright confusions and the round
Bell-cadences, are pealed
Over the frosty half-ploughed field.

Then swooping down self-confidently
From the fence-post or the tree,
He swaggers in pied feather coat
And slips the fat worms down his throat.

JAMES McAULEY

SPIDER ON THE SNOW

GOLD fire, blue glaze; thin tangle of cirrus thread;
No stir of air, no bird's flight overhead.
The fleece of snow sweats crystal in the sun;
And secretly a thousand rivulets run
Sinking through lichened rocks, gurgling beneath
The matted alpines of the springy heath,
Till the plateau fills full and begins to spill
Far down the sides. But up here I crouch still,
Watching in astonishment a small
Dark-bodied red-legged spider steadily crawl
Across the snow, with no concern at all.

JAMES McAULEY

JUDITH KELLY

CANTICLE

JAMES McAULEY

STILLNESS and splendour of the night,
When, after slow moonrise,
Swans beat their wings into the height,
Seeking the brilliant eyes
Of water, where the ponds and lakes
Look upward as the landscape wakes.

The loved one, turning to her lover,
Splendid, awake, and still,
Receives as the wild swans go over
The deep pulse of love's will.
She dies in her delight, and then
Renews her tender love again.

Where fragrant irises disclose
A kingdom to the sense,
The ceremony of pleasure goes
With stately precedence;
Like rich brocade it gleams and glooms
Through the heart's dim presence-rooms.

MAX DUPAIN

The wagtail in the myrtle-tree
Who cannot sleep for love
Sings all night long insistently
As if his song could prove
What wisdom whispered from the start,
That only love can fill the heart.

He sang under the boughs of youth,
Through twisted shadowed years;
He sings in this clear night of truth,
And now my spirit hears;
And sees, when beating wings have gone,
The lucid outline of the Swan.

GROUP FROM TARTARUS

A woman ripe with life, whose hand
flashed a wide wedding ring, had stopped
to greet two children not her own
who waiting for a parent hopped
bird-quick from slab to slab of stone.
Their father: and what sorrow spanned

love's light-through-eyeball race and flow
above the children's heads, what gift
this moment was from sweepstake fate
while the cloud-sliding watery drift
of winter hung above the weight
his children and her ring might show

of earlier love, no passer-by
except Professor Eisenbart
interpreted. He paused and read,
or seemed to read, the weather chart.
Still weary from his mistress' bed
he read at sight, from eye to eye,

their fugue of love and loss, and traced
the stretto of their parting words.
Lightly across the pavement slabs
a seagull walked. The sea-clean bird's
reptilian head made lightning stabs
gutterwards at some rotting waste.

Eisenbart felt, who prized his dry
indifference to love and luck,
uncharted cold that winter day
as a hard beak of anguish struck
the ripe waste of his heart's decay:
Too old to love, too young to die.

GWEN HARWOOD
1920-1995

201

IN THE MIDDLE OF LIFE

GWEN HARWOOD

HOPELESS in middle age to soften
those hearts long petrified by hate,
or melt from features loved so often
in friendship's warmth their desolate
mantle of self-sustaining spite.
We see ourselves, in callous light,

stripped of the vanity that conjured
for everyone an emperor's suit.
Who can drink flattery uninjured,
or banquet on illusion's fruit?
Unwelcome nourishment, but real,
is truth's unpalatable meal.

We need our enemies to teach us
what friends in kindness never show.
Where magnanimity can't reach us
the darts of hatred lodge and glow,
lighting our follies and pretensions,
our self-esteem's absurd dimensions.

Think of a still-life painter toiling
to keep the bloom of life intact,
fish, fruit and blossom slowly spoiling
while his brush holds the flowers erect,
the fruit unwrinkled, and the flesh
sea-lustred on the stinking fish.

SUBURBAN SONNET: BOXING DAY

GWEN HARWOOD

GOLD, silver, pink and blue, the globes distort her,
framed in the doorway: woman with a broom.
Wrappings and toys lie scattered round the room.
A glossy magazine the children bought her
lies open: *How to keep your husband's love*.
She stands and stares, as if in recollection,
at her own staring acid-pink reflection.
The simple fact is, she's too tired to move.

O where's the demon lover, the wild boy
who kissed the future to her flesh beneath
what skies, what stars, what space! and swore to love her
through hell's own fires? A child stretches above her
and, laughing, crowns her with a tinsel wreath.
She gathers up a new, dismembered toy.

A FINE THING

ROSEMARY DOBSON
1920–

TO BE a scarecrow
To lean all day in a bright field
With a hat full
Of bird's song
And a heart of gold straw;
With a sly wink for the farmer's daughter,
When no one sees, and small excursions;
Returning after
To a guiltless pose of indolence.

A fine thing
To be a figurehead
With a noble brow
On a ship's prow
And a look to the end of the world;
With the sad sounds of wind and water
And only a stir of air for thinking;
The timber cutting
The green waves, and the foam flashing.

To be a snowman
Lost all day in deep thought,
With a head full
Of snowflakes
And no troubles at all,
With an old pipe and six buttons,
And sometimes children in woollen gaiters;
But mostly lonely,
A simple fellow, with no troubles at all.

THE BIRTH

ROSEMARY DOBSON

A wreath of flowers as cold as snow
Breaks out in bloom upon the night:
That tree is rooted in the dark,
It draws from dew its breath of life,
It feeds on frost, it hangs in air
And like a glittering branch of stars
Receives, gives forth, its breathing light.

Eight times it flowered in the dark,
Eight times my hand reached out to break
That icy wreath to bear away
Its pointed flowers beneath my heart.
Sharp are the pains and long the way
Down, down into the depths of night
Where one goes for another's sake.

Once more it flowers, once more I go
In dream at midnight to that tree,
I stretch my hand and break the branch
And hold it to my human heart.
Now, as the petals of a rose
Those flowers unfold and grow to me—
I speak as of a mystery.

THE SHELL

ROSEMARY DOBSON

I MET A drowned man from the sea
His look was pale, his eyes were wild,
Sea-water ran upon his skin,
'Listen,' he said, and held a shell,
'Mine enemy is locked within.

'We fought. He pressed my eyeballs in
But I had strength enough for this—
To kick his flanks, and kicking rise
On a last gasping breath to air.
I stuffed him in this hollow shell.

'Hark, how he moans,' the drowned man said
And held the shell against my ear.
I heard the sullen captive roar
As though there beat upon a shore
Long thunders of Atlantic swell.

'I have an enemy,' I cried,
'And he is terrible and strong
Stronger than ocean, wilder far,
His name is Fear. I know him well.
How should I lock him in a shell?'

THE MOTHER

ROSEMARY DOBSON

SEEING her child shaken
By grief and wild passion
She knew again the tumult,
The storm that beat her branches
And stripped her of green graces
So many years ago.

How like a bird from heaven
Came then her dancing daughter,
A bird that rests from flying
Upon the sheltering branches
And stirs the tree's remembrance
Of sweet and rainy spring.

She has spun a garment
Of words for her daughter,
A coat she will throw over
To shelter her from evil,
From love, from life's mischances,
And keep her by her side.

But love knows no delaying
And grief will come too early:
She lacked the words to finish
The woven coat of comfort
And so her grieving daughter
Wears yet one wild bird's wing.

ARTHUR MURCH

207

CAPTAIN ARTHUR PHILLIP AND THE BIRDS

LEX BANNING
1921–1965

COPPER-GREEN Phillip,
with a beak like a hawk,
perches on his pedestal
and will not talk
to the stuttering starlings
fluttering around,
or the crumb-seeking pigeons
patterning the ground;
and though, daylong,
bird calls to bird,
copper-green Phillip
says never a word.

Copper-green Phillip
just stares and stands
with a scroll and a flag
in his strong bronze hands,
and the birds may wonder
what's on the scroll:
is it the *Sirius's*
pilgrims' roll;
or, perhaps, a commission;
or a declaration,
washing his hands
of the subsequent nation;
or, even, an inventory
of flocks and herds?
But Royal Navy captains
never talk to birds.

Copper-green Phillip
just stands and stares
away down the harbour
at the rolling years,
and the birds all gossip
of the nation's vices,
and of some of her virtues,
and of whom she entices;
but whether she's Magdalene,
or whether she's Martha,
It's all the same
to Captain Arthur.

THE TANTANOOLA TIGER

THERE in the bracken was the ominous spoor mark,
Huge, splayed, deadly, and quiet as breath,
And all around lay bloodied and dying,
Staring dumbly into their several eternities,
The rams that Mr Morphett loved as sons.

Not only at Tantanoola, but at Mount Schank
The claw welts patterned the saplings
With mysteries terrible as Egypt's demons,
More evil than the blueness of the Lakes,
And less than a mile from the homestead, too.

Sheep died more rapidly than the years
Which the tiger ruled in tooth and talk,
And it padded from Beachport to the Border,
While blood streamed down the minds of the folk
Of Mount Gambier, Tantanoola, and Casterton.

Oh this tiger was seen all right, grinning,
Yellow and gleaming with satin stripes:
Its body arched and undulated through the tea-tree:
In this land of dead volcanoes it was a flame.
It was a brightness, it was the glory of death:

It was fine, this tiger, a sweet shudder
In the heath and everlastings of the Border,
A roc bird up the ghostly ring-barked gums
Of Mingbool Swamp, a roaring fate
Descending on the mindless backs of grazing things.

Childhoods burned with its burning eyes,
Tantanoola was a magic playground word,
It rushed through young dreams like a river,
And it had lovers in Mr Morphett and Mr Marks
For the ten long hunting unbelieving years.

Troopers and blacks made safari, Africa-fashion;
Pastoral Quixotes swayed on their ambling mounts,
Lost on invisible trails. The red-faced
Young Lindsay Gordons of the Mount
Tormented their heartbeats in the rustling nights

While the tiger grew bigger, and clear as an axe.
'A circus once abandoned a tiger cub'—
This was the creed of the hunters and poets:
'A dingo that's got itself too far south,'
The grey old cynics thundered in their beers;

MAX HARRIS
1921–1995

DAVID MOORE

And blows were swapped and friendships broken;
Beauty burst on a loveless and dreary people,
And their monied minds broke into singing
A myth; these soured and tasteless settlers
Were Greeks and Trojans, billabong troubadours,

Plucking their themes at the picnic races
Around the kegs in the flapping canvas booths.
On the waistcoats sharks' teeth swung in time,
And old eyes, sharply seamed and squinting,
Opened mysteriously in misty musical surprise,

Until the day Jack Heffernan made camp
By a mob of sheep on the far slope of Mount Schank,
And woke to find the tiger on its haunches,
Bigger than a mountain, love, or imagination,
Grinning lazily down on a dying ewe;

And he drew a bead and shot it through the head.
Look down, oh mourners of history, poets,
Look down on the black and breeding volcanic soil,
Lean on your fork in this potato country,
Regard the yellowed fangs and quivering claws

Of a mangy and dying Siberian wolf.
It came as a fable or a natural image
To pace the bars of these sunless minds,
A small and unimpressive common wolf
In desperately poor and cold condition.

It howled to the wattle when it swam ashore
From the wreck of the foundered *Helena*,
Smelt death and black snakes and tight lips
On every fence-post and sliprail.
It was three foot six from head to tail.

Centuries will die like swatted blowflies
Before word of wolf will work a tremor
Of tenderness in the crusty knuckles
Around the glasses in the Tantanoola pub
Where its red bead eyes now stare towards the sun.

CANDLES

NAN McDONALD
1921–1974

A HUNDRED YEARS ago the sun-struck sails
Of a ship moved in the rolling plains of sea
On the great voyage out to New South Wales.

It was fair weather, white and gold and blue;
On deck the settlers drowsed in the long trough
Of peace between the old life and the new.

Suddenly fear jarred taut the sliding days
For a child hurt his eyes, the shade-deep brown
That still looked with a baby's solemn gaze.

These must be trusted, being so far from land,
To the ship's surgeon, frock-coat derelict—
Slurred learning, strong breath, and uncertain hand.

Nothing to do but pray that hand should find,
By the mercy of God, some memory of its skill—
And the hand fumbled, and the child was blind.

(Deep undersea the currents move, and swing
One ship out from the convoy, and she goes
South and yet south,over the icy ring

Into dark silences, where not again
The warm sun will rise up to blaze her course
To the mast-thick harbour and the tongues of men.)

He was too young to know he was alone;
This weary night was no more strange to him
Than the world of salt-scrubbed planks and bright spray blown,

Harsh ropes his small, fat hands would pat, the play
Of gleaming, following wings; and he sat still,
So patient now, but sometimes he would say,

Will they light the candles when we come to Sydney?

This she was called to endure, who would have done
Anything else, who would most willingly
Have burnt her own eyes out to light her son.

And when they came to Sydney, glided clean
Through the Heads on a blue day, saw shining sky
Arched over jewelled bays, and the hills between,

Each sun-shaft in green depths was a turned blade
And each thin, shimmering leaf on land a spear
In the open wound his echoing question made,

Asking of all this brilliance but the dim
Halo around a pointed yellow flame,
And this she could not even promise him.

That is the story. No one, listening, hears
More of that ship, of crew or passengers;
The roaring waters of a hundred years

Have drowned all but the little voice that yet
Floats on, slipping from wave to wave, because
No woman hearing it could quite forget.

THE WHITE EAGLE

NAN McDONALD

EVENING falls soon in the hills across the river,
Moving dark where the tree-tops gleamed a moment before,
Chilling to steel the lazy sweep of the reaches,
And at last, salt-cold, comes rippling in to our shore,

Where the gulls long since wheeled up and went flashing seaward,
With the tide's first ebb deserting the threatened land;
And the shag no longer sits where the bleaching driftwood
Thrusts from the slate-blue mud and damp white sand.

And the shadow climbs, and the clamorous gold-green thickets
Grow shrill with a brief unease that falls dulled to rest;
The thrush drops his gentle head, as in secret listening
To the freshets of silver locked in his soft grey breast.

And the lyre-bird too, that gay and skilful fellow,
Who set the dawn-fogged dew of the bush alight
With the opal glow of his soul and his art's rich cunning,
Can find no song for this other grey of night.

Now far and steeply above us the dusk has swallowed
The glint of the wiry grass that the boulders strew,
Echoing no more to the thronged black currawongs' calling
Where the rose-limbed trees twist out to pattern the blue.

But the light turns blazing at bay in its last high fortress
And the walls of yellow sandstone with glory run,
A crown for the night-gulfed slopes, and a golden footstool
For the lord of the rocks and the champion of the sun.

Stainless he rides on the swimming air, and below him
Roll the vast dim sea and the splendour of the world;
And the strength of his wing will be gilded, his breast still blinding
When the citadel falls with its blackened banners furled.

Tomorrow I too must be dropping down the river
With the screams of the flickering gulls for my parting words,
And in the thick town I shall be often thinking
Of the great hill darkening here, and my quiet birds.

I shall wish them all a still dusk and safe dreaming,
But the lift of my heart will follow my shining one
Where the high bright cliffs rise burning, and he beyond them,
All his white beauty warm in the eye of the sun.

REVERIE OF A MUM

HERE let me rest me feet!
The boys have gone to try
The shooting gallery, the girls
Are off to prospect for boys.
Here let me drop me bundle
Of bulging sample bags,
I was lucky to find this seat
In the shade, away from the noise.
We come on an early bus,
We seen the fruit and the jams,
The handicrafts and the flowers,
Bacon like marble, hams
Big as the side of a palace,
Wheels of golden cheese
Like off one of them olden chariots
From them spectacle films. And Jeez
The cakes done in royal icing!
There was one great galleon—clever!
All icing: sails, decks, ropes,
You could hardly credit. I never

NANCY KEESING
1923–1993

Seen such a cake. It took me
Back to that Spanish Gob
Off the Yankee ship in the war years
And a lying, promising slob
He turned out. Now my eldest, Marie,
Her eyes are funny but,
As hot and black as that little goat's feet
And she's a stuck-up slut.
She's got ideas of the stage now
Since we let her stay on at school
And they chose her for Cleopatra
In that play they done by the pool
In Hyde Park there. It's queer,
You marry and you settle down
Like they say, and you never think
Of the boys who done you brown.
Jeez! When I think of me hair
With frangipanis, and a high
Pompadour style—I used to swing
As if I'd of owned the sky.
There was that night in the Dom.
(I'd tan my kids if they went
Where we used ... war-time, but,)
And all around was the scent
Of gabardine coats and hair-oil
And frangipani in the night—
Whispers, rustling, and the giggles
When one Yank shinned up the light
And took out the bulb.... My God
But those boys knew what they wanted.
The whole world turned on velvet.
The sky came down and panted
Like a dog that's been running. Them fig-trees
Rattled that sky in their leaves.
Well, it isn't like that when you settle.
If my hubby knew! Funny though, I grieves
For them boys. Just sometimes. And the Vice Squad
Out on their surf-boat boots
Treading the Moreton Bay fig-leaves....
Fig-leaves! We up and we scoots
With my Spanish Yank having trouble,
It was funny giving coppers the slip,
The frangipani night laughed with us
As we dodged through the 'Loo to their ship.
We all took a sickie from the factory
When they sailed—'See youse again....'
Then the grey boys in jungle green come home.
And *that* was my castle in Spain.

THE SMALLEST SPROUT

A LIONESS killing a Nubian in a field of lotuses,
Made of ivory, gold, lapis lazuli and cornelian,
Four inches high, found in a well at Nimrud;
This torn from *The Illustrated London News*;
From the Adelaide *Chronicle*, 'how to make whitewash';
Next, a seedsman's catalogue, with 'This is *no good*'
Scribbled under one highly recommended camellia.
And in the drawer itself, the scent a smallest boy
Needed no opening of eyes to prove it hers.
And now no looking in any favourite place
Will find her, no telephone ringing at the most awkward moment
Will yield her voice, no mail a letter with news
Of the dogs, or the difficulties of painting a dying rose.

GEOFFREY
DUTTON
1922–

But walk on earth she walked, how much still grows.
She was not one to cut a single rose
Then watch the whole vast garden die.
She died between footfalls, in her own house,
A widow for thirty years, but never afraid
Of loneliness, nor of commanding what she thought was best.
However feminine, no Little Woman she,
She knew her place, and it was at the head;
A beauty old men did not forget, and the young noticed,
Which filled them less with sorrow or lust than awe,
Since like a judge's robes it symbolised the law,
An ordered life of strenuous principle,
Distrust of ease (at seventy striding on
While grown men ran behind), and dedication
To beauty itself, in flower or art or action
(With nothing but scorn for that self-pity
Which holds beauty irrelevant to this ugly age).
This was a beauty that soon left mirrors empty,
However often it returned to them.
Fingers that pressed on piano or violin
Could knead the compost round the hairs of roots
Or roll out pastry on a floury board;
Eyes that burnt as cold as salt in candleflame
Watched tenderly for the first crabapple blossom.

She knew the droughts, the country where they breed,
But she had looked beyond mirages of a gibber plain
And dry creeks running like cracks in a steer's skull
Towards the homestead, where the underground tank
Always keeps the pure rain water cool.
Only the sea she did not care to touch,
Admiring a moonlit bay, or an albatross
In flight, that smooth seismograph of storms,
But safe on land that could still fight off the sea
She was not going to walk back in again.

On the sea it is only by favour anyone has control,
But on the land a man is more or less in command,
A woman even more so. Once forced to fight
The wars she hates, she wins them, beating the guerrillas
Through knowing their jungles better than they do themselves.
Not only that, she lets the conquered see
That she was what they were really fighting for,
The earth itself, the swamps of intuition,
The tropic mountain snows and the fantastic butterflies,
Over which the solitary woman, trailing her beauty,
Flies like a bird of paradise to her own death,
Inviolable, no shout nor shot can halt her.

Achieved perfection is loveless, but she was loved.
Beauty, the vision vanishing beyond the trees,
Leaves a cold kiss on statues that do not change;
The mould is broken for lovers and for children.
She knew the earth was there for walking on;
It would have startled worshippers of her image
To have seen her tuck her skirts into her bloomers
And wade out laughing (rare occasion for the sea)
To scoop with a net the big blue crabs;
To hear her call a fart a fart; or flay
The snobbery of a visiting Englishwoman; or haul out
The steaming guts of a just-slaughtered fowl.

These were her robust and sometimes angry days,
But none of us could ever know her nights,
After she marked the page in Gibbon with a hairpin
And then turned off the light. The widow was a woman,
What agony for her never to be comforted;
Love's most heroic response is to the 3 a.m. despair.
Nor in such darkened moods is daylight any help;
Walking away from light one's shrinking shadow on the wall
Grows more nearly what one is, till it becomes
Nothing at all. Death eats what the self has left.

Life gone, there's left a kind of statue
That will not survive a living day, nor yet
Be beautiful uncovered in a thousand years
Like a miniature of ivory and precious stones.
It is only the taken body draws our tears;
Mortal beauty, once dragged down to earth
Is already a praise of life, the grave's no fear
For the grandchildren hunting for lizards under the crabapple trees.

Smooth ceremonies of black are suitable for strangers
And calculated for the praise of death, but for life
Any battered detail with a fingerprint will do,
Like her old car stacked full with flowers
Following behind the hearse, as someone said,
Like the General's charger. There were, in fact, on a hill
Not far from her open grave, some draught horses grazing,
A comfortable old piebald nipping and nuzzling
The big brown mare beside him. The grass around them
Showed in smallest sprouts the green of May.

220

SHEAF-TOSSER

THE lone crow caws from the tall dead gum:

ERIC ROLLS
1923–

Caw. Caw. Caw-diddle-daw.
And judges the stack with one watery eye,
Then turns the other to fix its lie.
Caw. Caw. Caw-diddle-daw.
There are four tiers of sheaves on the wagon yet
And one more loaded is standing by;
My arms are aching and I'm dripping sweat
But the sun is three axe-handles in the sky
And I must toss sheaves till dark.

It is fourteen feet from the ground to the eaves:
Caw. Caw. Caw-diddle-daw.
And two feet six to the third roof row,
Six feet high stands the load below:
Caw. Caw. Caw-diddle-daw.
Ten feet six now must I pitch,
Into the centre of the stack I throw
To the turner and the short-handled fork with which
He thrusts sheaves to the builder in monotonous flow,
Butts out and long-side down.

There are twenty-five crows on the old dry gum:
Caw. Caw. Caw-diddle-daw.
Thirteen on one branch and twelve on the other
And each one calls as loud as his brother,
Caw. Caw. Caw-diddle-daw.
My hands are blistered, my sore lips crack
And I wonder whether the turner would smother
If a hard throw knocked him off the stack
And a few sheaves slipped on top? But there'd come another
And I'd still toss sheaves.

There are thousands of crows on the gaunt white gum:
Caw. Caw. Caw-diddle-daw.
The reds are pale in the western sky
And the stack is more than sixty feet high:
Caw. Caw. Caw-diddle-daw.
My fork grows heavy as the light grows dim.
There are five sheaves left but I've fear of a whim
That one of the crows has an evil eye
And the five sheaves left will be there when I die,
For each bird's forgotten how to fly
Till he drives out my soul with the force of his cry:
Caw. Caw. Caw. Caw.
Caw. Caw. Caw. Caw.

DEATH SONG OF A MAD BUSH SHEPHERD

ERIC ROLLS

O LORD! the girl is dead
That lay to me in my bed.
O Lord, my Lord, her lips were red, her lips were
    red, so ruby red,
O Lord, my Lord, her lips were red, her lips were
    red, but now she is dead.

See, as her limbs unfold,
A beauty never told,
O Lord, but now my love is cold, my love is cold,
    so palely cold,
O Lord, but now my love is cold, and she to me
    would her limbs unfold.

At last there breaks the day
On the form that with me lay.
My love, my dreams, all fade away, my dreams and
    she all fade away,
My love, my dreams, all fade away, and, Lord, I am
    lonely in the day.

Must I take my sheep to water?
Must I take my sheep to slaughter?
There has been slaughter but there is no water,
    for Drought has been and Fire her daughter,
O Lord, give us water, for I am tired of slaughter,
    and the creeks are forlorn without any water.

I hear the curlews wail—
Such a melancholy tale.
When curlews wail in the moonlight pale, in fear I
quail in moonlight pale;
A story of horror in moonlight pale, in moonlight
pale when curlews wail.

At night I am racked by the howl
Of some unseen, shapeless owl.
For an owl is no owl but a monstrous ghoul, this
unseen owl is a monstrous ghoul;
A monstrous owl is a shapeless ghoul and, Lord,
I am tortured by its howl.

O Christ as I lie in pain
Foul death nibbles my brain.
And the noise of the nibbling waxes and wanes as
of frightened mice in a shed of grain;
And now it gnaws softly and now it gnaws loud,
champing and chewing—O Christ, the pain!

And now the plovers cry,
Telling me I die,
When plovers fly by night and cry, when plovers cry
at night and fly,
O God I know I surely die—there is a death-note
in their cry.

THE CREATURE IN THE CHAIR

LET some of the tranquillity of the cat
Curl into me. The creature, curled in my lap,
Has the world like a ball of wool in its purring eyes.
How many men, for the labour they are at,
Want the shapes of a caress or the gentle reward
Of curled-up animal generosities!

Let some of the calm presumption of the cat
Be mine. Amused at the comfort in its stare,
I stroke the nape of the world and start myself to stare:
Into the human possibility of what?—
Remonstrance brought to a sleep like a ball of wool
In the lap of a curled-up creature in a chair.

DAVID
ROWBOTHAM
1924–

THE OLD PRIEST

DAVID ROWBOTHAM

AND the old priest, dying, wept.
Grant me the purity of
The man: to be child again,
Stripped of the vestments of grave
Believing, dressed just in tears,
In the remnants of such an old
Cry! which—held by the feet—
We once let loose at the world.

As an entering child again,
Unknowing, and with no faith
More than the upside-down
Cry of deliverance,
The old priest, dying, wept—
For hands—foothold! Grant
Me remnants, to utter like this
The unwilled innocence.

CANBERRA IN APRIL

J.R. ROWLAND
1925–

VAST mild melancholy splendid
Day succeeds day, in august chairmanship
Presiding over autumn. Poplars in valleys
Unwavering candleflames, balance over candid
Rough-linen fields, against a screen of hills

Sending invisible smokes from far below
To those majestic nostrils. A Tuscan landscape
On a larger scale; for olives eucalypts
In drifts and dots on hillheads, magpie and crow
For fieldbirds, light less intimate, long slopes stripped

Bare of vine or village, the human imprint
Scarcely apparent; distances immense
And glowing at the rim, as if the land
Were floating, like the round leaf of a water-plant
In a bright meniscus. Opposite, near at hand,

Outcrops of redbrick houses, northern trees
In costume, office-buildings
Like quartz-blocks flashing many-crystalled windows
Across the air. Oblivious, on their knees,
Of time and setting, admirals pick tomatoes

In their back gardens, hearty
Bankers exchange golf-scores, civil servants
Their after-office beers; the colony
Of diplomats prepares its cocktail parties
And politicians their escape to Melbourne.

This clean suburbia, house-proud but servantless,
Is host to a multitude of children
Nightly conceived, born daily, riding bikes,
Requiring play-centres, schools and Progress
Associations: in cardigans and slacks

Their mothers polish kitchens, or in silk
White gloves and tight hats pour each other tea
In their best china, canvassing the merits
Of rival plumbers, grocers, Bega milk
And the cost of oil-fired heating or briquettes.

DOUGLAS DUNDAS

To every man his car; his wife's on Thursday
Plus one half-day she drops him at the office
(Air murmurous with typewriters) at eight-forty
To pick him up for lunch at home; one-thirty
Sees the streets gorged with his return to duty

And so the year revolves; files swell, are closed
And stored in basements, Parliaments adjourn
And reassemble, speeches are made and hooted.
Within the circle of the enfranchised
These invite those and are themselves invited,

At formal dinners, misprints of the *Times*
Compete with memories of Rome or Paris
For, after all, the capital is here.
The general populace sprays its roses, limes
Its vegetable patch and drinks its beer:

Golf at the week-end, gardening after five
Pictures on Saturday, radio day and night
T.V. to come, and shopping late on Friday—
As under glass the pattern of the hive
Swarms in its channels, purposeful and tidy

Tempting romantics to dismay and spite
Planners to satisfaction, both to heresy:
For everywhere, beyond the decent lawn
A visionary landscape wings the sight
And every child is rebel and unknown.

So long as daylight moon, night laced with stars
And luminous distance feed imagination
There's hope of strangeness to transcend, redeem
Purblind provincial comfort: summer fires
Under prodigious smokes, imperious storms,

A sense of the pale curving continent
That, though a cliché, may still work unseen
And, with its script of white-limbed trees, impart
A cure for habit, some beneficent
Simplicity or steadiness of heart.

PARENTS

MY FATHER asks me how I stand it all,
The work, the debts, the spite. My mother talks
As though I were a famous man and yet
Unguarded somehow, too fragile to touch.
It's their needs, not mine, that flutter here
In the questions and the anecdotes. I stare
At the rust encroaching on the walnut branches
Or the pile of litter where the biggest pine-tree
Used to stand, before my absence killed it.
Their door has a vine over it; they murmur
Endearments to the animals, and cry
At small wrongs. Which is the oldest of us three?

Facts sound like charges. The least important man
Is a legend in his neighbour's living-room,
Menacing and remarkable as the lightning
That ran from tree to tree about the house
So lately, like the shining of its ghosts.
I nod, but the names, perils, dates mean nothing,
And where that's true, the deepest bonds are lost.
How will the vine bear this year? I feel
My heart growing till my thoughts are hoarse
And the old branches pick at the heap of leavings.
There is so much I don't recall. They stand,
Timid, waving to watch me go, barely
Visible in the window's copper sheen.

VINCENT BUCKLEY
1925–1988

THIS RUNNER

FRANCIS WEBB
1925–1973

THIS runner on his final lap
Sucks wildly for elusive air;
Space is a vortex, time's a gap,
Seconds are shells that hiss and flare
Between red mist and cool white day
Four hundred throttling yards away.

Each spike-shod muscle, yelping nerve,
Worries, snaps at his stumbling weight;
He goes wide on this floating curve,
Cursing with crazy, hammering hate
A rival glued to inside ground
Who flogs his heart, forces him round.

Friends, here is your holiday;
Admire your image in this force
While years, books, flesh and mind give way
To the sheer fury of the source.
Here is your vicious, central shape
That has no need of cheer or tape.

SAM HOOD

FIVE DAYS OLD
(For Christopher John)

FRANCIS WEBB

CHRISTMAS is in the air.
You are given into my hands
Out of quietest, loneliest lands.
My trembling is all my prayer.
To blown straw was given
All the fullness of Heaven.

The tiny, not the immense,
Will teach our groping eyes.
So the absorbed skies
Bleed stars of innocence.
So cloud-voice in war and trouble
Is at last Christ in the stable.

Now wonderingly engrossed
In your fearless delicacies,
I am launched upon sacred seas,
Humbly and utterly lost
In the mystery of creation,
Bells, bells of ocean.

Too pure for my tongue to praise,
That sober, exquisite yawn
Or the gradual, generous dawn
At an eyelid, maker of days:
To shrive my thought for perfection
I must breathe old tempests of action

For the snowflake and face of love,
Windfall and word of truth,
Honour close to death.
O eternal truthfulness, Dove,
Tell me what I hold—
Myrrh? Frankincense? Gold?

If this is man, then the danger
And fear are as lights of the inn,
Faint and remote as sin
Out here by the manger.
In the sleeping, weeping weather
We shall all kneel down together.

LETTER FROM GARELLA BAY

R.F. BRISSENDEN
1928–1991

SUN-DAZZLE, bright
On blue water; trees
    That break the light;
Wet, salt sea-smell; the sea's
    Incessant voice
On rock, pebble, sand:
    It's a fine place
To escape to with a friend.
    Each day we talk
Poetry, fishing, life;
    Swim, drink, sun-bake;
Forget work and the wife.
    Recall instead
Free days, free girls: the times
    We really had
And those we might have—dreams,

A nostalgic boast
Or two, the odd lie: we
   Agree the coast
Inspires us: the same sea
   Sang round the rocks
On which Ulysses drove
   His battered wrecks
And told his lies, while love
   Herself was born
In the sea-foam: good talk
   Over the wine.
But each night as I walk
   Down to the stone
Hut near the water where
   I sleep alone
I remember how, just here,
   Four years ago,
Warm, happy, trembling we
   Renewed our love
And you smelt like the sea.

MAX DUPAIN

VERANDAS

for Monique Delamotte

R.F. BRISSENDEN THEY don't build houses like that any more—not
With verandas the way they used to: wide verandas
Running round three sides of the place, with vines
Growing up the posts and along the eaves—passion-
fruit, grape, wistaria—and maiden-hair fern in pots,
And a water-bag slung from the roof in the shade with the water
Always cool and clean and tasting of canvas.

Comfortable worn cane chairs and shabby lounges,
Beds for the kids to sleep in, a ping-pong table,
A cage for the cockatoo the boys had caught
Twenty years ago by the creek, a box for the cat
And a blanket for the old blind dog to doze on—
There was room for everything and everybody,
And you lived out on the veranda through the summer.

That's where the talking happened—over a cup
Of tea with fresh sponge cake and scones, or a drink
(A beer for the men and a shandy for the girls)
On Sunday afternoons or warm dry evenings:
Do you remember, it always began, do you
Remember?—How it was Grandpa who forged the hook
They used to catch the biggest cod in the Lachlan—

And didn't we laugh when Nell in her English voice
Said: 'Hark at the rain!'—And who was the bloke that married
Great-aunt Edith and drove the coach from Bourke?
And weren't they working up Queensland way in that pub
Frank Gardiner ran, and nobody twigged who he was
Even though they called him the Darkie—and they never
Found it, did they, the gold: nobody found it.

And they never will—just like that reef at Wyalong:
Nothing but quartz and mullock. But the fishing
Was good in those days, Tom, they'd say: remember
The ducks, the way we'd watch them in their hundreds
Flying along the billabong at sunset?
You won't see that any more—they're all fished out,
The water-holes, and the mallee-fowl have gone.

And in the dusk and under a rising moon
The yarning voices would drift and pause like a river
Eddying past the ears of the drowsing children
As they settled down in their beds and watched the possums
Playing high in the branches—and when they opened
Their eyes it would somehow always be morning with sunlight
Flooding level and bright along the veranda.

from LETTERS TO LIVE POETS

X

THE sou'wester whips the day awake.   BRUCE BEAVER
The pines are tossing 'monkey tails'   1928–
about the gardens and the streets.
The air hums and rushes overhead
and next-door the little girl
is calling out to it.
All week she has blown
a two-note whistle and called the tune
her own. The white and blue weather
excites her. The wind blows
back into her face the tune.

She catches it and feels it blown
about her hair and face.
It buzzes like wild bees;
it stings with specks of dust and sand.
Yet over it and under it is the cool
to warmer charm of the September breeze,
spiked with salt and mellowed with
the mild juice of new grass.

The sheets crack and flap a semaphore
among the red and blue and black of 'coloureds'.
She sits cross-legged beneath
the carousel of washing, fluting
and singing two notes, two words:
'I am, I am.' The mother
admonishes. She is thin and sallow,
without a man.
Has her reasons
all about her like an angry
counterpoint. All winter
she has yelled at the child who yells
back at herself 'I am, I am'.

But the divas of the air and sky
respond 'We are, we are' and lift her
over the yards and the thrumming pines,
past gargling crows and creaking gulls,
above the splintering enamel
of the blue and whitening bay
back to where she is with a man
out of the clouds. The 'he' who'll spank
her mother good and bring them all
toffee apples every day.

How she sings and makes the whistle
talk with her. When she goes
inside the house her hair will crackle
and float about. Her mother will lick
the corner of a handkerchief
and clean the corners of her eyes.
Then by herself again
she'll clean the whistle's gritty mouth
and listen to it humming to
itself.
        Do you hear them now?
Have I admitted something past
my manhood? Do we recollect
blowing up a sunny storm
all by ourselves once upon
a time in a backyard garden
near the sea?
Or is it that all women
learn to sing to themselves early
that some men, early or late,
may listen?

WHITE CAT AND BROWN GIRL

HOLDING a white cat arms' length high,   BRUCE BEAVER
The tail flicking, the eyes flashing;
Hugging it close until squirming free
It drops and sits, posing and licking
Impeccable paws at her broad brown feet,

Edie stands in the misty yard,
The trees weeping, the grass soaking;
Behind her move the incestuous herd
Of white goats munching and staring;
About her the mist falls bitter and sweet.

All morning she'll walk in the sun's esteem,
Drinking but little, eating nothing.
At noon the white cat and she will dream
Of the day's going, the evening's coming,
Of the dark that carpets the dusty street.

Then both will wake and stretch and dress,
The one in moon-fire, the other in denim,
And leave the house by separate ways
To the same meeting, the same parting
At both ends of the broken street.

The cat will flatten beside a fence
In darkness watching, in silence waiting
For a scent to set off the song and dance,
Then hating and loving he'll live until morning
Damps his white ashes with bitter and sweet.

And Edie will pass by the hostel and wait,
Hearing the babble and smelling the cooking
Of migrant workers young and hot
Who'll tell her they're lonely and drink to her only
And kiss before morning her broad brown feet.

LOVE AND MARRIAGE

RAY MATHEW
1929–

DESIRE that all men have is all my love.
But the girl reads magazines with glossy covers,
Denies the self-in-time that she might have,
Declares that she needs love and never lovers.

Habitual's the thing I most despise.
But the girl talks home and marriage, licensed lovers,
Denies the act, the play, the hope of prize,
Declares she needs what never love discovers.

I should have known, those loving-days ago,
The girl in her hid woman and not lover
For when we fell upon the floor to crow
She saw the carpet needed sweeping over

Though she said nothing then; I had my way.
But she it is who names the wedding-day.

PHAR LAP IN THE MELBOURNE MUSEUM

PETER PORTER
1929–

A MASTERPIECE of the taxidermist's art,
Australia's top patrician stares
Gravely ahead at crowded emptiness,
As if alive, the lustre of dead hairs,
Lozenged liquid eyes, black nostrils
Gently flared, otter-satin coat declares
That death cannot visit in this thin perfection.

The democratic hero full of guile,
Noble, handsome, gentle Houyhnhnm
(In both Paddock and St Leger difference is
Lost in the welter of money)—to see him win
Men sold farms, rode miles in floods,
Stole money, locked up wives, somehow got in:
First away, he led the field and easily won.

It was his simple excellence to be best.
Tough men owned him, their minds beset
By stakes, bookies' doubles, crooked jocks.
He soon became a byword, public asset,
A horse with a nation's soul upon his back—
Australia's Ark of the Covenant, set
Before the people, perfect, loved like God.

And like God to be betrayed by friends.
Sent to America, he died of poisoned food.
In Australia children cried to hear the news
(This Prince of Orange knew no bad or good).
It was, as people knew, a plot of life:
To live in strength, to excel and die too soon,
So they drained his body and they stuffed his skin.

Twenty years later on Sunday afternoons
You still can't see him for the rubbing crowds.
He shares with Bradman and Ned Kelly some
Of the dirty jokes always going around.
It is Australian innocence to love
The naturally excessive and be proud
Of a handsome chestnut gelding who ran fast.

LIFE-CYCLE
for Big Jim Phelan

WHEN children are born in Victoria
they are wrapped in the club colours, laid in beribboned cots,
having already begun a lifetime's barracking.

Carn, they cry, Carn . . . feebly at first
while parents playfully tussle with them
for possession of a rusk: Ah, he's a little Tiger! (And they are. . . .)

Hoisted shoulder-high at their first League game
they are like innocent monsters who have been years swimming
towards the daylight's roaring empyrean

Until, now, hearts shrapnelled with rapture,
they break surface and are for ever lost,
their minds rippling out like streamers

In the pure flood of sound, they are scarfed with light, a voice
like the voice of God booms from the stands
Ooohh you bludger and the covenant is sealed.

Hot pies and potato-crisps they will eat,
they will forswear the Demons, cling to the Saints
and behold their team going up the ladder into Heaven,

BRUCE
DAWE
1930–

239

And the tides of life will be the tides of the home team's fortunes
—the reckless proposal after the one-point win,
the wedding and honeymoon after the grand final. . . .

They will not grow old as those from more northern States grow old,
for them it will always be three-quarter-time
with the scores level and the wind advantage in the final term,

That passion persisting, like a race memory, through the welter of seasons,
enabling old-timers by boundary-fences to dream of resurgent lions
and centaur figures from the past to replenish continually the present,

So that mythology may be perpetually renewed
and Chicken Smallhorn return like the maize-god
in a thousand shapes, the dancers changing

But the dance for ever the same—the elderly still
loyally crying Carn. . . . Carn . . . (if feebly) unto the very end,
having seen in the six-foot recruit from Eaglehawk their hope of salvation.

HOMECOMING

BRUCE
DAWE

ALL DAY, day after day, they're bringing them home,
they're picking them up, those they can find, and bringing them home,
they're bringing them in, piled on the hulls of Grants, in trucks, in convoys,
they're zipping them up in green plastic bags,
they're tagging them now in Saigon, in the mortuary coolness
they're giving them names, they're rolling them out of
the deep-freeze lockers—on the tarmac at Tan Son Nhut
the noble jets are whining like hounds,
they are bringing them home
—curly-heads, kinky-hairs, crew-cuts, balding non-coms
—they're high, now, high and higher, over the land, the steaming *chow mein*,
their shadows are tracing the blue curve of the Pacific
with sorrowful quick fingers, heading south, heading east,
home, home, home—and the coasts swing upward, the old ridiculous curvatures
of earth, the knuckled hills, the mangrove-swamps, the desert emptiness . . .
in their sterile housing they tilt towards these like skiers
—taxiing in, on the long runways, the howl of their home-coming rises
surrounding them like their last moments (the mash, the splendour)
then fading at length as they move
on to small towns where dogs in the frozen sunset
raise muzzles in mute salute,
and on to cities in whose wide web of suburbs
telegrams tremble like leaves from a wintering tree
and the spider grief swings in his bitter geometry
—they're bringing them home, now, too late, too early.

240

PROVINCIAL CITY

Climbing the range
your ears pop like champagne
and your heart distends
with something other than relief.

You can smell the peace up here.
The proportion, the narrowness.
Traitor, traitor, whines that piano-wire voice
as you swing past the Welcome sign

To find nothing is changed.
Overhead the clouds boil past,
low, friendly, meaning no harm.
The thunder moving into position

BRUCE
DAWE

DAVID STRACHAN

Shortly after five o'clock is stolid
as a furniture removalist.
The lightning jerks its thumb:
Over here, Fred.

When it rains
the gutters run red
but it's innocent. Dogs and magpies
the red soil stains.

In season the currawongs in the camphor-laurels
cry like tin-shears.
(The jacarandas hang their sheets
of blue water in mid-air.)

Down James Street the semis hurtle
nightly, brutalising through the quiet
civilised dark like the Eumenides,
or conscience, or history.

Here the elderly come to convalesce
after life's anxious illness; the young
leave daily for the Cities of the Plain
where there is work (or the hope of it).

On the hillside at Drayton
the cemetery glitters like a dream;
asterisks of light
on the wind-screens of mourners' cars

Glint remotely as stars
in a heaven-deep well.
We will never get there.
This is a city which is all *present:*

It moves, but oh so slowly
you would have to sleep years,
waking suddenly once in a decade
to surprise it in the act of change.

Saturday night, in the main street kerb,
the angle-parked cars are full of watchers,
their feet on invisible accelerators,
going nowhere, *fast*

DAVID STRACHAN

A SUMMER DEATH
*(The speaker is a young mother who has
taken an overdose of sleeping tablets.)*

SORRY the windows aren't too clean: I never
managed to keep things as I like them—funny
that after living so messily so long
I should become as tidy as my mother,
or almost, or want to be. But lying
here on the unmade double bed, the sun
comes streaming in pretty much the same—
an odd time to be dying. Am I dying?
Very relaxed, more relaxed than for weeks,
for months, for years, I can't remember quite
being so absorbed in the mere play of light
across things, colours, shadows, the clear run
of weather that's so mild and yet so sunny.
Hard to remember now the constant bother
of marriage, the accusations and the lame
denials, the sour talk of love for ever,
the quarrels about bills, deposits, cheques,
because it's all so clear now, and so soon:
watching the curtains stream and blow apart,
I know that there's an end and a new start
now, about now, a lightness of the heart. . . .

Something is terribly wrong, terribly wrong—
I can't now even hear the children crying,
drowsily sinking in the summer afternoon.

EVAN JONES
1931–

243

HALF-HEARD

CHRISTOPHER
KOCH
1932–

ON the road through the hills I thought I heard it,
Something moving, coming with evening,
In its slow warm breathing through the paddock-land.
The few and spiteful houses there ignored it.

It had come from the coast. I stood on the coast,
Where gulls cried angrily for something that moved,
In the sun-plains across the sea.
The water there was heavy with its hand.

And one by one the evening waves caressed the sullen sand.
Quietly they pondered on nothing at all,
On the laying of their long quiet hands, perhaps,
Upon the waiting beach.

Considering carefully nothing at all,
They too ignored the bird's half-baffled cry.

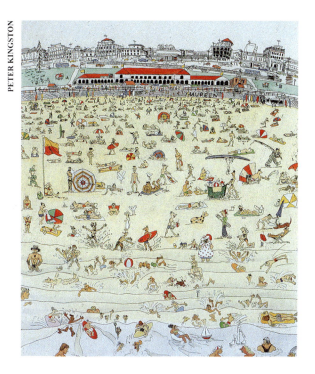

PETER KINGSTON

SUMMER SKETCHES: SYDNEY

i

City of yachts and underwater green
with blue hydrangeas fading in between
the walls of sloping gardens full of sails,
as sudden as a heart the sunlight fails
and over all the city falls again
a change of light, the neon's coloured rain.

VIVIAN SMITH
1933–

ii

Tourists in their lives of sudden ease
stare through dark glasses at the coral-trees
and know at once that only colour's true:
the red in green: within the green, the blue.

iii

At night the cool precision of the stars,
the neon glitter and the sexy cars,
the easy pick-up in the close green bars.

iv

A holiday like some smooth magazine;
how photos can improve the simplest scene.
They isolate the image that endures;
beyond the margins is the life that cures.
But when the surface gloss is thought away
some images survive through common day
and linger with a touch of tenderness:
the way you brushed your hair, your summer dress.

245

FAMILY ALBUM

VIVIAN SMITH

i

PLAYING with a tomahawk, a gun,
the children in the weeded formal garden
pitch their Christmas tents and just for fun
whet their axes and the blades they harden

chop off screams and squeals within the dusk
that splays each other's hair with pats of mud.
Upstairs the adolescent and athletic son
glimpses heaven from his tower of blood

and riding like his hero's motorbike
crashes into nowhere-all-is-well.
Mother calls the youngsters in to tea.
The light filters. Somewhere rings a bell.

ii

A bell rings. And father shuts his book.
A constipated blowfly sings the praise
of summer in its iridescent wings. . . .
Father notes the young ones' little ways

and how they've torn his prize azalea out;
is wise; remembers how he too was young;
and watering the roses he recalls
the tender taste of his wife's tongue—

and how he praised her body with his own
and made her flower like a burning tree;
and standing in the garden's fading green
dreams of a little sad adultery.

ADRIFT

ADRIFT in her Parker Knoll
rocking-chair, my mother
rocks this way and that
in this room and that room
of a stranger's house—the new
two-roomed flat she calls
her unit, never home.
A unit: but of what?
Where now is the whole?

And brought from the house
at Hamilton her solid
antique furniture—
chairs, bed-ends, a credenza
stacked against the wall,
piled up without thought
for use or for order.
Haphazard: an image of
the way things never were.

DAVID MALOUF
1934–

My sister's kids come brawling
around her knees, bring
bits of a jigsaw puzzle
to sort in her lap:
a dazzle of sea—or is it
sky? the bricks and mortar
of somebody's house.
Her own is tenanted
by strangers; who leave the lights

ablaze in empty rooms,
bang doors, let kittens pee
on cushions, scratch at chairs.
In a corner of afternoon
gilt-edged and insecure
since my father's tough heart slammed
and shut her out, she rocks
in the late sun, a ghost
the sun does not shine through.

OTHER PEOPLE

CHRIS WALLACE-CRABBE
1934–

IN the First World War they . . .
Who were *they*? Who cares any more? . . .
Killed four of my uncles,
So I discovered one day.

There were only four on that side of the family
And all swept away in a few bad years
In a war the historians tell us now
Was fought over nothing at all.

Four uncles, as one might say
A dozen apples or seven tons of dirt,
Swept away by the luck of history,
Closed off. Full stop.

Four is a lot for uncles,
A lot for lives, I should say.
Their chalk was wiped clean off the slate,
The War meant nothing at all.

War needs a lot of uncles,
And husbands, and brothers, and so on:
Someone must *want* to kill them,
Somebody needs them dead.

Who is it, I wonder. Me?
Or is it you there, reading away,
Or a chap with a small-arms factory?
Or is it only *they*?

MAX DUPAIN

A TASTE OF SALT WATER

THOMAS
SHAPCOTT
1935–

THIS cold glass on my desk contains salt water;
it is the sea water, bitter and rich to the taste,
carrying arguments and threats and signals
you would never hear in any booming shell
picked up and cleaned, long dead beyond dying.
It is the ocean, here, itself. I think of my grandmother.

When I was a boy at the edge of the scattering sea
where running laughter was an entire language
she was the mystery in the water under the jetty
and the finder of gifts in the seaweed treasuring the sand.
She was the shallow rockpools telling me stories
as I clambered into sunburnt salt-bright sleep
and drowned in the cool sheets, sandy and forgotten.

But I think I acknowledged her most of all
when I was washed across sandbanks into adolescence.
It is a time when parents are too distant and too close,
slashing at the wrong moment, infinitely vulnerable
in the blistering, freckling sunlight everywhere.
My grandmother then was a relaxed summer holiday,
moving outside any possible language of argument,
till it seemed to me she alone could show me
the deep water caves of infinite calm
down past the tease and glare of sun on my shallows,
deeper past the tidal channels where my father
clumsily foundered and tangled in worrying seaweed,
further down, where the long grasses of light
surged and filtered slowly and merged into greenness,
deeply and easily green, the pastures of wisdom for ever submarine.

But the ocean is all of it salt, it is all salt water.
I took from my grandmother this cold glass to drink
on the first day that I opened my eyes underwater
wanting to plunge down and search for her treasure.
In my mouth I choked on the taste of the raw ocean.
Once tasted, its bitterness stings in you for ever.

She lay more than a week dying. I was a man.
The tides rose and returned still in her breath,
but her body had beached up like a bare sandbank
and the dry wind ruffled its surface coldly and foreignly
scuffling for shells. The wind licked only
at the crusting salt and the brackish waste of tidestains.

I walked on that sandbank, and looked at the minute hand on my watch.
Her eyes were shut. She would not see, I knew,
whether I waited or not. We were old strangers.
Out of the broken driftwood I picked a stick
the shape of a bone, a fish, an anchor, a man.
I know that the sea taste in this one small glass
is not so much her bitter savour as my own.

MARRIAGE

THOMAS
SHAPCOTT

A COBWEB tangles dustily around the light bulb,
the ceiling points to my inefficient brushstrokes
and the evidence of so many forgotten weekends;
but it is home, it is our own. I watch you bathe

tonight, easing your limbs heavily to the water,
and your tired body, which should be familiar to me
as my own, becomes a serious instruction
in all the persistent mysteries of marriage.

Now that your belly distends and feeds on you,
and your breasts buoy up and are moist with the expectant milk,
I can see only your strong frailty. The pressure
kicks already. The curve of your back is vulnerable,
and your throat, as you stretch out to reach for soap,
denies and denies the trudging chains of kitchen,
ironing, and the disciplining children.
And should you look up and smile....
Come out, here is your towel.

No, do not look into the mirror, we only see
the flaws and abrasions there, cobwebs in a poor light.
If you would see yourself truly, look at me
and be afraid and joyful at the sight.

THE GHOST AT ANLABY
for Geoffrey and Ninette Dutton

RANDOLPH STOW
1935–

NOW sulkies come haunting softwheeled down the
leaves; on the cool veranda, over
whisky, wistaria, gentlemen admire
antwaisted, hamsleeved, bellskirted ladies
crossing the lawns with fishtailed racquets
intent on tennis. Heart, unlearn your fire.

Forget now, forget. Below the willows
Tom Roberts squatters, George Lambert ladies,
whose boats and fancy made this dam a lake,
speak of, remember, no visitant stranger.
Once time was a sportsman, and I the quarry,
who now would sleep with death, for sleep's kind sake.

But O whose fingers, soft as wistaria,
played with my watch-chain, under the crabapples;
under the lilacs in October flower
whose fingers like lingering tendrils twined in
my hair, my beard? What phantom remembers
that wicked, warm, Edwardian midday hour?

Rosella-plumed sun, go quickly down on
my afternoon ghosts. Let purple night that
brings all lovers to their billiard-rooms descend.
Click of the balls. Among wraiths of cigar-smoke,
with rib-nudging stories I died before telling,
I shall go haunting in search of a friend, a friend.

THE SLEEPERS
from 'Thailand Railway'

RANDOLPH STOW

LET the wick burn low: and suddenly I remember
(with tears in the throat, with anger, with disbelief)
that we are young.

These skeletons ribbed and tanned like droughtstruck sheep,
these monkey-faces, hooding their hot sunk eyeballs
—these are young men.

Limbs that the surf washed, lips that the girls farewelled,
fumble, shape words. I know these unaltering, nightly
homecomings. Dawn

will be heartbreak, exile, atrocities of light
on a tangle of rags and angled bones: but now
is years ago.

Thank God for sleep no captor steals indefinitely,
for death that brings a gift, the final privacy,
time to oneself.

My neighbour moans in his sleep, and I stretch my arm,
and he sighs and quietens under my arm like a child,
gaunt cheek on hand.

When I smashed my mirror his face still showed my face.
Thank God for a feeble light, for our phantom youth,
for need and tenderness.

MRS MACINTOSH

RODNEY HALL
1935–

MRS MACINTOSH so simply
has reduced the world's dilemmas
to her fixed obsession, birdcage buying.
Now exhibits fill her rooms:
some are miniature pagodas,
and one a jail of cells.
The smallest, made from a lost
girl's hand, is bones enmeshed
in silver wire. The largest
looks an anarchy of cleverness
the total snub to cage-convention
a cloud so frail and knobbled
it dangles crazily askew, high
against the inconvenience of a wall.

These, her eccentricities,
are cherished catalogued
paraded for the delectation
of any visiting evangelist
salesman or charity collector.
Her cages, Mrs Macintosh
is careful to point out, are empty.
Birds revolt her—frighten
her wrinkled eye with theirs
and mock her ways with harsh high
female voices; or sing so sweetly
they could almost lure her back
to join the world. Unbearable.
No, she likes her symbolism:
cages free of birds, pure captivity
that's innocent of pain.

All day her hymns escape the house.

ON TRYING TO REMEMBER SOMEONE

RODNEY HALL

THE MIND cannot hold fast to people,
the wholeness of their tissue
cannot be fused again:
the wholeness that we need to recreate.
Even our own wounds heal
to part of our accepted selves,
scars no more observable than wrinkles
cease to be wounds at all
much less a documentary of battle.
Memory even vivisects our friends—
each particular
in careful store, complete
with the tag of our response.

We go tap-tapping white sticks
about our phantom warehouse,
question woolly flesh,
catch at dust and kiss the shadows,
put every certainty to flight.
So now we search for unknown people
as living counterparts of those
digested by the mind—
hoping, perhaps, we'll learn who changed our lives.
Not that we want to be as once we were;
rather we want to know
what others did to us
and if there must be judgments.

RAINWATER TANK

EMPTY RINGS when tapped give tongue
rings that are tense with water talk:
as he sounds them, ring by rung,
Joe Mitchell's reddened knuckles walk.

The cattle dog's head sinks down a notch
and another notch, beside the tank,
and Mitchell's boy, with an old jack-plane,
lifts moustaches from a plank.

From the puddle that the tank has dripped
hens peck glimmerings and uptilt
their heads to shape the quickness down;
petunias live on what gets spilt.

The tankstand spider adds a spittle
thread to her portrait of her soul.
Pencil-grey and stacked like shillings
out of a banker's paper roll

stands the tank, roof-water drinker.
The downpipe stares drought into it.
Briefly the kitchen tap turns on
then off. But the tank says Debit, Debit.

LES MURRAY
1938–

257

JO MCINTYRE

AN ABSOLUTELY ORDINARY RAINBOW

LES MURRAY

THE word goes round Repins,
the murmur goes round Lorenzinis,
at Tattersalls, men look up from sheets of numbers,
the Stock Exchange scribblers forget the chalk in their hands
and men with bread in their pockets leave the Greek Club:
There's a fellow crying in Martin Place. They can't stop him.

The traffic in George Street is banked up for half a mile
and drained of motion. The crowds are edgy with talk
and more crowds come hurrying. Many run in the back streets
which minutes ago were busy main streets, pointing:
There's a fellow weeping down there. No one can stop him.

The man we surround, the man no one approaches
simply weeps, and does not cover it, weeps
not like a child, not like the wind, like a man
and does not declaim it, nor beat his breast, nor even
sob very loudly—yet the dignity of his weeping

holds us back from his space, the hollow he makes about him
in the midday light, in his pentagram of sorrow,
and uniforms back in the crowd who tried to seize him
stare out at him, and feel, with amazement, their minds
longing for tears as children for a rainbow.

Some will say, in the years to come, a halo
or force stood around him. There is no such thing.
Some will say they were shocked and would have stopped him
but they will not have been there. The fiercest manhood,
the toughest reserve, the slickest wit amongst us

trembles with silence, and burns with unexpected
judgments of peace. Some in the concourse scream
who thought themselves happy. Only the smallest children
and such as look out of Paradise come near him
and sit at his feet, with dogs and dusty pigeons.

Ridiculous, says a man near me, and stops
his mouth with his hands, as if it uttered vomit—
and I see a woman, shining, stretch her hand
and shake as she receives the gift of weeping;
as many as follow her also receive it

and many weep for sheer acceptance, and more
refuse to weep for fear of all acceptance,
but the weeping man, like the earth, requires nothing,
the man who weeps ignores us, and cries out
of his writhen face and ordinary body

not words, but grief, not messages, but sorrow
hard as the earth, sheer, present as the sea—
and when he stops, he simply walks between us
mopping his face with the dignity of one
man who has wept, and now has finished weeping.

Evading believers, he hurries off down Pitt Street.

THE BROAD BEAN SERMON

LES
MURRAY

BEANSTALKS, in any breeze, are a slack church parade
without belief, saying *trepass against us* in unison,
recruits in mint Air Force dacron, with unbuttoned leaves.

Upright with water like men, square in stem-section
they grow to great lengths, drink rain, keel over all ways,
kink down and grow up afresh, with proffered new greenstuff.

Above the cat-and-mouse floor of a thin bean forest
snails hang rapt in their food, ants hurry through several dimensions,
spiders tense and sag like little black flags in their cordage.

Going out to pick beans with the sun high as fence-tops, you find
plenty, and fetch them. An hour or a cloud later
you find shirtfuls more. At every hour of daylight

appear more that you missed: ripe, knobbly ones, fleshy-sided,
thin-straight, thin-crescent, frown-shaped, bird-shouldered, boat-keeled ones,
beans knuckled and single-bulged, minute green dolphins at suck,

beans upright like lecturing, outstretched like blessing fingers
in the incident light, and more still, oblique to your notice
that the noon glare or cloud-light or afternoon slants will uncover

till you ask yourself Could I have overlooked so many, or
do they form in an hour? unfolding into reality
like templates for subtly broad grins, like unique caught expressions,

like edible meanings, each sealed around with a string
and affixed to its moment, an unceasing colloquial assembly,
the portly, the stiff, and those lolling in pointed green slippers. . . .

Wondering who'll take the spare bagfuls, you grin with happiness
—it is your health—you vow to pick them all
even the last few, weeks off yet, misshapen as toes.

THE FUTURE

THERE is nothing about it. Much science fiction is set there
but is not about it. Prophecy is not about it.
It sways no yarrow stalks. And crystal is a mirror.
Even the man we nailed on a tree for a lookout
said little about it; he told us evil would come.
We see, by convention, a small living distance into it
but even that's a projection. And all our projections
fail to curve where it curves.
                              It is the black hole
out of which no radiation escapes to us.
The commonplace and magnificent roads of our lives
go on some way through cityscape and landscape
or steeply sloping, or scree, into that sheer fall
where everything will be that we have ever sent there,
compacted, spinning—except perhaps us, to see it.
It is said we see the start.
                              But from here, there's a blindness.

LES
MURRAY

The side-heaped chasm that will swallow all our present
blinds us to the normal sun that may be imagined
shining calmly away on the far side of it, for others
in their ordinary day. A day to which all our portraits,
ideals, revolutions, denim and deshabille
are quaintly heartrending. To see those people is impossible,
to greet them, mawkish. Nonetheless, I begin:
'When I was alive—'
                              and I am turned around
to find myself looking at a cheerful picnic party,
the women decently legless, in muslin and gloves,
the men in beards and weskits, with the long
cheroots and duck trousers of the better sort,
relaxing on a stone veranda. Ceylon, or Sydney.
And as I look, I know they are utterly gone,
each one on his day, with pillow, small bottles, mist,
with all the futures they dreamed or dealt in, going
down to that engulfment everything approaches;
with the man on the tree, they have vanished into the Future.

THE DOLPHINS

from 'Monologues for Marcus Furius Camillus, Governor of Africa'

I

GEOFFREY
LEHMANN
1940–

MY personal slave in Africa first told me
Of how they play with men and rub against one
(Though barnacles upon their backs may cause
Abrasions, even death)
And how they dive for bubbles and bright objects,
And mimic us with duck-like noises.

This slave once on a journey called to me.
I had my litter lowered, stepped out and followed him.
He ran down goat-tracks to a rocky cove
And whistled and a dolphin danced towards us
Across the flat grey sea. The slave
Threw off his tunic and his rope-soled sandals,
Swam to the dolphin with outlandish shouts,
Hugged it and bit it with a laugh.
Almost intelligible it clicked and whistled.

Months later, at the noon siesta,
He came to me distraught and led me wordless
Past bodies snoring in cool hallways
And over sand dunes to a beach.
A dolphin lay there, puffed with death, eyes squinting.
Making a sign to ward off evil spirits
He split the skull in with a flint. The brain
Lay large and lustrous, bigger than a man's,
A silvery pulp, marbled with tiny veins.
He pointed to it briefly, muttered hoarsely,
Then threw sand on the body.

That night he babbled to me about dolphins,
Their sea-lore and their songs and odysseys,
And how their minds excelled our own
And they would contact us one day and bring
Peace to the world.
                    The palm-leaves clashed,
As breezes fanned the peristyle.
Rubbing ash on his face he softly moaned
Of the dead dolphin and his passion for it,
The language they had shared
And the shrill music that its blow-hole uttered,
Inaudible to him, but causing dogs
To freeze and listen, muscles trembling.

He raved of dolphins until dawn,
Of feats of magic and strange medicaments,
And history dating back before our gods.

My head drooped and I drowsed off on my couch.

Soon afterwards he vanished. Fishermen
Maintained they saw him swimming out to sea
One dusk, a strange light in his salt-wet hair.

IV

Walking one evening by the sea I heard
Laughter and splashing and strange voices,
And in an inlet came upon nine dolphins
Leaping and frisking in the stillness,
With moonlight gleaming dully on their bodies.

I listened to their comic mimicry
Of human voices, high-pitched and distorted,
And thought I picked out
Snatches of speech from various languages.
Not just the rudimentary sounds they mimicked,
But also tones, inflexion, quirk of speech.
The voices threatened, laughed, were sad or boastful.
Face down upon a shelf of rock I lay
And yearned to stand and cry with arms outstretched,
'I am a man and you are dolphins, let
Us love each other.'
                            But I was afraid.

Bubbles and flakes of phosphorescence.
Hour-long I watched, and now
With voices dwindling in a wake of stillness
They headed out to sea still gossiping.

Exhausted my eyes shut and I woke next day
Amongst red rock and sun and sea-glare.

GERRIT FOKKEMA

THERE ARE SOME LUSTY VOICES SINGING
From 'Ross's Poems'

THERE are some lusty voices singing
and hands clapping
of fine Aboriginal ladies
(in tune with the juke-box)
as I go past their saloon.

The walls are dirty turquoise,
the floorboards sodden with beer and cigarette butts.
The girls entertain black and white friends,
fall pregnant,
and die of poverty and alcohol.

It's degrading, you say (so do I).
but there's something I like
about the vehemence of their despair,
the way they throw their bodies at life
and don't care.
Black people on a winter night
will sit on boxes and kerosene tins
around a big fire
beneath overcast skies that don't move.

You can tell from the way they sing together
they've more compassion
than most Christian congregations.
Walking past I'm stirred by the voices
of girls in the turquoise saloon,
singing and clapping above the juke-box
with such despair and joy—
something we have lost.

GEOFFREY LEHMANN

RUSSELL DRYSDALE

GRIT
A Doxology

I PRAISE the country women
of my mother's generation
who bred, brought up and boasted
six Australians each—
the nearest doctor fifty miles
on a road cut off by flood;
the women who by wordless men
were courted away from typewriters
and taught themselves to drive—
I praise their style
in the gravel corners.
I praise the snakes they broke in two
and the switch of wire they kept in a cupboard.
I praise what they keep and what they lose—
the long road in to the abattoirs,
the stare which cures
a stockman of shooting swans.
I praise the prints, the wide straw brims
they wore out to the clothes line;
I praise each oily crow that watched them.
I praise the tilting weather—
the dry creeks and the steady floods
and the few good weeks between.
I praise each column in the ledger
they kept up late by mosquito and lamp-light;
the temerity of the banker
reining them in at last—or trying;
the machinations for chequered paddocks
swung on the children's names;
the companies just one step ahead;
the tax clerk, in his way, also.
I praise each one of their six children
discovering in turn
the river in its tempers
the rapids and the river trees;
the children who grew up to horse sweat
and those who made it to the city.
I praise the stringy maxims
that served instead of prayers;
also the day that each child found
a slogan not enough,
surprising themselves in a camera flash
and bringing no extra paddocks.
I praise the boast of country women:
they could have been a wife

GEOFFREY PAGE
1940–

to any of a dozen men
and damn well made it work.
I praise what I have seen
to be much more than this.
I praise their politics of leather;
the ideologies in a line of cattle;
the minds that would not
stoop to whisky.
I praise their scorn
for the city of options, the scholars
in their turning chairs and air-conditioned theories.
I praise also that moment
when they headed off in tears—
the car in a toolshed failing to start,
a bootful of fencing wire.
I praise the forty years
when they did not. I praise
each day and evening of their lives—
that hard abundance year by year
mapped in a single word.

BONDI AFTERNOON 1915
Elioth Gruner

GEOFF PAGE

THE WIND plays through
the painted weather.

No cloud. The sea
and air, one blue.

A hemisphere
away from gunfire

an artist finds
his image for the year:

a girl in white
blown muslin, walking
in the last
clear afternoon.

APIS MELLIFICA

ROGER
McDONALD
1941–

IN a dreamlike fall, the long
spoon in the honey-jar descends—a bubble going

down, he thinks, a silver bell.
He stands there awhile,

humming, twisting the spoon
slowly from side to side. (The moon

drops from an amber-coloured cloud,
on the horizon a metal sphere rides

heavily over water, hunting the crushed ocean floor.)
Fifteen pounds of honey in the tall jar—

nectar, the fall of pollen, bees in the Yellow Box tree
filling that flowery head once a year

with a huge thought, all of it here.
Now the spoon climbs up as though something

is spoken by light
and shade in their alternating

vowels of movement, and held—as though what the tree thought
was taken away and stored,

deepened, like an old colour, and understood.

SICKLE BEACH

ROGER
McDONALD

Sickle beach,
bay like a wine glass.
Butterflies launch themselves
eastward from marram grass.

Lemon, the lower sky,
apricot air.
Who would believe a man
died close to here?

Came, on a blue day,
easy, on horseback.
Slipped, and broke his head
hard on a rock.

Blood in the rippled light,
a word of surprise:
Me? It is not true.
Thus a man dies.

Thus, in the empty hills,
blackberries increase,
rabbits and wild cats
run through the house.

JOURNEY: THE NORTH COAST

ROBERT GRAY
1945–

NEXT THING, I wake up in a swaying bunk,
as though on board a clipper
lying in the sea
and it's the train, that booms and cracks,
it tears the wind apart.
Now the man's gone
who had the bunk below me. I swing out,
cover his bed and rattle up the sash—
there's sunlight rotating
off the drab carpet. And the water sways
solidly in its silver basin, so cold
it joins together through my hand.
I see from where I'm bent
one of those bright crockery days
that belong to so much I remember.

The train's shadow, like a bird's,
flees on the blue and silver paddocks,
over fences that look split from stone,
and banks of fern,
a red clay bank, full of roots,
over a dark creek, with logs and leaves suspended,
and blackened tree trunks.
Down these slopes move, as a nude descends a staircase,
slender white gum trees,
and now the country bursts open on the sea—
across a calico beach, unfurling;
strewn with flakes of light
that make the whole compartment whirl.
Shuttering shadows. I rise into the mirror
rested. I'll leave my hair
ruffled a bit that way—fold the pyjamas,
stow the book and wash bag. Everything done,
press down the latches into the case,
that for twelve months I've watched standing out
of a morning, above the wardrobe
in a furnished room.

THE DUSK

A KANGAROO is standing up, and dwindling like a plant   ROBERT GRAY
with a single bud.
Fur combed into a crest
along the inside length of its body,
a bow-wave
under slanted light, out in the harbour.

And its fine unlined face is held on the cool air;
a face in which you feel
the small thrust-forward teeth lying in the lower jaw,
grass-stained and sharp.

Standing beyond a wire fence, in weeds,
against the bush that is like a wandering smoke.

Mushroom-coloured,
and its white chest, the underside of a growing mushroom,
in the last daylight.

273

The tail is trailing heavily as a lizard lying concealed.

It turns its head like a mannequin
toward the fibro shack,
and holds the forepaws
as though offering to have them bound.

An old man standing on a dirt path in his vegetable garden,
where a cabbage moth puppet-leaps and jiggles wildly
in the cooling sunbeams,
has the bucket still swinging in his hand.

And the kangaroo settles down, pronged,
then lifts itself
carefully, like a package passed over from both arms—

The now curved-up tail is rocking gently counterweight behind
as it flits hunched
amongst the stumps and scrub, into the dusk.

CATTLE

PETER SKRZYNECKI
1945-

WITH their boxing-glove muzzles
They will stand in your path, heads lowered,
Or run stumbling through bracken
And creeks for no reason,
The grass alive with their fear.

Their bodies heavy
With milk and beef—awkward
As felled timber, they live
Herded by dogs and whips,
By our curses and impatience.

In downpours and mists
They stand like mute sentinels—immobile
With solemn, wide-open eyes,
Staring through hills and fences.

At night they bellow
Across paddocks and gullies,
Wake us from sleep and reassure us
Of our dreams and homestead.

Branded with fire
They have plodded through
Grass, mud and water for centuries—
Leaving, across continents,
A cleft print

That man will decipher
As an omen of its final hunger.

THE BEGINNING

MARK
O'CONNOR
1945–

GOD HIMSELF
having that day planted a garden
walked through it at evening and knew
that Eden was not nearly complex enough.
And he said:
'Let species swarm like solutes in a colloid.
Let there be ten thousand species of plankton
and to eat them one thousand zoöplankton.
Let there be ten phyla of siphoning animals, and
one thousand finned vertebrate types, from
white-tipped reef shark to long-beaked coral fish,
and to each his proper niche,
and—no Raphael, I'm not quite finished yet—
you can add seals and sea-turtles & cone-shells & penguins
(if they care) and all the good seabirds your team can devise—
oh yes, and I nearly forgot it, I want a special place
for the crabs! And now for parasites to hold
the whole system in check, let. . . . '
'. . . In conclusion, I want,' he said,
'ten thousand mixed chains of predation—
none of your simple rabbit and coyote stuff!
This ocean shall have many mouths, many palates,
many means of ingestion. I want
one hundred means of death, and three thousand regenerations,
all in technicolour naturally. And oh yes, I nearly forgot,
we can use Eden again for the small coral cay in the centre.

'So now Raphael, if you please,
just draw out and marshal these species,
and we'll plant them all out in a twelve-hectare patch.'

So for five and a half days God laboured
and on the seventh he donned mask and snorkel
and a pair of bright yellow flippers.

And, later, the host all peered wistfully down
through the high safety fence around Heaven
and saw God with his favourites finning slowly over the coral
in the eternal shape of a grey nurse shark,
and they saw that it was very good indeed.

A policeman helped a man load
a mattress on his truck.
At a white railing we saw the brown water
boil off into the dark.
It rolled midstream higher than its banks
and people cheered when a cat on a crate
and a white fridge whizzed past.

II

Every summer morning at five-thirty in the dark
I rummaged for my swimming bag
among musty gym shoes and Mum's hats from 1940
in the brown hall cupboard.
And Dad and I purred down through the sweet, fresh morning
still cool, but getting rosy
at Paul's Ice Cream factory,
and turned left at the Gasworks for South Brisbane Baths.

The day I was knocked off my kickboard
by an aspiring Olympian aged ten
it was cool and quiet and green down on the bottom.
Above the swaying ceiling limbs like pink logs,
and knifing arms churned past.
I looked at a crack in the cream wall
as I descended and thought of nothing.
When all of a sudden
Dad's legs, covered in silver bubbles,
his khaki shorts and feet in thongs
plunged into view like a new aquatic animal.

I was happy driving home;
Dad in a borrowed shirt with red poinsettias
and the coach's light blue, shot-silk togs.

KING PARROTS

THEY'VE arrived.
That's all I am allowed to know.
Four, no six, they have materialised

trembling on the Mexican Hawthorn
as though the tree had just devised them,
six startling orchids,

or six jocund rascals, outrageous
in their green or crimson balaclavas
and crimson pantaloons,

ALAN GOULD
1949–

279

tucking away their conifer wings,
eating with greedy disdain
like babies or comic strip bandidos.

My lawn is rubbished with half-eaten crimson berries.
Vandals. Solferino angels:
how can my eye stray while they remain

in creaturely candelabra
on a sky of nursery blue?
It's like a siege.

One cocks its head, as though to say,
'Don't worry. We are too brilliant to be real',
then goes on eating from my tree.

They're gone. The branch skitters into stillness.
And I could spend a year behind this glass
longing for their return.

PORTRAIT OF THE ARTIST AS AN OLD MAN

MICHAEL
DRANSFIELD
1948–1973

IN my father's house are many cobwebs.
I prefer not to live there—the ghosts
disturb me. I sleep in a loft
over the coach-house, and each morning cross
through a rearguard of hedges to wander in the house.
It looks as though it grew out of the ground
among its oaks and pines, under the great
ark of Moreton Bay figs.
My study is the largest room upstairs;
there, on wet days, I write
archaic poems at a cedar table.
Only portraits and spiders inhabit the hall
Of Courland Penders . . . however,
I check the place each day for new arrivals.
Once, in the summerhouse, I found a pair
of diamond sparrows nesting on a sofa
among warped racquets and abandoned things.
Nobody visits Courland Penders; the town
is miles downriver, and few know me there.
Once there were houses near by. They are gone
wherever houses go when they
fall down or burn down or are taken away on lorries.
It is peaceful enough. Birdsong flutes from the trees
seeking me among memories and clocks.
When night or winter comes, I light a fire
and watch the flames
rise and fall like waves. I regret nothing.

MAX DUPAIN

INGREDIENTS OF THE BALLAD

MICHAEL DRANSFIELD

I WENT to see an alchemist
he kept the wind in bottles
he made a storm by pulling corks
made rain with brine on a hot stone

i went to see reality
i had to pay to get inside
it was no better than my dreams
but more expensive, being real

i went to see the holy lands
i had to pay to get inside
a war was going when i left
with prizes for the church that won

i went to see a girl i knew
i had to pay to get inside
but when i left she gave me love
as if it were of value.

THE MEMBERS OF THE ORCHESTRA

WALK onto the dark stage dressed for a funeral
or a wedding and we, the anxious ones, quieten
as we wait to discover which it will be tonight:

they sit or stand before thin books written
in a foreign script, more alien than Chinese,
but its secret contents will be revealed now

as at the reading of a dead relation's will,
for the last member has entered, slightly late
as befits his honour, like a famous lecturer

with a new theory and a pointer to make it clear.
Alas, he too cannot talk except in the language
of the deaf and dumb, but as he waves his hands

the members of the orchestra commence their act
of complicated ventriloquism, each making
his instrument speak our long-forgotten native tongue.

Now one violin reaches above the rest, rehearsing
the articulate sorrow of things in this world
where we have suddenly woken to find a music

KEVIN HART
1954–

MAX DUPAIN

283

as curious as the relation between an object
and its name. We are taken by the hand and led
through the old darkness that separates us

from things in themselves, through the soft fold
of evening that keeps two days apart. And now
each instrument tells its story in details

that become the whole, the entire forest contained
within a leaf: the orchestra is quickly building
a city of living air about us where we can live

and know ourselves at last, for we have given up
our selves, as at our wedding or our funeral,
to take on something new, something that was always there.

A HISTORY OF THE FUTURE

KEVIN HART

THERE will be cities and mountains
as there are now,

and steeled armies
marching through abandoned Squares
as they have always done.

There will be fields to plough,
the wind will shake the trees, acorns
will fall,

and plates will still crack
for no apparent reason.

And that is all we can truly know.

The future is over the horizon, we cannot hear
a word its people say,

and even if they shout to us
to make us cease
bombing their lands, destroying their cities,

a shout from there would sound like an acorn
dropped on cement,

or a plate on the shelf
beginning to crack.

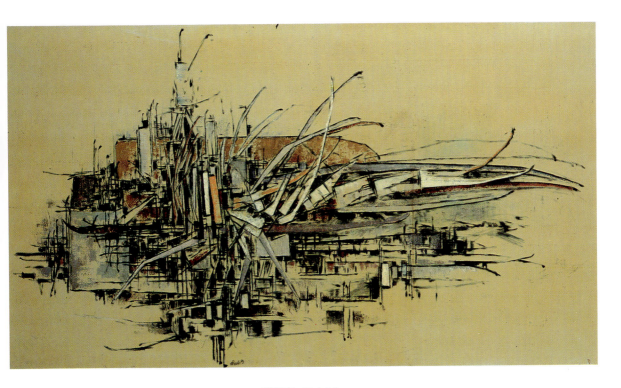

THE DAM

THE dam at the end of the deep green field
is a metre of brown wrapping paper
covering the clay that has not congealed.
In the days before the excavator
two men with shovels dug it in a week.
When I was five I nearly drove the tractor in.
A load of fodder held us back.
In summer it's popular with the herd
who muck it up by floating green cow pats
and come out caked, with leeches on their teats.
In winter it's the spot for shooting birds.
Two ibises stand on the rim like taps.

PHILIP HODGINS
1959–1995

LEAVING

SHE left the hospital quietly at night.
The lights were out and only a skeleton staff
remained in the office on her first floor ward.

Outside the streets were dark with drizzle
and there were only a few cars around,
making a smooth tearing sound as they passed.

PHILIP HODGINS

She noticed that the cars were very old, pre-war,
but were shining in good condition anyway
and that the city centre had a human scale,

the sort of scale it used to have when she
first came here with her parents sixty years ago.
The highest objects were the crosses on the spires.

By the time she reached the station the sun was up
and the platform was a rather frightening place
with its cross-currents of adults dressed for work.

A train had just arrived and from its van
men in overalls were unloading wooden crates.
She held her mother's hand as she'd been told to.

The station building hadn't changed a bit.
Its famous row of clocks under the copper dome,
its tiled floors and timber ceilings were all intact.

Moving off, the train whistled and she saw again
the enamel platform sign, cast iron framed,
which had cast her mind's image of that number.

It only took a few suburbs before the train
was out in a landscape of fifty acre farms
where harnessed horses and small grey tractors

both worked the paddocks, and where the roads,
even the main ones back to town, weren't sealed.
Sometimes she saw a farmer waving at the train.

Her carriage creaked and swayed like an old bed.
It seemed to her the further away they went
the more she recognized the farms and little towns.

The home stop, when it came, was feverishly hot
and the light was very harsh. She squinted
with interest at the lack of progress in this town.

It was here as a girl she had first seen life
away from the formality of her parents' farm.
Nothing since had been as new as that look.

The station was as crowded as it had been then.
Most of the population seemed to be there
for it was the railway that kept the town alive.

Soon the train began to take on new passengers.
She waited until she had to give up her place
and then stepped out into the terrible light.

FIVE THOUSAND ACRE PADDOCK

THERE was only one   PHILIP HODGINS
tree in all that space and he
drove straight into it.

THE FISH MARKETS

JEMAL SHARAH
1969–

ONLY the sea escapes this enclosed space,
its shimmer, like pigeons rising, leaning away
from the cement-encircled place's
mortuary chill. In those low buildings
is a humming crowd of people, come to gaze
in swarms, upon a harlequinade
of fishes: obdurate mussels, prawns
with a gasflame flicker at each tail, fish
patterned with newsprint, smeared
like wet road with oily rainbows,
mottled, marbled, freckled with colour
and glazed with ice and water:
the fins' feathery lines cling like tear-wet lashes.
So clean a carnage—preserved on banks of ice:
a massacre, bloodless, white as innocence
and so fresh you'd think the victims were alive,
but for the stillness, the look of faint surprise
that death deals out, the fingermarks on the eyes.
You imagine a trawler raising its great draught
of moons and crescents, ungainly in the dark,
releasing its gasping load into the holds
for bringing here: the asphalt desolation
of this site, with the indifferent sea
and air with its scent of manifold ends;
the haul heaped, piled, swimming
in voluptuous death.

NEW-FOUND LAND

JEMAL SHARAH

SHOULDERS slope like dunes
across my sight:
warm as a lonely beach
in the afternoon light.

Shells slipping into sand,
the spine's ridge: small clenches
of bone. Smooth beneath my hand,
driftwood branches.

After ambling through years
my feet found this track.
The ways are mined now;
I can't go back.

INDEX OF
AUTHORS

WITH BRIEF BIOGRAPHIES AND SELECT BIBLIOGRAPHIES

ETHEL ANDERSON

ETHEL Louise Anderson (*née* Mason) was born of Australian parents in 1883 at Leamington, Warwickshire, and died in Sydney in 1958. Her childhood home was at Rangamatty, near Picton (NSW), and she was educated at the Church of England Girls' Grammar School, Sydney. After her marriage to the British Army officer Austin Anderson (later Brigadier-General) she spent ten years on the Indian frontier, returning in 1924 to Australia where her husband became aide to various NSW Governors before his appointment as aide to the Governor-General, Lord Gowrie. A witty and idiosyncratic writer, she published essays and short stories (notably *Indian Tales*, 1948, and *At Parramatta*, 1956) as well as verse.

Squatters' Luck, 1942; *Sunday at Yarralumla*, 1947; *The Song of Hagar*, 1957.

Page 119

DOROTHY
AUCHTERLONIE

BORN on 28 May 1915 at Sunderland, Durham, England, Dorothy Auchterlonie was brought to Australia at the age of twelve and educated at North Sydney High School and the University of Sydney. After taking an MA degree she worked as a teacher and a journalist before marrying the eminent critic and literary historian, H.M. Green. For some years she was co-principal of the Presbyterian Girls' College, Warwick (Q), and in 1961 she became the first woman lecturer at Monash University (Melbourne). Later she taught at the Australian National University and at the Royal Military College, Duntroon which became the Australian Defence Force Academy in 1984. A distinguished scholar and critic, her major work is *Ulysses Bound*, 1974, a landmark in the study of the novelist Henry Handel Richardson. She died in 1991.

Kaleidoscope, 1940; *The Dolphin*, 1967.

Pages 195–196

LEX BANNING

LEX (A.A.) Banning was born in Sydney in 1921. After graduating in Arts at the University of Sydney he became a freelance journalist, reviewing books and writing for films and radio. Later he became librarian at the Spastic Centre in Mosman, Sydney. He had produced three books of perceptive and sardonic verse before his death on 2 November 1965.

Every Man His Own Hamlet, 1951; *The Instant's Clarity*, 1952; *Apocalypse in Springtime*, 1956.

Page 208

BORN on 14 February 1928 at Manly, NSW, Bruce Beaver was educated at Manly Public School and at the Sydney Boys' High School, then worked in a variety of occupations—as a labourer, clerk, fruit-picker, proof-reader, as well as in radio and occasional journalism—until he went to New Zealand in 1958, spent six months on Norfolk Island in 1959, and returned to Australia in 1962. Since 1961 he has published many volumes of verse with a great variety of modes and themes, as well as a novel, *You Can't Come Back* (1966). Bruce Beaver lives at Manly.

Under the Bridge, 1961; *Seawall and Shoreline*, 1964; *Open at Random*, 1967; *Letters to Live Poets*, 1969; *Lauds and Plaints*, 1974; *Odes and Days*, 1975; *Death's Directives*, 1978; *As It Was*, 1979; *Selected Poems*, 1979; *Headlands*, 1986; *Charmed Lives*, 1988; *New and Selected Poems*, 1991; *Anima and Other Poems*, 1994.

Pages 233–236

BORN at Unley, SA, on 30 July 1913, John Blight was educated at Brisbane High School and lived in Queensland ever since. He worked as an orchardist, then qualified as an accountant, and, after hard times on the track during the Depression, became a public servant. In 1949 he was appointed a member of a Government Commission of Inquiry into the timber industry in Queensland. He became secretary, then director, of a sawmilling company with mills along the north-west coast of Queensland. Best known for his sonnets about the seashore and its creatures, from the seventies he turned a philosophic eye on the cities and suburbs. An original and personal poet, he was aptly called 'an illuminator' by Douglas Stewart. He died in 1995.

The Old Pianist, 1945; *The Two Suns Met*, 1954; *A Beachcomber's Diary*, 1963; *My Beachcombing Days*, 1968; *Hart*, 1975; *Selected Poems, 1939–1975*, 1976; *Pageantry for a Lost Empire*, 1977; *The New City Poems*, 1980; *Holiday Sea Sonnets*, 1985; *Selected Poems*, 1991.

Pages 165–166

BARCROFT Boake began to write poetry only towards the end of his short life of 26 years and he is remembered mainly for the poem 'Where the Dead Men Lie'. He was born in Sydney on 26 March 1866 and educated (after several years in Noumea as a small child) at Sydney Grammar School. He worked as a surveyor's assistant in the Monaro district, then as a drover and boundary rider. Life in the bush was, to him, the only life worth living: he was fascinated by horses and horsemanship and inspired by the verse of Adam Lindsay Gordon. He was a melancholy, moody young man who suffered from deep depression. At home in

Sydney, and out of work, he hanged himself with his stockwhip from the limb of a gumtree on the shore of Long Bay, Middle Harbour. This was on 2 May 1892. His one book was published after his death with a memoir by A.G. Stephens.

Where the Dead Men Lie and Other Poems, 1897.

Pages 63–64

E.J. BRADY

EDWIN James Brady was born on 7 August 1869 at Carcoar, NSW. His father was an Irish-American who had been a whaler in the South Seas and the Arctic and Brady's education began in the United States. He returned to Australia in 1882 and attended the Marist Brothers' High School in Sydney. Working first as a shipping clerk, then as a farmer and a journalist, he travelled widely in Australia, finally settling at Mallacoota on the eastern coast of Victoria. His vigorous ballads of the sea are thought to be the best of his work. He died in 1952.

The Ways of Many Waters, 1899; *The Earthen Floor*, 1902; *Bushland Ballads*, 1910; *Bells and Hobbles*, 1911; *The House of the Winds*, 1919; *Wardens of the Seas*, 1933.

Pages 83–85

CHRISTOPHER BRENNAN

BORN in Sydney on 1 November 1870 of Irish parents, Christopher John Brennan was educated at St Ignatius (Riverview) College and the University of Sydney where he took an honours degree, then an MA, before winning a scholarship to Germany. Intended for the priesthood, he fell in love with his landlady's daughter, Anna Werth, who came to Sydney in 1897 to marry him. He was employed in the Sydney Public Library and in 1908 became a teacher of Latin, French, and German at the University of Sydney. In 1920 he was appointed Associate Professor of German and Comparative Literature, a post he held for five years until he was dismissed owing to his alcoholism and the break-up of his marriage. He managed to live by teaching and coaching and a small Commonwealth pension until he died of cancer on 5 October 1932. Brennan was a legend to all who knew him. Influenced by the French Symbolists, he was an intellectual of wide-ranging scholarship.

XVIII Poems, 1897; *XXI Poems: Towards the Source*, 1897; *Poems 1913*, 1914; *A Chant of Doom and Other Verses*, 1918; *XXIII Poems*, 1938; *The Burden of Tyre*, 1953; *The Verse of Christopher Brennan*, ed. A.R. Chisholm and J.J. Quinn, 1960.

Pages 89–91

BORN at Wentworthville, NSW, on 13 March 1928, Robert Francis Brissenden was educated at Cowra High School and the universities of Sydney (MA) and Leeds (PhD). He began his career as Tutor in English at the University of Melbourne, then lectured in English at the Canberra University College and the Australian National University. Brissenden was a specialist in eighteenth-century literature—his *Virtue in Distress* (1974) is a critical study of the novel in that period—and was joint editor of *Studies in the Eighteenth Century*. He was Chairman of the Literature Board of the Australia Council from 1978 to 1981. In 1985 he was forced to retire from the ANU when he contracted Parkinson's disease, but he then embarked on a new career as a writer of thrillers. He died on 7 April 1991.

Winter Matins, 1971; *Elegies*, 1974; *Building a Terrace*, 1975; *The Whale in Darkness*, 1980; *Sacred Sites*, 1990.

Pages 230–233

BORN of Irish parents at Romsey (Vic.) on 8 July 1925, Vincent Buckley was educated in Melbourne by the Jesuit Fathers and then at the university where he obtained an MA. Having served briefly in the RAAF during World War II, he became a public servant before joining the staff of the University of Melbourne as lecturer, then Reader, in English, becoming Professor in 1967. As a critic, poet, teacher, and committed Roman Catholic, he is thought to have had a wide influence on his contemporaries. Apart from his books of verse he published several volumes of critical essays defining his standards and his beliefs, and he was working on his anthology *The Faber Book of Modern Australian Verse* when he died in 1988.

The World's Flesh, 1954; *Masters in Israel*, 1961; *Arcady and Other Places*, 1966; *Golden Builders and Other Poems*, 1976; *The Pattern*, 1979; *Late Winter Child*, 1979; *Last Poems*, 1991.

Page 227

DAVID Campbell was born on 16 July 1915 at Ellerslie station near Adelong, NSW, and educated at The King's School, Parramatta, and at Cambridge (Jesus College). An outstanding athlete, he played football for England against Ireland and Wales. In World War II he served as a pilot in the RAAF, becoming Squadron Leader commanding Nos 1 and 2 Squadrons and being awarded the DFC and bar. A childhood spent on an isolated station is celebrated in the stories *Evening Under Lamplight* (1959). This background and life as a grazier on properties near

Canberra provide material for beautiful lyrics set in the Monaro landscape. David Campbell added artistry and poetic insight to themes treated by the balladists. He died on 28 July 1979.

Speak with the Sun, 1949; *The Miracle of Mullion Hill*, 1956; *Poems*, 1962; *Selected Poems 1942–1968*, 1968; *The Branch of Dodona and Other Poems 1969–1970*, 1970; *Devil's Rock and Other Poems 1970–1972*, 1974; *Deaths and Pretty Cousins*, 1975; *Words with a Black Orpington*, 1978; *The Man in the Honeysuckle*, 1979; *Collected Poems*, ed. Leonie Kramer, 1989.

Pages 187–193

VICTOR DALEY

BORN on 5 September 1858 at Navan, County of Meath, Ireland, Victor Daley was taken after his father's death to Devonport, England, and educated at the Christian Brothers' school. After working as a railway employee at Plymouth, he came to Australia in 1878, earning a living as a clerk and then as a freelance journalist in Melbourne and Sydney, where he settled in 1898, the year his first book of verse was published. He wrote for the *Bulletin* and for the Melbourne labour journal, the *Tocsin*, under the name 'Creeve Roe'. Daley died of tuberculosis on 29 December 1905 at Waitara, a suburb of Sydney. He was a romantic whose verse has a charming individual voice.

At Dawn and Dusk, 1898; *Wine and Roses*, edited with a memoir by Bertram Stevens, 1911; *Creeve Roe*, ed. Muir Holborn and Marjorie Pizer, 1947.

Pages 38–39

BEATRICE DAVIS

BEATRICE Davis was born in Bendigo in 1909. She studied music at the Sydney Conservatorium and graduated from Sydney University in 1929. After she had worked for the *Medical Journal of Australia* for a number of years, she joined Angus & Robertson as their full-time editor in 1937. She married a few months later, but her husband died after only eight years had passed. For a long time she was the only full-time book editor in Australia, but she continued to be regarded as the finest book editor in the country when the growth of indigenous publishing provided a standard against which her work could be measured. Her reputation survived her dismissal by Angus & Robertson's new management in 1973, and continued until her death on 23 May 1992. She worked with many of Australia's most celebrated poets, from Mary Gilmore to Les Murray, but she preferred as far as possible to remain anonymous. Yet, as Douglas Stewart wrote, she 'as much as anyone else, and more than most . . . kept Australian literature alive for more than a quarter of a century'.

BORN in Geelong, Vic., on 15 February 1930, Bruce Dawe left High School when he was sixteen and worked in various unskilled jobs before he joined the RAAF. While doing an Arts course at the University of Melbourne he became converted to Roman Catholicism; and after he graduated he joined the staff of the Darling Downs College of Education at Toowoomba, Q., where he continued to teach as it evolved into the University of Southern Queensland, until his early retirement in January 1993. When his verse was first published in the 1960s Bruce Dawe was seen as one of the few contemporary poets with a popular voice. Dealing with themes common to modern civilisation, he writes in an unaffectedly colloquial style that is unmistakably Australian.

No Fixed Address, 1962; *A Need of Similar Name*, 1964; *An Eye for a Tooth*, 1968; *Beyond the Subdivisions*, 1969; *Condolences of the Season*, 1971; *Sometimes Gladness: Collected Poems 1954–1978*, 1978, 1988; *Toward Sunrise*, 1986; *This Side of Silence*, 1990; *Mortal Instruments*, 1995.

Pages 239–241

BORN on 7 September 1876 at Auburn, SA, Clarence Michael James Dennis (known to his friends as 'Den') was educated at the Gladstone State School and at the Christian Brothers' College in Adelaide. He worked as a clerk, a barman, a carpenter, and edited the satirical magazine the *Gadfly* before going to Melbourne in 1906, then to Toolangi in the hill country. It was with the publication in 1915 of *The Sentimental Bloke* that his immense popularity as a comic writer was established and continued to grow. As a contributor or on the staff, he was associated with the Melbourne *Herald* from 1922 to 1938. He died on 21 June 1938.

Backblock Ballads, 1913; *The Songs of a Sentimental Bloke*, 1915; *The Austra—laise: A Marching Song*, 1915; *The Moods of Ginger Mick*, 1916; *The Glugs of Gosh*, 1917; *Random Verse*, 1952.

Pages 98–108

BORN in Sydney on 18 June 1920, Rosemary De Brissac Dobson was educated at Frensham, Mittagong, NSW, and at the University of Sydney. Having studied, and later taught, art, she joined the editorial staff of Angus & Robertson, publishers, and continued to do freelance work after her marriage in 1951 to A.T. Bolton, who was until his retirement director of Publications to the National Library, Canberra. Five books of poems were followed by *Selected Poems* (1973), since revised and reprinted. Translated into French by Diesendorf/Dautheuil, her poems have been published bilingually by Seghers, Paris, in the series 'Aughor du Monde'. Later publications include versions of poems from the Russian (with David Campbell), a study of the artist, Ray Crooke, a selection of poems called *Over the Frontier*, and two sequences of poems published by the Brindabella Press. A sensitive and original writer, Rosemary Dobson has a wide range of theme and mood, from the deeply personal to the elegant humour and wit of her poems on classical works of art.

In a Convex Mirror, 1944; *The Ship of Ice*, 1948; *Child with a Cockatoo*; *Cock Crow*, 1965; *Selected Poems*, 1973; *Over the Frontier*, 1978; *The Three Fates*, 1984; *Collected Poems*, 1992; *Untold Lives*, 1992.

Pages 203–207

MICHAEL
DRANSFIELD

BORN on 12 September 1948, Michael Dransfield was a colourful figure among the young poets of the late sixties and early seventies, not only because of the quality of his work but because of his candour in declaring himself a drug taker and describing the effects of his addiction. He wrote prolifically from the age of nineteen and became a cult figure among the young of the hippy generation. He was obviously unsuited to the jobs he briefly took in the public service and as a cadet journalist, and led a wandering life buying and selling small country properties. Being attracted by ritual, he thought of becoming a monk; and he studied heraldry with a view to establishing his family's aristocratic lineage. He had published three books of verse before his death on 20 April 1973, and further volumes appeared posthumously.

Streets of the Long Voyage, 1970; *The Inspector of Tides*, 1972; *Drug Poems*, 1972; *Memoirs of a Velvet Urinal*, 1973; *Voyage into Solitude*, 1978; *Collected Poems*, 1987.

Pages 280–282

GEOFFREY DUTTON

GEOFFREY Piers Dutton, a prominent figure in the Australian literary scene, was born on 2 August 1922 at Anlaby station, Kapunda, SA, and educated at Geelong Grammar School and the University of Adelaide. After serving as a pilot with the RAAF in World War II, he went to study at Magdalen College, Oxford, and to travel abroad. From 1955 to 1962 he lectured in English at the University of Adelaide. A poet, critic, historian, editor and publisher, he has written prolifically since the 1940s. He was involved in the founding of *Angry Penguins*, of *Australian Letters*, and of the *Australian Book Review*; he edited an Australian series for Penguin Books; he founded the series Sun Books and was its editorial director for many years; was editor of the *Bulletin* Literary Supplement; and was for a time Literary Editor of *The Australian*. Apart from his many books of verse, he has written novels, short stories, biographies, travel books and books on Australian literature and artists and authors.

Night Flight and Sunrise, 1944; *Antipodes in Shoes*, 1958; *Flowers and Fury*, 1962; *Poems Soft and Loud*, 1967; *Findings and Keepings*, 1970; *A Body of Words*, 1977; *Selective Affinities*, 1985; *New and Selected Poems*, 1993.

Pages 217–219

EDWARD George Dyson was born in 1865 near Ballarat, Vic., his father being a mining engineer on the goldfields. At the age of twelve he was working for a travelling draper; then he worked in and around the mines before going to Melbourne where he was employed in a factory. Getting a job in a newspaper office, Dyson was to spend most of his life as a journalist, and after the publication of his first book of verse in 1896 he turned to fiction. He wrote many comic novels and short stories, *Fact'ry 'Ands* (1906) being the best remembered of these. Dyson died on 22 August 1931.

EDWARD DYSON

Rhymes from the Mines, 1896; *'Hello Soldier': Khaki Verse*, 1919.

Pages 51–53

GEORGE Essex Evans was born in London on 18 June 1863, came to Queensland in 1881 and, then eighteen years old, began as a farmer on the Darling Downs; this enterprise failing, he became a teacher, a journalist and then a public servant. Having been agricultural editor of the *Queenslander* and edited (with A.B. Paterson) the magazine the *Antipodean*, he was literary director of the Tourist Bureau of Queensland. He died on 10 November 1909 at Toowoomba, where a monument to his memory was built: his first book of verse having been published in 1891, he was well known and popular in Queensland.

G. ESSEX EVANS

The Repentance of Magdalene Despar, 1891; *Loraine and Other Verses*, 1898; *The Sword of Pain*, 1905; *The Secret Key and Other Verses*, 1906; *Collected Verse*, 1928.

Pages 50–51

ROBERT David FitzGerald was born on 22 February 1902 at Hunter's Hill, Sydney, and educated at Sydney Grammar School and the University of Sydney, where he studied science. Descended on his father's side from a family of surveyors and on his mother's side from the Le Gay Breretons, he qualified in 1925 as a land surveyor and got a job

R.D. FitzGERALD

297

with the Native Lands Commission in Fiji. He returned to Australia in 1936 to become a senior surveyor in the Commonwealth Department of the Interior. Since the 1920s FitzGerald has been recognised as a major figure in Australian poetry, an intellectual with a positive philosophy and a moral force who celebrates the value of the man of action and the significance of the past in the modern world . He died in 1987.

The Greater Apollo, 1927; *To Meet the Sun*, 1929; *Moonlight Acre*, 1938; *Between Two Tides*, 1952; *This Night's Orbit*, 1953; *Southmost Twelve*, 1963; *Forty Years' Poems*, 1965; *Product*, 1978.

Pages 134–139

MARY HANNAY FOOTT

MARY Hannay Foott (*née* Black) was born on 26 September 1846 in Glasgow and brought to Australia by her parents in 1853. She was educated in Melbourne and was a student at the National Art Gallery School. In 1874 she married T.W. Foott and lived on a property he managed and part owned on the Paroo River in south-west Queensland. After his death in 1884 she became, for ten years, the social and literary editor of the *Queenslander*. She retired to Bundaberg and died there in September 1918. H.M. Green sees her as a forerunner of the balladists of the nineties.

Where the Pelican Builds and Other Poems, 1885; *Morna Lee and Other Poems*, 1890.

Page 36

MARY FULLERTON ('E')

MARY Elizabeth Fullerton was born in 1868 at Glenmaggie, North Gippsland, Vic., and left Australia to live in England in 1921. She was a novelist, descriptive writer, and journalist as well as a poet and, like her close friend Miles Franklin, had a liking for using pseudonyms. Her early verse, written in Australia, was published under her own name; her two later books, written in London, under the pen-name 'E'. She died in 1946.

Moods and Melodies, 1908; *The Breaking Furrow*, 1921; *Moles Do So Little with Their Privacy*, 1942; *The Wonder and the Apple*, 1946.

Pages 82–83

LEON GELLERT

LEON Maxwell Gellert was born in 1892 at Walkerville, SA, and educated at the Adelaide High School and the University of Adelaide. He left schoolteaching to enlist in World War I and was at the landing at Gallipoli, where he was wounded and invalided to England. He became director and co-editor of *Art in Australia*, and also edited *Home* magazine. On the staff of the *Sydney Morning Herald* he wrote humorous articles and became literary editor. He retired to live in Adelaide where he died on 22 August 1977.

Songs of a Campaign, 1917; *The Isle of San*, 1919; *Desperate Measures*, 1928.

Page 120

NÉE Mary Jean Cameron, Mary Gilmore was born near Goulburn, NSW, on 16 August 1865 and died in Sydney on 3 December 1962. She was created a Dame of the Order of the British Empire in 1936 for services to Australian literature. She worked as a teacher in country schools and then in Sydney where she met William Lane and joined his group of hopeful idealists who went to Paraguay to found the 'New Australia'. There, in 1897, she married William Alexander Gilmore. She returned to Australia in 1902, and in 1908 founded the Women's Page of the Sydney *Worker*, which she edited for the next 23 years. She was indeed a woman of the people—not in any political sense, but through the warmth of her intuitive sympathy for anyone who suffered.

MARY GILMORE

Marri'd and Other Verses, 1910; *The Passionate Heart*, 1918; *The Wild Swan*, 1930; *The Rue Tree*, 1931; *Under the Wilgas*, 1932; *Battlefields*, 1939; *The Disinherited*, 1941; *Pro Patria Australia*, 1945; *Fourteen Men*, 1954; *Selected Verse* (ed. R.D. FitzGerald), 1969.

Pages 54–62

THE son of a retired Indian Army officer, Adam Lindsay Gordon was born on 19 October 1833 in the Azores and taken to England when he was seven years old. He was sent to Cheltenham College, then the Military Academy at Woolwich. High-spirited and headstrong, he showed no interest in a military career, and in 1853 his father sent him to Adelaide. Disdaining to use any family influence, he spent two years with the Mounted Police, then became an itinerant horse-trainer, was briefly a member of the South Australian Parliament, and invested inherited money in enterprises that invariably failed, the last being a livery stable at Ballarat. Gordon had read widely and took his verse writing seriously; but horses and horsemanship were his life. He rode brilliantly, with reckless courage, despite the defective eyesight that caused him many spills. In Melbourne in 1868 he rode three steeplechase winners in one day. He settled in the Melbourne suburb of Brighton in 1869, and came to know Kendall and Marcus Clarke at the Yorick Club. By now he had published three books of verse and a fourth was on the way. Suffering from head injuries caused by riding accidents,

ADAM LINDSAY GORDON

an emotional instability inherited from his mother, and a constant burden of debts, he shot himself at Brighton on 24 June 1870, the day after his last book of verse was published.

The Feud, 1864; *Astaroch*, 1867; *Sea Spray and Smoke Drift*, 1867; *Bush Ballads and Galloping Rhymes*, 1870.

Pages 24–27

ALAN GOULD

BORN in London on 22 March 1949, Alan Gould lived in Ireland, Iceland, and Singapore before he arrived in Australia in 1966. He now lives in Canberra and is a part-time teacher. Founding editor of the now defunct *Canberra Poetry*, he is an accomplished critic and essayist as well as being a highly-regarded, prize-winning novelist. He has also published nine books of verse. His mother was Icelandic, and Nordic legend, as well as the lore of early sailing ships, inspired much of his early work; more recently, his interests have expanded, and he has become an alert and witty observer of the contemporary world.

The Skald Mosaic, 1975; *Icelandic Solitaries*, 1978; *Astral Sea*, 1981; *The Pausing of the Hours*, 1984; *The Twofold Place*, 1986; *Years Found in Likeness*, 1988; *Formerlight—Selected Poems*, 1992; *Momentum*, 1992; *Mermaid*, 1996.

Pages 279–280

ROBERT GRAY

BORN on 23 February 1945, Robert Gray grew up at Coffs Harbour in Northern NSW. He left school early and has worked mainly in advertising agencies and bookshops. He has been well known as a critic and reviewer of poetry and was co-editor with Geoffrey Lehmann both of *The Younger Australian Poets* (1983) and *Australian Poetry in the Twentieth Century* (1992). Influenced at first by the poetry of D.H. Lawrence and William Carlos Williams, Gray writes verse that is notable for its clarity and precision, and for the visual brilliance of its imagery. In his latest books he has explored the possibilities of more formal verse structures, without forgoing his interest in Taoist, Buddhist, and other philosophy.

Introspect, Retrospect, 1970; *Creekwater Journal*, 1974; *Grass Script*, 1979; *The Skylight*, 1984; *Selected Poems*, 1985; *Piano*, 1988; *Certain Things*, 1993; *New and Selected Poems*, 1995.

Pages 272–274

RODNEY HALL

BORN in Solihull, Warwickshire, on 18 November 1935, Rodney Hall was brought to Queensland by his widowed Australian mother and educated at the Brisbane Boys' College. He was more than happy to leave school at 16 to become a scriptwriter for radio and TV, an actor, and a musician. From 1967 to 1978 he was poetry editor of the *Australian*. Since his first book of verse appeared in 1961 he has published many further collections, including *Selected Poems* (1975); he has also published novels and biographies and prepared five anthologies. Two of his novels have won the Miles Franklin Award, *Just Relations* in 1982 and *The Grisly Wife* in 1994. Rodney Hall is an expert in renaissance and baroque music. He lives at Bermagui on the south coast of NSW. He was Chairman of the Australia Council from 1991 to 1994.

Penniless Till Doomsday, 1961; *Forty Beads on a Hangman's Rope*, 1963; *Eye Witness*, 1967; *The Autobiography of a Gorgon*, 1968; *The Law of Karma*, 1968; *Heaven in a Way*, 1970; *A Soapbox Omnibus*, 1973; *Selected Poems*, 1975; *Black Bagatelles*, 1978; *The Most Beautiful World*, 1981.

Pages 254–256

THE son of ex-convicts, Charles Harpur was born on 23 January 1813 at Windsor, NSW, where his father, Joseph, was schoolmaster and parish clerk. In the 1830s the family moved to Sydney where Charles worked as a clerk in the post office from 1837 to 1839. In the 1840s he was farming in the Hunter River district: then he became a schoolteacher at Jerry's Plains where, in 1850, he married Mary Doyle (the 'Rosa' of his sonnet sequence). In 1859 he was appointed a Gold Commissioner at Araluen, a position he held until 1866, living on his South Coast farm Euroma. Misfortunes followed the abolition of this appointment: his son killed in a shooting accident, his farm damaged by floods, and poverty a constant anxiety. He died of tuberculosis on 10 June 1868. Harpur described himself as poetry's 'first high priest in this bright southern clime'; Douglas Sladen called him 'the grey forefather of Australian poets'. Immersed in the English tradition, he never quite spoke with an Australian voice.

CHARLES HARPUR

Thoughts: A Series of Sonnets, 1845; *The Bushrangers: A Play and Other Poems*, 1853; *A Poet's Home*, 1862; *The Tower of the Dream*, 1865; *Poems*, 1883.

Page 29

MAX Harris was born on 13 April 1921 in Adelaide where he went to St Peter's College and graduated from the university. From the early 1940s he played a variety of roles in the literary life of Australia: poet, novelist, editor, publisher, bookseller, critic. He was co-founder of the publishing firm Reed and Harris; he was editor of the avant-garde magazine *Angry Penguins* (1941–46) in which the work of 'Ern Malley' was first published; he was co-editor and founder of the quarterly *Australian Letters* and of the *Australian Book Review*; he directed and expanded the famous Mary Martin's Bookshop; and he published a novel and four books of verse. For many years he wrote for the *Australian* and the *Bulletin*, a forthright and amusing critic of literature and life. He died on 13 January 1995.

MAX HARRIS

The Gift of Blood, 1940; *Dramas of the Sky*, 1942; *The Coorong and Other Poems*, 1955; *A Window at Night*, 1967.

Pages 209–211

KEVIN HART

KEVIN Hart was born in London on 5 July 1954 and was brought to live in Brisbane at the age of ten. He graduated from the Australian National University in philosophy and had a Stanford Writing Fellowship in 1977. Having gained a doctorate from the University of Melbourne, he is now Associate Professor of English at Monash University. His work has been influenced by the modern European poets and by his conversion to Roman Catholicism.

The Departure, 1978; *The Lines of the Hand*, 1981; *Your Shadow*, 1984; *Peniel*, 1991; *New and Selected Poems*, 1995.

Pages 283–284

P.J. HARTIGAN ('JOHN O'BRIEN')

THE Very Rev. Mgr Patrick Joseph Hartigan, who adopted the pen-name 'John O'Brien', was born at Yass, NSW, on 12 October 1879 and died on 27 December 1952. Educated at St Patrick's College, Goulburn, and Manly, he was parish priest at Narrandera, NSW, inspector of Catholic Schools at Goulburn, and chaplain at the convent of the Sisters of the Sacred Heart, Rose Bay, Sydney. His humorous ballads deal mainly with the Roman Catholic Irish-Australian farmers who were his parishioners for so many years.

Around the Boree Log and Other Verses, 1921.

Pages 109–112

WILLIAM HART-SMITH

BORN on 23 November 1911 at Tunbridge Wells, England, William Hart-Smith arrived in New Zealand when he was twelve and attended the Seddon Memorial Technical College in Auckland. He came to Australia in 1936 and worked in radio as a copywriter, announcer, and freelance journalist until he enlisted for World War II in 1940. After the war he spent some years in New Zealand as Adult Education tutor in South Canterbury. Later he lived in Darwin, Sydney, and Perth, before returning to Auckland where he died on 15 April 1990.

Columbus Goes West, 1943; *Harvest*, 1945; *The Unceasing Ground*, 1946; *Christopher Columbus*, 1948; *On the Level*, 1950; *Poems of Discovery*, 1959; *The Talking Clothes*, 1966; *Selected Poems*, 1985.

Pages 157–158

GWEN HARWOOD

GWEN Harwood was born in Brisbane on 8 June 1920. After leaving the Brisbane Girls' Grammar School, she continued her studies in music and taught music. Married, with four children, she moved to Tasmania with her husband in 1945. When her work began to appear in literary magazines she used a variety of pen-names—Walter Lehmann, Miriam Stone, T.F. Kline, Francis Geyer; and her first book, under her own name, did not appear until 1963. Hers is personal poetry of a high order. She has written the libretti for two operas composed by Larry Sitsky: *The Fall of the House of Usher* (1965) and *Lenz* (1974), while *Blessed City* is a selection of wartime letters to her friend Thomas Riddell. She died on 5 December 1995.

Poems, 1963; *Poems/Volume Two*, 1968; *Selected Poems*, 1975; *The Lion's Bride*, 1981; *Bone Scan*, 1988; *Collected Poems*, 1991; *The Present Tense*, 1995.

Pages 201–203

BORN on 28 January 1959, Philip Hodgins grew up on a dairy farm at Katandra West in Victoria's Goulburn Valley. He attended Geelong College as a boarder, and then worked in publishing until he contracted chronic myeloid leukemia at the age of 24, and was told he could expect to live only for three years. This alarming news prompted his prize-winning first book *Blood and Bone*, but for some years he outlived the prognosis, and continued to produce verse of high quality at an exceptional speed. He moved to a house near Maryborough in Victoria after he married the fiction writer Janet Shaw; they had two children before he died on 18 August 1995.

PHILIP HODGINS

Blood and Bone, 1986; *Down the Lake with Half a Chook*, 1988; *Animal Warmth*, 1990; *A Kick of the Footy*, 1990; *The End of the Season*, 1992; *Up On All Fours*, 1993; *Dispossessed*, 1994; *Things Happen*, 1995.

Pages 285–287

THE son of a Presbyterian clergyman, Alec Derwent Hope was born at Cooma, NSW, on 21 July 1907. He was educated at Lesley House School, Hobart, and at Bathurst and Sydney High Schools, then at the University of Sydney and at Oxford, to which he won a travelling scholarship. After teaching from 1932 to 1938 at State schools in the country, he became a lecturer at the Sydney Teachers' College, then a senior lecturer in the University of Melbourne. He became Professor of English at the Australian National University, Canberra (1951–68) and has now retired as Emeritus Professor. An intellectual who adheres to classical forms, A.D. Hope is a brilliant satirist and a poet of considerable importance. As well as many books of verse, he has published collections of essays and critical studies, among them *The New Cratylus: Notes on the Craft of Poetry* (1979).

A.D. HOPE

The Wandering Islands, 1955; *Poems*, 1960; *Selected Poems*, 1963; *New Poems 1965–1969*, 1969; *Dunciad Minor*, 1970; *Collected Poems 1930–1970*, 1972; *Antechinus: Poems 1975–1980*, 1981; *Orpheus*, 1991.

Pages 139–145

EVAN JONES

EVAN Jones was born in Melbourne on 20 November 1931 and educated at Melbourne High School and the University of Melbourne. After lecturing there in history, he went on a Writing Fellowship to Stanford University (California) in 1958. On his return in 1960 he lectured in English at the Australian National University, and then at the University of Melbourne. He is now an Associate of the English Department at Melbourne.

Inside the Whale, 1960; *Understandings*, 1967; *Recognitions*, 1978; *Left at the Post*, 1984.

Page 243

NANCY KEESING

BORN in Sydney on 7 September 1923, Nancy Keesing (Mrs Mark Hertzberg) was educated at Sydney Church of England Girls' Grammar School and at Frensham before taking a diploma in Social Studies at the University of Sydney. A poet, critic, anthologist and researcher in social and literary history, she also wrote short stories and books for children. She first became widely known as the editor, with Douglas Stewart, of the anthologies *Australian Bush Ballads* (1955) and *Old Bush Songs* (1957). She was Chairman of the Literature Board of the Australia Council (1974–77) and Chairman of the NSW Committee of the National Book Council (1981–84). She died on 19 January 1993.

Imminent Summer, 1951; *Three Men and Sydney*, 1955; *Showground Sketchbook*, 1968; *Hails and Farewells*, 1977.

Pages 215–216

HENRY KENDALL

BORN on 18 April 1839 at Kirmington on the South Coast of NSW, Henry Kendall was the son of a small farmer who moved north with his family to the Clarence River district. He was thirteen when his father died in 1851 and his mother took her children back to the South Coast to live near Wollongong. In 1855, as a cabin boy, he went to the South Seas on a whaling brig owned by an uncle. Two years later he was breadwinner for the family in Sydney: errand boy, shop assistant, solicitor's clerk (at Grafton), public servant. He married in 1868, and went to Melbourne in 1869, hoping to make a living by writing; but here he failed, as he did when he returned to Sydney in 1870, a victim of poverty and drink. He was in desperate straits in 1873 when the timber merchants, George and Michael Fagan, took charge of him and cared for him until he was well enough to be employed as storekeeper in their timber business at Camden Haven, near Port Macquarie (NSW). His wife and two sons (they had been living apart) rejoined him here in

1876, and another son and a daughter were born. When Kendall was appointed Inspector of Forests, at Cundletown on the Manning River, the travelling this involved proved too much for him and he died of tuberculosis on 1 August 1882. While acknowledging his faults, T. Inglis Moore said of him: 'He had a gift of song and remains one of the sweetest of our singers.'

Poems and Songs, 1862; *Leaves from Australian Forests*, 1869; *Songs from the Mountains*, 1880; *Orara*, 1881; *Selected Poems*, 1957.

Pages 30–33

CHRISTOPHER Koch is best known as a novelist, as his third novel, *The Year of Living Dangerously*, was successfully filmed, while *The Doubleman*, his fourth, won the Miles Franklin award. The evocative verse he wrote in his youth has appeared in magazines and anthologies. He was born in Hobart on 16 July 1932 and educated at St Virgil's College, Hobart High School, and the University of Tasmania. He had various jobs in Hobart, Sydney, and Melbourne, then in London when he went abroad for two years. In Sydney again, he was Schools Broadcasts producer for the Australian Broadcasting Commission from 1957 to 1959; then there were travels in the United States and in Italy, and he returned to take a position with the ABC in Melbourne. Since 1976 he has been a full-time writer, moving between Launceston and various parts of Sydney.

CHRISTOPHER KOCH

Page 244

EVE Langley is best known as the author of *The Pea Pickers* (1942), which shared the S.H. Prior Memorial Prize in 1941. She was born near Forbes, NSW, on 1 September 1908 (the year of her birth is uncertain) and educated at Fiefield school until her family moved to Molong, then to Gippsland, Vic., and the Dandenongs. In 1932 she followed the family to New Zealand, working as proof-reader, librarian, and freelance journalist; and there she married Hilary Clark and had two sons and a daughter. She returned to Australia and a second novel, *White Topee*, was published in 1954. She lived in the Blue Mountains, NSW, for some years before her death in June 1974: her body was discovered in the derelict shack where she lived alone. Her poems have appeared in magazines and anthologies.

EVE LANGLEY

Page 147

THE son of Peter Larsen, a Norwegian seaman turned gold-digger, Henry Lawson was born on 17 June 1867 in a tent at Grenfell, NSW. He was brought up on a selection at Eurunderee, near Mudgee, and went to

HENRY LAWSON

school there, and later at Mudgee. Leaving school at fourteen, he worked with his father until failure to make a living on the land drove the family to Sydney. Here he worked as a painter while his mother, Louisa, a strong-minded woman who became a pioneer in women's suffrage, founded the *Dawn* newspaper. He began to write and, at night, helped his mother with the paper and attended evening classes. His first story was accepted by the *Bulletin* in 1888, a few days before his father died. He earned a few guineas from his contributions to the *Bulletin* and between 1889 and 1893 he travelled to Albany, WA, to Brisbane, and to Wellington, NZ, in search of employment. His first book was published by his mother in 1894 and he began to make literary friends (J. Le Gay Brereton, Mary Gilmore, Victor Daley). In 1896 his first book of verse was published by Angus & Robertson. He married Bertha Bredt in 1896 and took her to Western Australia, then to New Zealand; and in 1900, with the help of Earl Beauchamp, he took his family to London, where two books were accepted by Blackwood. He returned to Australia in 1902 and, beginning to drink heavily, was separated from his wife and family in 1903. He had constant difficulties with drinking and poverty, and, apart from a holiday in 1910 at Mallacoota, Vic., and a period at Leeton on the Yanco Irrigation Settlement, remained in Sydney until his death at Abbotsford on 22 September 1922. He was given a State funeral.

In the Days When the World Was Wide, 1896; *Verses, Popular and Humorous*, 1900; *When I Was King*, 1905; *The Skyline Rider*, 1910; *My Army, O My Army, Song of the Dardanelles*, 1915; *Selected Poems of Henry Lawson*, 1918; *Poetical Works of Henry Lawson*, 1925.

Pages 66–81

GEOFFREY LEHMANN   BORN in Sydney on 28 June 1940, Geoffrey Lehmann went to the Sydney Church of England Grammar School before studying Arts-Law at the University of Sydney where he co-edited the university magazines *Arna* and *Hermes*. He practised as a solicitor for some years before becoming a lecturer in tax and law at the University of New South Wales; he is now a partner in the accountancy firm Price Waterhouse, and a widely-consulted commentator on tax law. As well as verse, he has published a novel, a book of art criticism, an anthology of comic verse, a children's book, and a book on Taxation Law in Australia. With Robert Gray, he has edited two anthologies. He has married twice, and has five children.

The Ilex Tree (with Les A. Murray), 1965; *A Voyage of Lions*, 1968; *Conversation with a Rider*, 1973; *Selected Poems*, 1976; *Ross' Poems*, 1978; *Nero's Poems*, 1982; *Children's Games*, 1990; *Spring Forest*, 1992; *Collected Poems*, 1996.

Pages 262–265

FREDERICK T. Macartney was born in Melbourne on 27 September 1887 and died there on 2 September 1980. He worked as a clerk, a reporter, and a freelance journalist, then spent two years as bookkeeper on a Riverina station. In 1921 he joined the Northern Territory public service and became Clerk of Courts, Sheriff, and Public Trustee at Darwin. In 1933 he returned to Melbourne and lectured on Australian literature for the Melbourne University Extension Board and for the Commonwealth Literary Fund. He edited and compiled the revision of E. Morris Miller's *Australian Literature: A Bibliography to 1938*, extending it to 1950 (1956).

Poems, 1920; *Preferences*, 1941; *Gaily the Troubadour*, 1946; *Tripod for Homeward Incense*, 1947; *Selected Poems*, 1961.

Page 121

Page 121

FREDERICK
T. MACARTNEY

JAMES McAuley was born at Lakemba, NSW, on 12 October 1917 and educated at Fort Street High School and the University of Sydney. From 1938 to 1942 he was a schoolteacher then (during World War II) served in the Australian Army Directorate of Research and Civil Affairs. His next appointment was with the Australian School of Pacific Administration. He was converted to Roman Catholicism in 1952. In 1956 he became the founding editor of the magazine *Quadrant*. In 1961 he accepted an invitation to become Reader in Poetry at the University of Tasmania. He was subsequently appointed Professor of English at that university. He died on 15 October 1976. During the 1940s, in collaboration with Harold Stewart, he invented the poet 'Ern Malley' whose sequence 'The Darkening Ecliptic' first appeared in the magazine *Angry Penguins*: this hoax was a protest against the obscurity of its avant-garde contributors, and against obscure modern writing in general.

Under Aldebaran, 1946; *A Vision of Ceremony*, 1956; *Captain Quiros*, 1964; *Surprises of the Sun*, 1969; *Collected Poems 1936–1970*, 1971; *Music Late at Night*, 1976; *A World of Its Own*, 1977; *Collected Poems*, ed. Leonie Kramer, 1994.

Pages 196–201

Pages 196–201

JAMES McAULEY

SON of George Gordon McCrae, poet and man of letters, Hugh McCrae was born in Melbourne on 4 October 1876 and educated at Hawthorn Grammar School. After studying art, he was articled to an architect; but he soon tired of this and turned to freelance writing and illustrating as a means of earning a living. In 1914 he decided to go on the stage, went to New York with the Granville Barker company, and returned to act in a film and in stage productions in Australia. After ventures as a magazine

HUGH McCRAE

307

editor, a dramatic critic and a lecturer, he went to live near Camden, then moved to Sydney, where he died in 1958. Fascinated by the style of the eighteenth century, he wrote verse, an operatic fantasy, short stories, reminiscences, and an imaginary biography. He was a fine craftsman and lyricist, ebullient and witty.

Satyrs and Sunlight, 1909; *Colombine*, 1920; *Idyllia*, 1922; *The Mimshi Maiden*, 1938; *Poems*, 1939; *Forests of Pan*, 1944, *Voice of the Forest*, 1945; *The Best Poems of Hugh McCrae*, ed. R.G. Howarth, 1961.

Pages 97–98

RONALD McCUAIG

RONALD McCuaig was born at Newcastle, NSW, on 2 April 1908. He worked in radio journalism for the *Wireless Weekly*, then the *ABC Weekly*, before joining the staff of *Smith's Weekly* and then the *Sydney Morning Herald*. After this he spent twelve years on the literary staff of the *Bulletin*, which he left in 1961 to take a position with the Australian Commonwealth News and Information Bureau. Most of his verse is light-hearted, witty and satirical. He died in Sydney on March 1 1993.

Vaudeville, 1938; *The Wanton Goldfish*, 1941; *Quod Ronald McCuaig*, 1946; *The Ballad of Bloodthirsty Bessie and Other Poems*, 1961; *Selected Poems*, 1992.

Pages 148–153

NAN McDONALD

BORN at Eastwood, a suburb of Sydney, on 25 December 1921, Nan McDonald was educated at Hornsby High School and the University of Sydney where she graduated with an honours BA. She joined the editorial staff of Angus & Robertson in 1943 and remained in that position for thirty years: a distinguished and imaginative editor. She died at Mount Keira, near Wollongong, NSW, on 7 January 1974.

Pacific Sea, 1947; *The Lonely Fire*, 1954; *The Lighthouse*, 1959; *Selected Poems*, 1969.

Pages 212–214

ROGER McDONALD

BORN at Young, NSW, on 23 June 1941, Roger McDonald is a graduate of the University of Sydney. After working as a schoolteacher, he became a producer of feature programmes for the Australian Broadcasting Commission, then a publisher's editor with the University of Queensland Press. In this capacity (1969–1979) he was responsible for the Press's poetry programme and the series Paperback Poets. Roger

McDonald has become widely known as a novelist since *1915*, his novel of World War I, was filmed. He lived on a farm near Braidwood from 1980, until it was acquired by the Water Board in 1993; he now lives in Sydney.

Citizens of Mist, 1968; *Airship*, 1975.

Pages 270–271

ISOBEL Marion Dorothea Mackellar, daughter of Sir Charles Mackellar, was born in Sydney in 1885 and died on 14 January 1968. She travelled widely and her verse includes translations from European languages, especially from the Spanish. She also wrote a novel and two books for children (with Ruth Bedford). The poem 'My Country', said to have been written when she was nineteen, first appeared in 1908 in the *Spectator* (England), then in 1911 in her first published book of verse.

The Closed Door and Other Verses, 1911; *The Witch Maid and Other Verses*, 1914; *Dreamharbour and Other Verses*, 1923; *Fancy Dress and Other Verses*, 1926; *My Country and Other Poems* (illus. Rhys Williams), 1945.

Pages 116–117

DOROTHEA MACKELLAR

BORN in Perth, WA, on 25 September 1913, Kenneth Ivo Mackenzie was brought up in the country at Pinjarra and educated at the Guildford Grammar School, the Muresk Agricultural College, and the University of Western Australia where he studied Arts and Law. In 1934 he moved to Sydney where he married and worked as a newspaper and radio journalist for six years. During World War II he served in the prison garrison at Cowra where he witnessed the outbreak of the Japanese—the subject of the novel *Dead Men Rising*, 1951. Helped by Commonwealth Literary Fund Fellowships, he retired to his property at Kurrajong in the Blue Mountains where he wrote and worked on the land. He was drowned in Tallong Creek, near Goulburn, NSW, on 19 January 1955. The poem 'Heat' could be said to foreshadow his death. As 'Seaforth Mackenzie' he wrote four novels.

Our Earth, 1937; *The Moonlit Doorway*, 1944; *Selected Verse*, ed. Douglas Stewart, 1961; *The Poems of Kenneth Mackenzie*, ed. Evan Jones and Geoffrey Little, 1972.

Pages 162–163

KENNETH MACKENZIE

RHYLL McMaster was born in Brisbane on 13 August 1947. While married to the poet and novelist Roger McDonald, she lived on the land at Braidwood, near Canberra, and the time-consuming occupation of

RHYLL McMASTER

farming and raising three children meant she was not in that time a pro-
lific poet, but her work is highly regarded, as her books have won several
major literary prizes. She now lives in Braidwood, and has remarried.

The Brineshrimp, 1972; *Washing the Money*, 1986; *On My Empty Feet*, 1993;
Flying the Coop: New and Selected Poems, 1994.

Pages 278–279

DAVID MALOUF

HIS mother from England, his father from Lebanon, David Malouf was
born in Brisbane on 20 March 1934. He was educated at the University
of Queensland, where he later taught for two years before going to live in
England in 1959. Nearly ten years later he returned to become a lecturer
in English at the University of Sydney. He resigned in 1977 to become a
full-time writer, and he now divides his time between Italy and Sydney,
an internationally-acclaimed writer of fiction, memoirs and librettos. His
sixth novel *The Great World* won the Miles Franklin award in 1990.

Bicycle and Other Poems, 1970; *Neighbours in a Thicket, 1974; Wild Lemons*,
1980; First Things Last, 1981; *Selected Poems*, 1981, 1992; *Poems 1959–
1989*, 1992.

Pages 247–248

JOHN MANIFOLD

BORN in Melbourne on 21 April 1915, John Manifold was the eldest son
of one of Australia's wealthiest pastoralists. He grew up on the family
properties in the Western District of Victoria, and was educated as a
boarder at Geelong Grammar School. When he was 18 his father
informed him that he was not to inherit the family property; instead it
was bequeathed to his younger brothers, who were not as intellectually
gifted and hence less assured of earning a living. Manifold reacted by
becoming a communist. In 1934 he went to Cambridge University,
where he formally joined the Communist Party; unlike his fellow
students Burgess, Maclean, Philby and Blunt, he did not conceal his
membership, though like them he received a life-long pension from the
Soviet government. John Manifold was a musician as well as a poet, an
authority on Australian folk songs and the tunes that were used with the
old bush ballads, well known for his performances. He edited the *Penguin
Australian Song Book* (1964). He died in Brisbane on 19 April 1985.

The Death of Ned Kelly and Other Ballads, 1941; *Trident*, 1944; *Selected Verse*,
1946; *Nightmares and Sunhorses*, 1961; *Collected Verse*, 1978.

Pages 194–195

RAY MATHEW

BORN in Sydney on 14 April 1929, Ray Mathew was educated at Sydney
High School and the Sydney Teachers' College and taught for several

years in country schools. He left teaching in 1952 as he launched a successful, if precocious, career as a playwright and actor. He then went to England to further his development, but after initial success he met with disappointment. He now lives in sight of Central Park in New York.

With Cypress Pine, 1951; *Song and Dance*, 1956; *South of the Equator*, 1961.

Page 236

FRANK Wilmot, who used the pen-name 'Furnley Maurice', was born in Collingwood, Melbourne, on 6 April 1881. As a boy he went to work for E.W. Cole and rose to be manager of the famous Book Arcade. In 1932 he was appointed manager of the Melbourne University Press, a position he held until his death on 22 February 1942. Wilmot's father had been secretary of the first Socialist group in Victoria, and Wilmot himself had strong socialist views as well as a belief that vernacular and everyday language should be used in verse. He was appointed a member of the Commonwealth Literary Fund Advisory Board; and in 1940, sponsored by the Fund, he gave lectures on Australian literature at various universities.

To God: From the Weary Nations, 1917; *Eyes of Vigilance*, 1920; *Ways and Means*, 1920; *Arrows of Longing*, 1921; *The Gully*, 1925; *Melbourne Odes*, 1934; *Poems*, 1944.

Pages 113–114

'FURNLEY MAURICE' (FRANK WILMOT)

LITTLE is known about Jack Moses except that he was a close friend of Henry Lawson and contributed 'The Clot of Gold' to *Henry Lawson and His Mates* (1931). He was born in 1860 and died in 1945. *The Bulletin Book of Verses and Recitations* (1920) was dedicated to him as 'a *Bulletin* reciter in the Bush'.

Nine Miles from Gundagai, 1938.

Pages 36–37

JACK MOSES

IAN Mudie was born at Hawthorn, SA, on 1 March 1911, and educated at Scotch College, Adelaide. He worked at various jobs—freelance journalist, farm-hand, manager of a real-estate agency—and, with Rex Ingamells, was closely associated with the Jindyworobak movement that began in Adelaide. Later, he spent six years as editor for the publishing firm of Rigby, Adelaide, then retired to write full time. He died in England, during a trip abroad, on 25 October 1976. Ian Mudie is the author of many prose works—notably *Riverboats* (1961) and *The Heroic Journey of John McDouall Stuart* (1968).

IAN MUDIE

Corroboree to the Sun, 1940; *This Is Australia*, 1941; *The Australian Dream*, 1943; *Their Seven Stars Unseen*, 1943; *Poems 1934–1944*, 1945; *The Blue Crane*, 1959; *The Northbound Rider*, 1963; *Look, The Kingfisher*, 1970; *Selected Poems 1934–1974*, 1976.

Page 164

LES A. MURRAY

LES Murray was born on 17 October 1938 at Bunyah on the north coast of NSW and brought up there on his father's dairy farm. He attended various country schools before going to the University of Sydney where he studied languages and went on to work with the Western languages translation unit at the Australian National University. He then went overseas, returning to work with The Prime Minister's Department. In 1971 he retired to make writing his full-time career. He has since clearly revealed himself to be first among Australia's poets with his breadth of vision and his popular appeal. For twenty years he lived in Chatswood, a suburb of Sydney, acting as poetry adviser for his publisher of the time, Angus & Robertson, before he returned to live in Bunyah in 1985.

The Ilex Tree (with Geoffrey Lehmann), 1965; *The Weatherboard Cathedral*, 1969; *Poems against Economics*, 1972; *Lunch & Counter Lunch*, 1974; *Selected Poems: The Vernacular Republic* 1976 (revised edition, *Poems 1961–1981*, 1982); *Ethnic Radio*, 1977; *The Boys Who Stole the Funeral*, 1980; *The People's Otherworld*, 1983; *The Daylight Moon*, 1987; *Dog Fox Field*, 1990; *Collected Poems*, 1991; *Translations from the Natural World*, 1992; *Subhuman Redneck Poems*, 1996.

Pages 257–262

SHAW NEILSON

JOHN Shaw Neilson was born at Penola, SA, on 22 February 1872 and died in Melbourne on 12 May 1942. His father was born in Scotland, his mother in Victoria, of Scottish descent. He had less than three years' schooling at Penola and at Minimay (over the Victorian border) where he worked with his father on a selection until misfortune forced the family to move to Nhill (Vic.)—where again it was hard physical labour: shearing, harvesting, fencing, scrub-cutting. Encouraged by his father, who also wrote verse, Neilson was writing beautiful lyrics in his thirties: but his eyesight was failing and he had to dictate his poems to fellow workers. When he was fifty he was given a Commonwealth literary pension of £1 a week; and in 1928 a job was found for him in a government department. But he was never happy in cities: he needed to be out of doors. In the nineties his verse began to appear in the *Bulletin*, and he owed much to the encouragement of A.G. Stephens, as he did to the friendship of James Devaney when his health broke down in the 1940s. The magic of Neilson's delicately beautiful lyrics is beyond description.

Old Granny Sullivan, 1916; *Heart of Spring*, 1919; *Ballads and Lyrical Poems*, 1923; *New Poems*, 1927; *Collected Poems*, 1934; *Beauty Imposes*, 1938; *Unpublished Poems* (ed. James Devaney), 1947; *Selected Poems*, 1963; *Poems* (ed. A.R. Chisholm), 1965; *Selected Poems* (ed. Robert Gray), 1993.

Pages 91–96

MARK O'Connor was born in Shepparton, Vic., on 19 March 1945, and lived at Ararat before going to the University of Melbourne where he began an engineering course and left with an honours degree in Arts. Graduating in 1966, he had appointments first at the University of Western Australia, then at the Australian National University. He worked as a diver for the Maritime Services Board, and it was through his discovery of the Great Barrier Reef at One Tree Island (off Gladstone, Q.) that he became a writer. Since the publication of his first book, *Reef Poems*, in 1976, he has maintained himself as a writer. He is now living in Canberra, after extensive travel overseas and throughout Australia.

Reef Poems, 1976; *The Eating Tree*, 1980; *The Fiesta of Men*, 1983; *Poetry in Pictures: The Great Barrier Reef*, 1986; *Selected Poems*, 1986; *Poetry of the Mountains*, 1988; *The Great Forest*, 1989; *Firestick Farming*, 1990.

Page 276

WILLIAM Henry Ogilvie was born at Kelso, Scotland, on 21 August 1869. He came to Australia when he was twenty, drawn by his admiration for Adam Lindsay Gordon and his love for horses. He spent twelve years, until he returned to Scotland in 1901, droving, horse-breaking, and feeling himself to be truly Australian. His nostalgia for Australia is shown in the many books of verse he published after his return. He died in 1963.

Fair Girls and Gray Horses, 1898, 1958; *Hearts of Gold*, 1903; *The Australian*, 1916; *From Sunset to Dawn*, 1946; *Saddle for a Throne*, 1952.

Pages 86–88

BORN at Grafton, NSW, on 7 July 1940, Geoff Page was brought up in the country and educated at the Armidale School and the University of New England. For many years he has been a schoolteacher in Canberra, but he is also a novelist, an anthologist, a translator, and a prolific and well-respected reviewer.

Smalltown Memorials, 1975; *Collecting the Weather*, 1978; *Cassandra Paddocks*, 1980; *Clairvoyant in Autumn*, 1983; *Collected Lives*, 1986; *Footwork*, 1988; *Selected Poems*, 1991; *Gravel Corners*, 1992; *Human Interest*, 1994.

Pages 267–268

A.B. ('BANJO')
PATERSON

ANDREW Barton Paterson was born on 17 February 1864 at Narrambla, near Orange, NSW, and educated at Sydney Grammar School. Qualifying as a solicitor, he worked in a lawyer's office, at the same time contributing verse to the *Bulletin* under the pen-name 'The Banjo'— verse about the country life he had been brought up to. His verse was immediately popular and he soon forsook law for journalism. He was a war correspondent in South Africa in 1899, returning in 1900. He then went to China and to London, and in 1902 he was lecturing in Australia on the Boer War. He was editor of the Sydney *Evening News* (1904) and of the *Town and Country Journal* (1907–8), then spent six years as a pastoralist on the upper Murrumbidgee. In World War I he was an Ambulance Driver in France, a Remount Officer in Egypt, and again a war correspondent, returning to live in Sydney in 1919. He wrote novels and short stories and collected and edited *Old Bush Songs* (1905). The immense and lasting popularity of Paterson's verse is sufficient tribute to his magical skill as a balladist. He died in Sydney on 4 February 1941.

The Man from Snowy River and Other Verses, 1895; *Rio Grande's Last Race and Other Verses*, 1902; *Saltbush Bill, J.P., and Other Verses*, 1917; *The Collected Verse of A.B. Paterson*, 1921; *The Animals Noah Forgot*, 1933.

Pages 40–49

HAL PORTER

BORN on 16 February 1911 at Albert Park, Melbourne, Hal Porter was educated at Kensington and Bairnsdale (Gippsland). He became a schoolteacher and was resident master at schools in South Australia, Tasmania, NSW, and Victoria. After World War II he spent two years in Japan at Nijimura, where he taught children of the Occupation Forces and lectured to senior pupils in Japanese schools. From 1954 to 1961 he was librarian at Bairnsdale, then at Shepparton (Vic.). He retired to live at Garvoc, near Warrnambool, becoming a full-time writer. In 1981 he moved to live in Ballarat where, in 1983, he was seriously injured in a motor-car accident. He died as a result of his injuries in the next year. As well as three books of verse, Hal Porter published seven books of short stories, two novels, three volumes of autobiography and four plays.

The Hexagon, 1956; *Elijah's Ravens*, 1968; *In an Australian Country Graveyard and Other Poems*, 1974.

Pages 159–161

BORN in Brisbane on 16 February 1929, Peter Porter has had many occupations—cadet reporter, clerk, bookshop salesman, advertising copywriter. He has been writing poetry since his teens, and has gained a considerable reputation among contemporary English poets: for he is an expatriate who has lived in London for over forty years. He has visited Australia with growing frequency since 1974.

Once Bitten Twice Bitten, 1961; *Poems Ancient and Modern*, 1965; *A Porter Folio*, 1969; *The Last of England*, 1970; *Preaching to the Converted*, 1972; *Living in a Calm Country*, 1975; *The Cost of Seriousness*, 1978; *English Subtitles*, 1981; *Collected Poems*, 1983; *Fast Forward*, 1984; *The Automatic Oracle*, 1987; *Possible Worlds*, 1989; *Selected Poems*, 1989; *The Chair of Babel*, 1992; *Millennial Fables*, 1994.

Page 238

RODERIC Quinn was born in Sydney on 26 November 1867 and died there on 15 August 1949. His parents were from Ireland and he was educated at various Catholic schools. He read for the law, taught in a country State school, had a job in the public service, then became editor of the *North Sydney News*. He appears to have lived mainly through his verse and prose contributions to the *Bulletin* and other journals.

The Hidden Tide, 1899; *The Circling Hearths*, 1901; *Poems*, 1920.

Pages 65–66

BORN at Napier, New Zealand, on 21 March 1909, Elizabeth Riddell (Mrs E.N. Greatorex) came to Australia in 1930 to work as a journalist with *Smith's Weekly* and the Sydney *Sunday Sun*. Then she spent some years overseas, travelling widely and holding posts in London and New York before returning to Australia. In 1950 she was appointed editor of the magazine *Woman*, then moved on to other fields. She is now a freelance journalist, greatly respected for her perceptive book reviews.

The Untrammelled, 1940; *Poems*, 1948; *Forbears*, 1961; *Occasions of Birds*, 1987; *From the Midnight Courtyard*, 1989; *Selected Poems*, 1992; *The Difficult Island*, 1994.

Pages 153–156

ROLAND Robinson was born on 14 June 1912 at Belbriggan, County Clare, Ireland and was brought to Australia when he was nine years old. He went to school at Blakehurst, NSW, and left when he was fourteen to work on a sheep station in western NSW as rouseabout, boundary-rider, and sometimes a jockey at country race meetings. By chance he became a ballet dancer, a member of the Kirsova Ballet for three years. He was later a railway fettler, a script-writer, a green-keeper, and travelled widely in outback Australia, particularly in the Northern Territory and the Centre, absorbing the lore of the Aborigines. In the 1940s he was associated with the Jindyworobak movement, and in the 1950s was largely responsible for the publishing venture of the Lyre Bird Writers. He died at Belmont, NSW, on 8 February 1992.

Beyond the Grass-Tree Spears, 1944; *Language of the Sand*, 1949; *Tumult of the Swans*, 1953; *Deep Well*, 1962; *Grendel*, 1967; *Selected Poems*, 1971; *The Hooded Lamp*, 1976; *Selected Poems*, 1983.

Pages 168–169

ERIC ROLLS

BORN at Grenfell, NSW, on 25 April 1923, Eric Rolls began his education with the NSW Correspondence School and then attended Fort Street High School. During World War II he went from school to serve with the AIF in New Guinea and Bougainville. A farmer, first at Narrabri, then at Boggabri, and later at Baradine (NSW), he has published two important studies of the country environment, *They All Ran Wild* (1969) and *A Million Wild Acres* (1981). He has now retired from farming and lives in Sydney, writing a weekly column for the *Sun-Herald*.

Sheaf Tosser, 1967; *The Green Mosaic: Memories of New Guinea*, 1977; *Miss Strawberry* (for children), 1979; *Selected Poems*, 1990.

Pages 221–223

DAVID ROWBOTHAM

BORN on 27 August 1924 at Toowoomba, Q., David Rowbotham was educated at the Toowoomba Grammar School and at the universities of Queensland and Sydney. Having been a journalist in Sydney and in London, he joined the staff of the Brisbane *Courier-Mail* (1955–64), lectured in English at the University of Queensland (1965–69), and became literary and theatre critic of the *Courier-Mail* (1969–80), then its literary editor from 1980 to his retirement in 1987. He has travelled as guest lecturer to Hawaii, the United States, Japan, and Italy.

Ploughman and Poet, 1954; *Inland*, 1958; *All the Room*, 1964; *Bungalow and Hurricane*, 1967; *The Makers of the Ark*, 1970; *The Pen of Feathers*, 1971; *Mighty Like a Harp*, 1974; *Selected Poems*, 1975; *Maydays*, 1980; *New and Selected Poems*, 1994.

Pages 223–224

J.R. ROWLAND

JOHN Russell Rowland was born at Armidale, NSW, on 10 February 1925 and educated at Cranbrook school and the University of Sydney. After graduation he joined the Department of External Affairs and was given various postings before he became Ambassador to the USSR (1965–68), High Commissioner to Malaysia (1969–72), Ambassador to Austria, Czechoslovakia and Hungary (1973–75), Secretary of the Department of Foreign Affairs in Canberra (1976–78), then Ambassador to France until his retirement.

The Feast of Ancestors, 1965; *Snow*, 1970; *Times and Places*, 1975; *The Clock Inside*, 1979; *Sixty*, 1985.

Pages 224–226

THOMAS W. SHAPCOTT

BORN at Ipswich, Q., on 21 March 1935, Thomas William Shapcott is the younger of twin boys. He went to the Ipswich Grammar School until he was fifteen, then studied accountancy. He practised for many years as an accountant in Brisbane and he has been writing poetry steadily and in various forms ever since his first poem appeared in the *Bulletin* in 1956. He sold his accountancy practice in 1978 to become a full-time writer. From 1983 to 1990 he served as Director of the Literature Board of the Australia Council; he then became Director of the National Book Council.

Time on Fire, 1961; *The Mankind Thing*, 1964; *Sonnets*, 1960–63, 1964; *A Taste of Salt Water*, 1967; *Inwards to the Sun*, 1969; *Fingers of Air*, 1970; *Begin with Walking*, 1972; *Shabbytown Calendar*, 1975; *Selected Poems*, 1978; *Turning Full Circle*, 1979; *Welcome!*, 1983; *Travel Dice*, 1987; *The City of Home*, 1995.

Pages 250–252

JEMAL SHARAH

BORN in Canberra on 23 January 1969, Jemal Sharah began life with exceptional literary credentials, as her godfather was the poet Les Murray. Her father was killed in a car accident in 1975, and subsequently she moved to Sydney where she attended Sydney Girls High School and Sydney University. She began to write poems of exceptional promise before she had even left school: the poem 'The Fish Markets', which has appeared in several anthologies, was written at the age of 17. She now works for the Department of Foreign Affairs, and spent most of 1995 in Jordan.

Path of Ghosts, 1994.

Pages 287–288

PETER SKRZYNECKI

BORN in Europe on 6 April 1945 of Polish-Ukranian parents. Peter Skrzynecki was brought to Australia in 1949 and educated at St Patrick's College, Strathfield, NSW, and at the Sydney Teachers' College. He is a graduate of the University of New England and was a teacher with the Education Department of NSW before becoming a lecturer in English at the University of Western Sydney.

Behind the Lids, 1970; *Head Waters*, 1972; *Immigrant Chronicle*, 1975; *The Aviary*, 1978; *The Polish Immigrant: Migrant Poems 1972–82*, 1982; *Night Swim*, 1989; *Easter Sunday*, 1993.

Pages 274–275

KENNETH SLESSOR

BORN at Orange, NSW, on 27 March 1901, Kenneth Slessor was educated at the Sydney Church of England Grammar School and began his career as a journalist in 1920 as a reporter with the Sydney *Sun*. He held various jobs in Sydney and Melbourne as sub-editor and feature writer before he became editor of *Smith's Weekly* (1935–39). With the outbreak of World War II, he was appointed Australian Official War Correspondent (1940–44). In 1944 he returned from overseas to join the Sydney *Sun* as leader writer and literary editor (1944–57); and in 1957 he became leader writer and book reviewer for the Sydney *Daily Telegraph*. He was appointed to the Advisory Committee of the Commonwealth Literary Fund in 1953; and he edited the literary magazine *Southerly* from 1956 to 1961. He added only one poem to the collected work published in 1944: the haunting El Alamein threnody 'Beach Burial'. Kenneth Slessor died on 30 June 1971. Richness of imagery and the music of his verse make him one of the most rewarding of Australian poets.

Thief of the Moon, 1924; *Earth-Visitors*, 1926; *Five Visions of Captain Cook* (in *Trio: A Book of Poems*, by K. Slessor, H. Matthews, and C. Simpson), 1931; *Cuckooz Contrey*, 1932; *Darlinghurst Nights and Morning Glories*, 1933; *Five Bells: XX Poems*, 1939; *One Hundred Poems*, 1944; *Poems*, 1957; *Collected Poems*, ed. Dennis Haskell and Geoffrey Dutton, 1994.

Pages 121–133

VIVIAN SMITH

VIVIAN Smith was born in Hobart on 3 June 1933, and educated at the Hobart High School and the University of Tasmania, where he became a lecturer in French. In 1967 he moved to Sydney where his doctorate was awarded for a thesis on Vance and Nettie Palmer. He is now Reader in English at the University of Sydney. His poetry is distinctive for its quiet precision.

The Other Meaning, 1956; *An Island South*, 1967; *Familiar Places*, 1978; *Tide Country, 1983; Selected Poems*, 1985; *New Selected Poems*, 1995.

Pages 245–246

THOMAS E. SPENCER

THOMAS Edward Spencer was born in London in 1845. Having visited Australia briefly as a youth, he returned to live in Sydney in 1875. He was a successful builder and contractor. A popular humorist in his day, he wrote a novel and short stories as well as the ballads that became favourite recitation pieces. He died in 1910.

How McDougal Topped the Score, 1906; *Budgeree Ballads*, 1908; *Why Doherty Died*, 1910.

Page 33–35

DOUGLAS Alexander Stewart was born at Eltham, New Zealand, on 6 May 1913 and educated at Eltham Public School, the New Plymouth Boys' High School, and Victoria University College. He was editor of the Red Page of the *Bulletin* from 1939 to 1961 and published most of the leading poets and short-story writers of that period; and he served as poetry adviser on the committee of the Commonwealth Literary Fund from 1955 till 1972. In 1961 he joined the editorial staff of Angus & Robertson and continued as literary adviser until 1974. As poet, dramatist, short-story writer, as critic, biographer and anthologist, he has played an important part in the literary life of Australia. Having already published four books of verse, Douglas Stewart became more widely known for his verse plays, *Ned Kelly* (1943), *The Fire on the Snow*, and *the Golden Lover* (1944). Then, apart from his verse, there are the books of critical essays—*The Flesh and the Spirit* (1948), *The Broad Stream* (1975); the reminiscences—*The Seven Rivers* (1966), *Springtime in Taranaki* (1983); and the studies of Norman Lindsay and Kenneth Slessor. Douglas Stewart was the most versatile of writers; and in the range and variety of his lyric talent one of Australia's finest poets. He died in 1985.

Green Lions, 1936; *The White Cry*, 1939; *Elegy for an Airman*, 1940; *Sonnets to the Unknown Soldier*, 1941; *The Dosser in Springtime*, 1946; *Glencoe*, 1947; *Sun Orchids*, 1952; *The Birdsville Track*, 1955; *Rutherford*, 1962; *Selected Poems*, 1963; *Collected Poems*, 1967.

Pages 170–178

DOUGLAS STEWART

BORN on 28 November 1935 at Geraldton, WA, Randolph Stow was educated at Guildford Grammar School and the University of Western Australia. After graduation he joined a mission in the north-west of the state, then worked in New Guinea as an anthropologist, compiling a dictionary of the language of the Trobriand Islanders. He has lived in East Anglia, in the Highlands of Scotland, and in Malta, and has lectured in English in the universities of Adelaide, Leeds, and Western Australia. Randolph Stow is a novelist as well as a poet.

Act One, 1957; *Outrider: Poems 1956–62*, 1962; *A Counterfeit Silence: Selected Poems*, 1969.

Pages 252–254

RANDOLPH STOW

CHRIS WALLACE-CRABBE

BORN on 6 May 1934 at Richmond, Vic., Chris Wallace-Crabbe was educated at Scotch College and the University of Melbourne. He became Lockie Fellow in Australian Literature and Creative Writing at the university and has since had a successful academic career while engaging in a wide variety of literary and journalistic projects. He is now Professor of English at the University of Melbourne.

The Music of Division, 1959; *In Light and Darkness*, 1963; *The Rebel General*, 1967; *Where the Wind Came*, 1971; *Selected Poems*, 1973; *The Shapes of Gallipoli*, 1975; *The Emotions Are Not Skilled Workers*, 1979; *The Amorous Cannibal*, 1985; *I'm Deadly Serious*, 1988; *For Crying Out Loud*, 1990; *Rungs of Time*, 1993; *Selected Poems, 1956–1994*, 1995.

Pages 248–249

FRANCIS WEBB

FRANCIS Webb was born in Adelaide on 8 February 1925 and educated at Christian Brothers' Schools at Chatswood and Lewisham, Sydney. He served with the RAAF in Canada during World War II His work was first published in the *Bulletin* and the appearance in book form of 'A Drum for Ben Boyd', written when he was only 22, showed him to be a poet of unusual power and maturity. Suffering from bouts of mental illness, he died in Callan Park Hospital on 22 November 1973.

A Drum for Ben Boyd, 1948; *Leichhardt in Theatre*, 1952; *Birthday*, 1953; *Socrates*, 1961; *The Ghost of the Cock*, 1964; *Collected Poems*, 1969; *Cap and Bells: The Poetry of Francis Webb*, ed. Michael Griffith and James McGlade, 1991.

Pages 228–230

JUDITH WRIGHT

JUDITH Wright (Mrs J.P. McKinney) was born at Thalgarrah station near Armidale, NSW, on 31 May 1915. She was brought up on the land and educated by Correspondence School before going to the New England Girls' School and the University of Sydney. When her brothers enlisted in World War II she worked with her father on the land. After her husband's death she moved from Mount Tamborine, Q., to Canberra, and now lives in Braidwood. She was immediately recognised as an outstanding poet when her first book (*The Moving Image*) appeared in 1946 and her reputation continued to grow: no other poet can surpass her in expressing the spirit of Australia in such depth and with such artistry. Judith Wright's two major prose works are *Generations of Men* (1959) and *The Cry for the Dead* (1981). Concerned with the relationship of man to his environment, she is a tireless advocate of conservation.

The Moving Image, 1946; *Woman to Man*, 1949; *The Gateway*, 1953; *The Two Fires*, 1955; *Birds*, 1962; *Five Senses: Selected Poems*, 1963; *City Sunrise*, 1964; *The Other Half*, 1966; *Collected Poems 1942–1970*, 1971; *Alive: Poems 1971–1972*, 1973; *Fourth Quarter*, 1976; *The Double Tree: Selected Poems 1942–1976*, 1978; *Phantom Dwelling*, 1985; *A Human Pattern: Selected Poems*, 1990; *Collected Poems*, 1994.

Pages 180–187

ACKNOWLEDGMENT OF SOURCES

Thanks are due to the publishers and copyright owners concerned for permission to include copyright material. For future editions, we should be grateful to receive any correction of sources wrongly credited.

ETHEL ANDERSON

Afternoon in the Garden: *Sunday at Yarralumla*, Angus & Robertson, 1947.

ANONYMOUS

The Wild Colonial Boy; The Dying Stockman; Click Go the Shears; The Numerella Shore; Bold Jack Donahoe: *Old Bush Songs*, ed. Douglas Stewart and Nancy Keesing, Angus & Robertson, 1957.

DOROTHY AUCHTERLONIE

A Problem of Language; Release: *The Dolphin*, Australian National University Press, 1967. By courtesy of Andrew Green.

LEX BANNING

Captain Phillip and the Birds: *Apocalypse in Springtime*, Edwards & Shaw, 1956. By courtesy of Anna Banning.

BRUCE BEAVER

Letters to Live Poets: X: *Letters to Live Poets*, South Head Press, 1969. White Cat and Brown Girl: *Under the Bridge*, Beaujon Press, 1961. By courtesy of the author.

JOHN BLIGHT

Ear Shell: *My Beachcombing Days*, Angus & Robertson, 1968. Old Man and Tree: *Pageantry for a Lost Empire*, Nelson, 1977. Death of a Whale: *A Beachcomber's Diary*, Angus & Robertson, 1963.

BARCROFT BOAKE

Where the Dead Men Lie: *Where the Dead Men Lie and Other Poems*, Angus & Robertson, 1897.

E.J. BRADY

The Coachman's Yarn: *Australian Bush Ballads*, ed. Douglas Stewart and Nancy Keesing, Angus & Robertson, 1955. By courtesy of Mrs E.J. Brady.

CHRISTOPHER BRENNAN

I Am Shut Out of Mine Own Heart; My Heart Was Wandering in the Sands: *The Verse of Christopher Brennan*, ed. A.R. Chisholm and J.J. Quinn, Angus & Robertson, 1960.

R.F. BRISSENDEN

Letter from Garella Bay: *Winter Matins*, Angus & Robertson, 1971.
Verandas: *The Whale in Darkness*, Australian National University Press,
1980. By courtesy of Mrs R.L. Brissenden.

VINCENT BUCKLEY

Parents: *Arcady and Other Poems*, Melbourne University Press, 1966. By
courtesy of P. Buckley.

DAVID CAMPBELL

The Australian Dream; Night Sowing; Windy Gap; On Frosty Days;
The Stockman; Mothers and Daughters: *Selected Poems 1942–1968*,
Angus & Robertson, 1968.

VICTOR DALEY

The Call of the City: *Wine and Roses*, ed. Bertram Stevens, Angus &
Robertson, 1911.

BRUCE DAWE

Life-cycle: *Condolences of the Season*, F.W. Cheshire, 1971.
Homecoming: *Beyond the Subdivisions*, F.W. Cheshire, 1969.
Provincial City: *An Eye for a Tooth*, F.W. Cheshire, 1968.

C.J. DENNIS

The Intro: The Play: *The Songs of a Sentimental Bloke*, Angus &
Robertson, 1915.
The Austral—aise: *The Austral—aise: A Marching Song*, Ideal Press,
1915.
Permission given by Angus & Robertson.
Country Fellows: *Random Verse*, Hallcroft Publications, 1952.
Permission given by the Herald & Weekly Times, Melbourne.

ROSEMARY DOBSON

A Fine Thing; The Birth; The Shell; The Mother: *Selected Poems*,
Angus & Robertson, 1973.

MICHAEL DRANSFIELD

Portrait of the Artist as an Old Man: *Streets of the Long Voyage*,
University of Queensland Press, 1970.
Ingredients of the Ballad: *The Inspector of Tides*, University of
Queensland Press, 1972.

GEOFFREY DUTTON

The Smallest Sprout: *Poems Soft and Hard*, F.W. Cheshire, 1967. By
courtesy of the author.

EDWARD DYSON

The Old Whim-Horse: *Rhymes from the Mines*, Angus & Robertson,
1896.

G. ESSEX EVANS
The Women of the West: *Collected Verse*, Angus & Robertson, 1928.

ROBERT D. FitzGERALD
Legend; The Wind at Your Door: *Forty Years' Poems*, Angus & Robertson, 1965.

MARY HANNAY FOOTT
Where the Pelican Builds: *Where the Pelican Builds and Other Poems*, Gordon & Gotch, Brisbane, 1885.

MARY FULLERTON
Lovers: *Moles Do So Little with Their Privacy*, Angus & Robertson, 1942.
Stupidity: *The Wonder and the Apple*. Angus & Robertson, 1946.

LEON GELLERT
Through a Porthole; Anzac Cove: *Songs of a Campaign*, Angus & Robertson, 1917.

MARY GILMORE
Eve-Song: Nationality; Never Admit the Pain; Nurse No Long Grief; The Shepherd; The Brucedale Scandal: *Mary Gilmore: Selected Verse*, ed. R.D. FitzGerald, Angus & Robertson, 1969.
Old Botany Bay: *The Passionate Heart*, Angus & Robertson, 1918.
Fourteen Men: *Fourteen men*, Angus & Robertson, 1954.

ADAM LINDSAY GORDON
Ye Weary Wayfarer; The Sick Stockrider: *Poems of Adam Lindsay Gordon*, Oxford University Press (Humphrey Milford), 1929.

ALAN GOULD
King Parrots: *The Pausing of the Hours*, Angus & Robertson, 1984.
Permission granted by Margaret Connolly and Associates.

ROBERT GRAY
Journey: The North Coast: *Selected Poems*, Angus & Robertson, 1990.
The Dusk: *Grass Script*, Angus & Robertson, 1979.
Permission granted by Margaret Connolly and Associates.

RODNEY HALL
Mrs Macintosh; On Trying to Remember Someone: *Selected Poems 1959–1973*, University of Queensland Press, 1975. By courtesy of the author.

CHARLES HARPUR
A Midsummer Noon in the Australian Forest: *Charles Harpur*, ed. Adrian Mitchell, Sun Books, 1973.

MAX HARRIS
The Tantanoola Tiger: *A Window at Night*, ABR Publications, 1967. By courtesy of the author.

KEVIN HART
The Members of the Orchestra: *The Members of the Orchestra and Other Poems*, ed. Paul Kavanagh, University of Newcastle, 1981.
A History of the Future: *The Lines of the Hand*, Angus & Robertson, 1981. By courtesy of the author.

P.J. HARTIGAN ('JOHN O'BRIEN')
Said Hanrahan; Tangmalangaloo: *Around the Boree Log*, Angus & Robertson, 1921.

WILLIAM HART-SMITH
Space; The Waterspout (Two poems from Christopher Columbus); Boomerang: *Poems of Discovery*, Angus & Robertson, 1959.

GWEN HARWOOD
Group from Tartarus: *Poems*, Angus & Robertson, 1963.
In the Middle of Life: *Selected Poems*, Angus & Robertson, 1975.
Suburban Sonnet: Boxing Day: *Poems/Volume Two*, Angus & Robertson, 1968.

PHILIP HODGINS
The Dam: *Blood and Bone*, Angus & Robertson, 1986.
Leaving: *Up On All Fours*, Angus & Robertson, 1993.
Five Thousand Acre Paddock: *Animal Warmth*, Angus & Robertson, 1990.

A.D. HOPE
Imperial Adam; Sonnets to Baudelaire (vii); Australia; Chorale; The House of God: The Death of a Bird: *Collected Poems 1930–1970*, Angus & Robertson, 1972.

EVAN JONES
A Summer Death: *Recognitions*, Australian National University Press, 1978. By courtesy of the author.

NANCY KEESING
Reverie of a Mum: *Showground Sketchbook*, Angus & Robertson, 1968.

HENRY KENDALL
Bellbirds; September in Australia; The Last of His Tribe: *The Poems of Henry Kendall*, Angus & Robertson, 1920.

CHRISTOPHER KOCH

Half-heard: *The Penguin Book of Australian Verse*, ed. John Thompson, Kenneth Slessor, and R.G. Howarth, Penguin Books, 1958. Permission granted by the author.

EVE LANGLEY

Native Born: *Poetry in Australia, Volume II: Modern Australian Verse*, ed. Douglas Stewart, Angus & Robertson, 1964.

HENRY LAWSON

Faces in the Street; Ballad of the Drover; When Your Pants Begin to Go; Reedy River; Andy's Gone with Cattle; Waratah and Wattle; The Shearer's Dream; The Never-Never Land; To Jim; Bill: *Poetical Works of Henry Lawson*, Angus & Robertson, 1925.

GEOFFREY LEHMANN

The Dolphins: *A Voyage of Lions*, Angus & Robertson, 1968. There Are Some Lusty Voices Singing: *Ross' Poems*, Angus & Robertson, 1978. Permission granted by Curtis Brown (Australia).

FREDERICK T. MACARTNEY

Only Gods Forget: *Selected Poems*, Angus & Robertson, 1961.

JAMES McAULEY

Because; Pastoral; The Magpie; Spider in the Snow; Canticle: *Collected Poems 1936–1970*, Angus & Robertson, 1971.

HUGH McCRAE

I Blow My Pipes; Song of the Rain: *Poems*, Angus & Robertson, 1939.

RONALD McCUAIG

The Commercial Traveller's Wife; Love Me and Never Leave Me; The Letter; The Passionate Clerk to His Love: *The Ballad of Bloodthirsty Bessie and Other Poems*, Angus & Robertson, 1961.

NAN McDONALD

Candles; The White Eagle: *Pacific Sea*, Angus & Robertson, 1947.

ROGER McDONALD

Apis Mellifica: *The Younger Australian Poets*, ed. Robert Gray and Geoffrey Lehmann, Hale & Iremonger, 1983. Sickle Beach: *Airship*, University of Queensland Press, 1975. By courtesy of the author.

DOROTHEA MACKELLAR

My Country: *The Closed Door and Other Verses*, Australasian Authors' Agency, 1911. Permission given by Curtis Brown (Aust.)

KENNETH MACKENZIE

Friendship and Love; Heat: *The Poems of Kenneth Mackenzie*, ed. Evan
Jones and Geoffrey Little, Angus & Robertson, 1972.

RHYLL McMASTER

Profiles of My Father: *The Younger Australian Poets*, ed. Robert Gray
and Geoffrey Lehmann, Hale & Iremonger, 1983. By courtesy of the
author and Cameron Creswell Associates.

DAVID MALOUF

Adrift: *Neighbours in a Thicket*, University of Queensland Press, 1974.
By courtesy of the author.

JOHN MANIFOLD

The Bunyip and the Whistling Kettle: *Collected Verse*, University of
Queensland Press, 1978. By courtesy of the author.

RAY MATHEW

Love and Marriage: *South of the Equator*, Angus & Robertson, 1962.

'FURNLEY MAURICE' (FRANK WILMOT)

The Victoria Markets Recollected in Tranquillity: *Melbourne Odes*,
Lothian, 1934.

JACK MOSES

Nine Miles from Gundagai: *Nine Miles from Gundagai*, Angus &
Robertson, 1938.

IAN MUDIE

Who Me, Mate?: *Selected Poems 1934–1974*, Nelson, 1976. By courtesy of
the family of the late Ian Mudie.

LES MURRAY

Rainwater Tank; An Absolutely Ordinary Rainbow; The Broad Bean
Sermon; The Future: *The Vernacular Republic: Poems 1961–1981*, Angus
& Robertson, 1982.
Permission granted by Margaret Connolly & Associates.

SHAW NEILSON

Song Be Delicate; Love's Coming; The Orange Tree; Beauty Imposes;
May; 'Tis the White Plum Tree: *The Poems of Shaw Neilson*, ed. A.R.
Chisholm, Angus & Robertson, 1965. Permission granted by Lothian
Publishing Company, Melbourne, for all poems except 'Beauty
Imposes'.

MARK O'CONNOR

The Beginning: *Reef Poems*, University of Queensland Press, 1974. By
courtesy of the author.

WILL H. OGILVIE
The Death of Ben Hall: *Australian Bush Ballads*, ed. Douglas Stewart and Nancy Keesing, 1955.

GEOFF PAGE
Grit: A Doxology: *Cassandra Paddocks*, Angus & Robertson, 1980.
Bondi Afternoon 1915: *Smalltown Memorials*, University of Queensland Press, 1975. By courtesy of the author.

A.B. ('BANJO') PATERSON
Waltzing Matilda; The Man from Snowy River; The Man from Ironbark; The Travelling Post Office; Clancy of the Overflow; Over the Range: *The Collected Verse of A.B. Paterson*, Angus & Robertson, 1921 (32nd printing, 1965). Permission granted by Retrusa Pty Ltd.

HAL PORTER
Sheep: *The Hexagon*, Angus & Robertson, 1956.
The Married Couple: *In an Australian Country Graveyard*, Nelson, 1974. By courtesy of John F. Porter.

PETER PORTER
Phar Lap in the Melbourne Museum: *A Porter Selected: Poems 1959–1989*, Oxford University Press, 1987. By courtesy of the author.

RODERIC QUINN
The Fisher: *The Hidden Tide*, Bulletin Newspaper Co., 1899. Permission granted by Angus & Robertson.

ELIZABETH RIDDELL
The Train in the Night (from Travellers' Joy); Wakeful in the Township; Suburban Song: *Forbears*, Angus & Robertson, 1961.

ROLAND ROBINSON
The Wanderer: *Selected Poems*, Angus & Robertson, 1971.
Rock-Lily: *Tumult of the Swans*, Edwards & Shaw, 1953. Permission given by Angus & Robertson.

ERIC ROLLS
Sheaf Tosser; Death Song of a Mad Bush Shepherd: *Sheaf Tosser*, Angus & Robertson, 1967.

DAVID ROWBOTHAM
The Creature in the Chair: *New and Selected Poems 1945–1993*, Penguin Books Australia Ltd, 1994. The Old Priest: *Selected Poems*, University of Queensland Press, 1975. By courtesy of the author.

J.R. ROWLAND
Canberra in April: *The Feast of Ancestors*, Angus & Robertson, 1965.

THOMAS SHAPCOTT
A Taste of Salt Water; Marriage: *A Taste of Salt Water*, Angus & Robertson, 1967. By courtesy of the author.

JEMAL SHARAH
The Fish Markets; New-Found Land: Courtesy of the author.

PETER SKRZYNECKI
Cattle: *Immigrant Chronicle*, University of Queensland Press, 1975. By courtesy of the author.

KENNETH SLESSOR
Five Bells; Country Towns; Captain Dobbin; Polarities; Sleep; Metempsychosis; Beach Burial: *Poems* (2nd edition), Angus & Robertson, 1957.

VIVIAN SMITH
Summer Sketches: Sydney; Family Album: *An Island South*, Angus & Robertson, 1967.

THOMAS E. SPENCER
How McDougal Topped the Score: *How McDougal Topped the Score*, NSW Bookstall Co., 1908.

DOUGLAS STEWART
The Dosser in Springtime; Two Englishmen; Place Names; Brindabella; The Snow-Gum; Lady Feeding the Cats; Glencoe: *Collected Poems 1936–1967*, Angus & Robertson, 1967.
Between the Night and Morning: *Overland*, August, 1983.
Domestic Poem: *Southerly*, No. 2, 1983.
Permission given by Curtis Brown (Aust.) for the last two poems.

RANDOLPH STOW
The Ghost at Anlaby; The Sleepers: *A Counterfeit Silence*, Angus & Robertson, 1969. © Randolph Stow 1969.

CHRIS WALLACE-CRABBE
Other People: *Where the Wind Came*, Angus & Robertson, 1971. By courtesy of the author.

FRANCIS WEBB
This Runner; Five Days Old: *Collected Poems*, Angus & Robertson, 1969.

JUDITH WRIGHT
Woman to Man; Magpies; Our Love Is So Natural; Woman's Song; The Flame-Tree; Australia 1970: *Collected Poems*, Angus & Robertson, 1971.
Finale: *Australian Poetry in the 20th Century*, William Heinemann Australia, 1991. By courtesy of the author.

SOURCES OF ILLUSTRATIONS

The illustrative works used in this book could not have been obtained without the help and co-operation of numerous people and organisations.

ART GALLERY OF NEW SOUTH WALES: p.17 *Bailed Up*, T. Roberts, 1985; p.79 *An Interior*, J. Wolinksi, 1898; p.97 *The Music Lesson*, Sydney Long, 1904; p.108 *An Easter Holiday*, John D. Moore, 1925; p.126 *Wharfies, Circular Quay*, Harold Cazneaux; p.156 *Breakfast Piece*, Herbert Badham, 1936; p.170 *Hermit's Camp*, N.J. Caire; p.175 *Dawn – Snowy Regions N.S.W.*, Norman Deck, 1960; p.182 *Woman in Kitchen*, Charles Kerry, c.1895–1910; p.190 *Nearing Their Journey's End*, Henri Mallard, c.1920s; p.191 *Cattle Tracks*, John B. Eaton, c.1934; p.194 *My Camp*, Henri Bastin, 1966; p.215 *The Whelk Stall*, J.N. Kilgour, 1939; p.241 *Landscape, Hill End*, David Strachan, 1961; p.243 *The Sick Girl*, David Strachan, c.1945; p.263 *The Ever-Restless Sea*, W. Lister Lister, 1892; p.269 *Afternoon, Bondi*, Elioth Grüner, 1915; p.275 *Spring Frost*, Elioth Grüner, 1919.

ART GALLERY OF SOUTH AUSTRALIA: p.176 *Reconstruction*, Sali Herman, 1950; p.266 *Woman in a Landscape*, Sir Russell Drysdale, 1949.

AUSTRALIAN NATIONAL BOTANIC GARDENS: p.84 *Illawarra Flame Tree*, Sydney Botanic Gardens, © Murray Fagg, 1982.

AUSTRALIAN NATIONAL GALLERY: p.19 *Night*, S.T. Gill, 1870; p.65 *Ripples and Reeds*, Max Dupain, c.1928; p.155 *Backyard – Foster*, Max Dupain, 1940.

AUSTRALIAN WAR MEMORIAL: p.133 *Burying Party Western Desert*, 1942.

BALLARAT ART GALLERY: p.206 *Lovers and Shell*, David Strachan, c.1945–46.

BATTYE LIBRARY, STATE LIBRARY OF WESTERN AUSTRALIA: p.161 *The End of the War*.

CAZNEAUX FAMILY: p.132 *A Relic of the Past*, Harold Cazneaux; p.141 *Bathing Baby*, Harold Cazneaux.

CHAPMAN COLLECTION: p.34; p.227; p.246a; p.246b.

GULIANO DATIS: p.157 'Lettera' 1493 – *Columbus Landing in the Indies.*

DIXSON LIBRARY, STATE LIBRARY OF NEW SOUTH WALES: p.54 *Stockman's Hut Victoria,* S.T. Gill; p.58 *A Bush Funeral,* S.T. Gill, 1856.

DIXSON GALLERY, STATE LIBRARY OF NEW SOUTH WALES: p.40 *Swagman on the Road Mount Charlson,* S.T. Gill.

MAX DUPAIN: p.90 *Souvenir of Newport Beach,* 1978; p.99; p.146 *Souvenir of the Entrance,* 1976; p.149; p.165 *Shell-Nautilus,* 1954; p.167 *Out of work, Sydney Domain,* 1938; p.168; p.169; p.181; p.189; p.200; p.202 *Meat Queue,* 1946; p.205; p.229 *Baby Protesting,* 1946; p.231 *South West Rocks,* 1978; p.250 *Sunrise at Newport,* 1974; p.278 *Floater;* p.281; p.282; p.283.

GEOFFREY DUTTON: p.217 *Mrs Dutton By An Old Ruined Cottage Near Sandy Creek;* p.253 *The Water Tower at Anlaby,* 'Anlaby: Pastoral Homes of Australia' p.3.

GENERAL REFERENCE LIBRARY, STATE LIBRARY OF NEW SOUTH WALES: p.43 'Illustrated Australian News', 1870; p.60; p.67 *Thumb-Nail Sketches at Street Corners,* 'Australasian Sketcher', 19 April 1873; p.71 'Illustrated Australian News', 2 December 1876; p.73 *View on the Clarence River, N.S.W.,* 'Australasian Sketcher', 17 May 1873, p.33.

ROBERT MCFARLANE: p.247.

MITCHELL LIBRARY, STATE LIBRARY OF NEW SOUTH WALES: p.1 *Kangaroos,* possibly by J.W. Lewin, c.1819; p.2 *Sunbaker,* Max Dupain, 1937; p.14 *The Criminal,* David Strachan, from 'Accent and Hazard', 1951; p.22 *Bullock Team,* W. Strutt, c.1869; p. 23 *Waiting for the mail, N.S.W.,* S.T. Gill; p.25; p.28 *Illawarra,* Conrad Martens, 1848; p.30 *Harnett's Falls, Mosman Bay,* S.T. Gill, 1874; p.32 *One of the N.S.W. aborigines befriended by Governor Macquarie,* c.1810–1821; p.37 *Bush Scenes – Boundary Rider,* S.T. Gill; p.38 *Hunter Street from Bligh Street,* 1931; p.46 *Scone N.S.W.,* 1906; p.47 *Overlanders,* S.T. Gill; p.50 *Cottage, Hill End,* B.O. Holtermann, c.1872; p.52 *Old Bendigo,* George Rowe, 1857; p.55 *The* Sirius *and Convoy Sail into Botany Bay where the* Supply *and Transports are already at Anchor,* William Bradley's 'Journal', 1788; p.56 *Boundary Rider's Home,* J.S. Prout; p.57 *Might Versus Right,* S.T. Gill; p.62 *Ironpot Creek, Craigie Range, Granite;* p.76 *Federation Day January 1st, 1901, Centennial Park, Sydney;* p.64 *In the Australian desert,* S.T. Gill, 1870; p.75 *Droving,* S.T. Gill, c.1870; p.78 *Breakfast in a Drover's Camp,* Charles Kerry; p.81 *Portrait of Mr J.A. Macartney,* J.A. Macartney – 'Rockhampton Fifty Years Ago' f/piece, 1890; p.82 *Wind Cave, Blackheath,* E. Morris, 'Cassell's Picturesque Australasia', 1888; p.84 *Coaching in N.S.W.,* 'Illustrated Sydney News', 18

August 1877; p.87 SPF; p.89 *North Head, Port Jackson*, Conrad Martens, 1854; p.93 *Pye's Orange Grove, Parramatta*, 'Picturesque Atlas of Australia' Vol.1, p.119, 1886; p.94 *Stockyard near Jamberoo*, Charles Condor, 1886; p.103 *Rose of Persia*, J.C. Williamson, Theatre Royal, Sydney, c.1900; p.107 SPF *N.S.W. Artillery*; p.110 *Floodwaters, Echuca, Victoria*, 1906; p.112 *Race meeting at Petersham*, 1845; p.115 *Old Market George Street* No.2, Lionel Lindsay; p.116 *Elephant Mountain*, Eugène Von Guérard, 1845; p.120 SPF *Anzac Cove*, 1915; p.122 *Mosman Bay at Dusk*, Max Dupain, 1937; p.125 *Tenterfield, N.S.W.*, 1910; p.131 *Jean Lorraine*, Max Dupain, 1937; p.134 *Portrait of an unknown woman*, I. Brook, c.1804; p.137 *Convict Flogging*, R.S. William, 'The Fell Tyrant' f/piece, London 1837; p.142 *The South Australian Alps as first seen by Messrs Hovell and Hume on 8th November 1824*; p.144 *Point Perpendicular*, c.1936; p.150 SPF *Mail Services*; p.159 *A sheep station in Tasmania*, John Glover, 1833; p.164 *Martin Place, Sydney*, 1937; p.179 *A glimpse of Sydney from Darlinghurst*, 'Picturesque Atlas of Australasia' Vol.1, p. 85,1886; p.180 *Cover*, David Strachan, 'Accent and Hazard'; p.186 *Crater of Extinct Volcano*, S.T. Gill, c.1845; p.192 *Droving*; p.198 *Near Cox's farm, Mudgee*, Conrad Martens; p.213 *Landing of Emigrants in Queensland*, Danish emigrant, 'Missing Friends' p.55; p.220 *Wyola, WA*, 1987; p.222 *The Muse*, David Strachan, 'Accent and Hazard', 1951; p.228 *School sports*, Sam Hood, 1930s; p.232 *Views from Admiralty House*, 1939; p.237 *Bridal couple and guests on steps of church*, Sam Hood, 1930s; p.239 *Victoria versus WA*, Sam Hood, 1930s; p.244 *View from Bald Hill, Stanwell Park N.S.W.*, 1935; p.245 *Busy Bondi*, Peter Kingston, 1985; p.249 *Military funeral procession of 12/16th Battalion, Muswellbrook, N.S.W.*, c.1919; p.255 *Wanaaring, N.S.W.*, 1905; p.256 *Lady in her Bower*, Conrad Martens, c.1841; p.257 *Private home: Shellharbour N.S.W.*, 1949; p.265 *Beverley and Christie at the Queens Head pub, Wilcannia*, Gerrit Fokkema, 1983; p.270 *The Darling River*, Gerrit Fokkema, 1983; p.272 *Near Byron Bay NSW*, 1936; p.286 *The Fool (The Idiot)*, David Strachan, 'Accent and Hazard', 1951.

DAVID MOORE: p.210 *Hill End Interior*, 1966.

NATIONAL FILM & SOUND ARCHIVE: p.100 *The Sentimental Bloke*, 1919.

NATIONAL GALLERY OF VICTORIA: p.95 *The Clearing, Gembrook*, Arthur Streeton, 1888; p.152 *Interior with Blue Painting*, Grace Cossington-Smith, 1965; p.225 *The Avenue Canberra*, Douglas Dundas, 1948.

NATIONAL LIBRARY OF AUSTRALIA: p.20 *November*, S.T. Gill, c.1847; p.44 *Shearer's Hut, Seven Creeks Station, Near Longwood*, C. Nettleton; p.49 *Native Diving into Pool*, S.T. Gill.

NEWCASTLE REGION ART GALLERY: front jacket *Summer at Carcoar*, Brett Whiteley, 1977.

NEW ENGLAND REGIONAL ART MUSEUM: p.185 *The wave*, Margaret Coen. 1940.

PRIVATE COLLECTION: back jacket *Beatrice Davis*, 1982; p.96 *Blossom by a country house*, Margaret Coen, 1970s; p.174 *Brindabella*, Margaret Coen, 1940s; p.197 *Belmont, at Raglan Victoria*, 1910; p.199 *Winter sun, Crackenback*, Judith Kelly, 1981; p.207 *Mother and child*, Arthur Murch; p.234 *Country autumn*, Margaret Coen, c.1970; p.258 *Smile, Sydney*, Jo McIntyre, 1980; p.261 *From the Cahill Expressway*, Margaret Coen, 1970s.

QUEENSLAND ART GALLERY: p.285 *Construction in Space*, William Rose, 1930.

ROGER STEENE: p.277 *Great Barrier Reef*.

MRS PAMELA STRACHAN: p.193 *Head of a Girl*, David Strachan, 1947.

PETER WATTS: p.118 *Belmont*.